SECRETS OF A SUITCASE

PAULINE TERREEHORST

Secrets of a Suitcase

*The Countess, the Nazis,
and Middle Europe's Lost Nobility*

Translated from the Dutch by
BRENT ANNABLE

HURST & COMPANY, LONDON

First published in the United Kingdom in 2024 by
C. Hurst & Co. (Publishers) Ltd.,
New Wing, Somerset House, Strand, London, WC2R 1LA
© Pauline Terreehorst, 2024
English-language translation © Brent Annable, 2024
All rights reserved.

Distributed in the United States, Canada and Latin America by
Oxford University Press, 198 Madison Avenue, New York, NY 10016,
United States of America.

The right of Pauline Terreehorst to be identified as the author
of this publication is asserted by her in accordance with the
Copyright, Designs and Patents Act, 1988.

The right of Brent Annable to be identified as the translator of this
English-language publication is asserted by him in accordance with the
Copyright, Designs and Patents Act, 1988.

Originally published in 2020 as Het geheim van de Gucci-koffer by
Uitgeverij Prometheus, Amsterdam.

The publisher gratefully acknowledges the support of the
Dutch Foundation for Literature.

Nederlands
N letterenfonds
dutch foundation
for literature

A Cataloguing-in-Publication data record for this book
is available from the British Library.

ISBN: 9781911723394

This book is printed using paper from registered sustainable
and anaged sources.

www.hurstpublishers.com

Printed and bound in Great Britain by Bell & Bain Ltd, Glasgow

For my mother
(1929–2019)

CONTENTS

Map	ix
Family trees	x

PART ONE

The September Auction	3
Palatial Homes	11
Finstergrün	21
A Good Girl	31
A Good Name	39
Where It Was	49
Will and Fate	57
Modern Women	65
A Crumbling Empire	81
Double-Entry Bookkeeping	91

PART TWO

The Roaring Twenties	103
Noblesse Oblige?	121
Paying Guests	133
Unwanted Guests	147
Going Once, Going Twice	159
The Collector	167
Displaced Persons	179
A Royal Wedding	187
Afterword	203

Acknowledgements	215
Notes	217
Sources and Further Reading	235
List of Illustrations	241
Index of Names	243
Index	251

Henckel von Donnersmarck family tree (Catholic Beuthen branch)

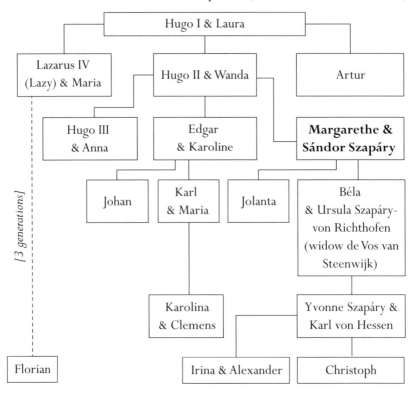

Szapáry marriage into the royal houses of Greece and Hesse

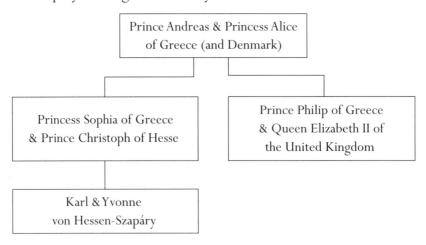

PART ONE

THE SEPTEMBER AUCTION

When Sotheby's still had an auction house in Amsterdam, I would sometimes visit to browse through their estate sales. I enjoyed seeing these pieces of furniture, sometimes very grand, in a moment of limbo, when they had left their homes and were waiting for a new owner. You could even touch them if you wanted to, or ask one of the assistants to open up a chest or cupboard. If you liked, you could sit down on a chair or sofa, and daydream about what had inspired the previous owners when decorating their homes. I rarely ever made a purchase; the prices were just too high, unless the item needed a lot of work. Thankfully, not all of the lots were sagging chaise longues, worn from the weight of nineteenth-century ladies reclining languidly as they recovered from tiresome conversations with overbearing gentlemen. Leafing through the catalogue of the 2004 autumn auction, my eye fell on a lot titled *Various travel accessories* that included a Gucci suitcase.

Gucci had regained popularity in the late twentieth century, due in part to recollections of the company's rich Italian heritage. In this, they were following in the footsteps of Prada, the venerable leather-goods specialist, which had given itself a major overhaul to become one of the best-known fashion brands at that time. Hermès and Louis Vuitton in France had jumped on the same bandwagon. They too had a rich history in the industry, associated with high-class equestrian sports like hunting and with early nineteenth-century tourism, as the well-to-do began taking international train journeys in luxury carriages. The bags, suitcases and scarves offered by these brands gave buyers instant access to that illustrious past, without having to mount a horse or travel the world.

In the later series, the iconic Gucci logo and red-and-green strap were featured even more prominently. The leather suitcase I was eyeing up among the *Various travel accessories* had this red-and-green-strap, a vintage sixties model.

SECRETS OF A SUITCASE

During the bidding, I had some unexpected competition from a young man—I ended up having to pay double what I'd originally intended. But I'd simply set my mind on this suitcase. When I went round the back to collect it, there were some other belongings too. Two boxes stood beside the case: they contained riding jackets, riding boots, a whip, hunting hats, four cocktail dresses, a fur stole and two fur collars, boxes of black and white lace, a green leather jewellery box from Paris containing glittering buttons taken from a garment, and a collection of gold-coloured curtain tiebacks. A third box contained a number of large albums, which on closer inspection held postcards. I took everything with me.

As I walked off, I was approached by my young nemesis from the auction. It turned out he was an Englishman, and had bid on the collection specifically for the riding jackets. He asked me what I was planning to do with them. I had no idea. They looked moth-eaten to me. He wanted to buy them, and I thought that I could at least recoup some of my losses after his bids had made the suitcase so much more expensive than planned. Curious about his interest in the worn-out jackets, I asked him what he wanted to do with them. 'Sell them!' he said excitedly. He explained that there was great demand for classic European garments at Japanese art academies, where they would be painstakingly analysed, picked apart, copied, and incorporated into new designs. For these jackets, he could earn many times the one hundred Euros he was paying me for them. Japanese fashion was still influential in those days, and many students admired the great Japanese designers such as Issey Miyake, Rei Kawakubo and Yohji Yamamoto. As head of a fashion school, I knew all about this; they, too, made use of old tailoring techniques.

At home, I stowed the boxes away in the attic, with a vague notion of doing 'something' with them one day. The moths plagued us for years afterwards.

I was, of course, intrigued by the contents of the suitcase and the boxes. My interest was drawn first to the dresses. They looked like they had been made by an expert seamstress in the sixties—they were almost couture, and must have belonged to a petite, slender woman, around a size six. On my initial survey of the items,

THE SEPTEMBER AUCTION

I encountered the name 'Gräfin (Countess) Jolanta Szápary.' My daughters and I thus took to calling them 'the countess's dresses.' The lace items—edgings, voiles and collars—had all been carefully preserved. The loose threads showed where they had been stitched on and removed multiple times, and divided in two. A beautiful hand had labelled the boxes *schwarz* (black) and *weiß* (white), which would have been important for finding the boxes quickly, in a time when death often came unexpectedly, and family members needed to dress themselves in black on short notice. The boxes themselves had also been repurposed: one, from Vienna, had contained Kaiser cough lozenges. The other was from a hairdresser in Dresden—Kellner & Sohn, according to the label—and had apparently held 'mourning flowers.' The salon would most likely have perished during the horrific bombing in 1945, I thought, and likewise the lady who had used this box to store her beloved lace so carefully.

The postcards remained in their albums. Many years later, when I unexpectedly had more time on my hands, I decided to turn them over and take a look at the writing sides. They were often blank, as though they had been purchased as holiday souvenirs. But occasionally they bore messages from various women, blowing paper kisses to 'Comtesse' Jolanta Szapáry. Most were written in the 1920s and '30s, and revealed the conventional way Jolanta and her friends addressed one another: with the title customarily reserved for unmarried women during the Habsburg era. But that monarchy had disappeared over a decade earlier.

I also found postcards from English and Scottish women, and a large number from Jolanta's mother that were signed *Deine alte Mama* ('your old mama'). When I looked up the names on the postcards, my preconceptions about the family of 'my' countess soon began to show cracks. I had originally assumed the simplest explanation for how the suitcase and boxes had ended up at Sotheby's in Amsterdam: that Jolanta Szapáry had moved to the Netherlands at some point. But things were not that straightforward.

The questions kept coming: was it even Jolanta who had worn those dresses and put on that stole, or pinned the black lace veils to her hat? The collection suggested otherwise. The postcards painted a picture of a pious woman, a paediatric nurse, who had lived with her mother in Austria and studied in London in the 1920s. But far more information was available on her mother, Margarethe Szapáry—or Margit, as the postcards sometimes called her.

This is how my journey through the history of Central Europe began: with a Gucci suitcase, lot number 0379, from Sotheby's German Noble Sale on 21 September 2004.

In one of the boxes, I found an album from 1914 titled *Offizielles Album für Kriegsbildkarten* (Official Album for War Postcards). The cover showed an image of two soldiers standing on either side of what looked like a theatre stage. Cannons had been placed behind them, and they were holding a banner. Arranged between them were portraits of the Austrian Emperor Franz Joseph I and the German Kaiser Wilhelm II, the two men who had initiated the first of Europe's two bloody world wars. Both leaders appear heroic and resolute on the cover, with their moustaches, mutton-chops, and rows of medallions pinned to their chests.

According to the label, this album had been made for the collection of 'official cards' issued by the Red Cross in support of their work for soldiers and their families. But inside, I saw nothing that resembled any kind of official war memorabilia—only cards depicting peaceful villages and landscapes of mediaeval tranquillity.

The photos contained no people. The inside cover concealed a few loose, restored shots of Austrian and Slovenian castles, perched atop high cliffs with views of lakes and wooded vistas. The postcards that were blank on the writing side, which seemed to be souvenirs from holidays to England and Scotland, were interspersed with others received from girlfriends and other acquaintances in the 1920s and '30s. This collection had nothing whatsoever to do with the First World War. The album must have been reused to save money, which was common in those days.

The rest of the postcard collection was bound in a far simpler manner: between two pieces of white cardboard, tied together with string. They seemed to have functioned as an alternative to holiday snaps. Many years later, I would discover that Jolanta's mother had gifted her a camera for Christmas in 1925, but she can't have used it much at all. The photos produced by amateur devices from that era were far too small—the Sotheby's boxes did contain several, but they were taken in the mountains, and by others. The names of the people in the photographs were written on the backs in pencil. In addition to *ich* ('me'), a certain 'Eleonore Schwarzenberg' features on horseback; at a picnic table somewhere in the Alps, two men in hunting hats are seated with Jolanta, their names recorded as 'Toni' and 'Rudl.' Another photograph shows a very fashionable man, standing proudly beside an open-topped automobile, goggles on his forehead. The back says, 'Béla in Canada 1928.' I would later learn that this was Jolanta's brother.

But these personal photos had fallen out of smaller boxes, which also contained buttons. The albums themselves contained only perfect shots taken by professional postcard photographers, whose superior equipment ensured that the churches, landscapes and castle ruins were rendered in crisp detail, even from the air. I found, for example, an aerial photograph of Walter Scott's castle, Kenilworth— a marvel of the day, and in a far more impressive view than one could ever photograph oneself.

They had been collected during a time when it had become a popular hobby not only to send postcards to loved ones—a nineteenth-century invention of the German postal service—but to buy them for oneself, giving travellers some post-holiday enjoyment after they had returned home. Card-collecting must have been a passion of Jolanta Szapáry's. Almost all of the cards that had been written on were addressed to 'Finstergrün Castle, Ramingstein, Salzburg Province, Austria', or occasionally simply to 'Countess Szapáry, Ramingstein'. Evidently this was indication enough, since the postcards had all arrived safely and been neatly arranged in the albums.

In addition to the England and Scotland album, there was another with pictures from France, and one from Italy. Occasionally cards from Austria itself were added. But, as international as the cards were, there was clearly a dominant theme: mediaeval and Gothic buildings and their interiors, primarily castles and churches, interspersed with details of saints' statues, altarpieces or doors with special woodcarvings. Jolanta seems to have been searching for familial connections among all these specimens of outstanding mediaeval architecture and craftsmanship, as well as links to the castle where she and her mother Margarethe lived.

Except one thing was strange: Finstergrün is *not* an old castle. Searching for information about the place, I found that it was built between 1900 and 1904, as a brand-new edifice adjacent to an existing ruin. But from the postcard photographer's distance, it was impossible to tell—the newness is only evident on closer inspection.

And so it was that, in April 2011, I took the train to Vienna and from there to the Lungau region, situated on a large plateau to the south of Salzburg, bounded by the Tauern mountain ranges. The Szapáry family probably made the same journey often, as the mountains permit no direct train connection to Salzburg. There's only a bus, which takes three hours and makes four trips daily.

The landscape was like something I'd only ever seen in model train sets, and the houses looked like the miniature versions I had so fondly assembled as a child. Scenes from *The Sound of Music* came to mind. Further off to the north, I could imagine the forests and lakes that had inspired Bruckner and Mahler to use birdsong and cowbells in their symphonies at the Wiener Musikverein at the turn of the twentieth century—works familiar-sounding, yet otherworldly.

The first thing I noticed on arriving at Finstergrün was a small exhibition dedicated to Margarethe (Margit) Szapáry, who had lived there with her daughter Jolanta. They pronounce her surname there with an Austrian accent, 'cha-PAH-ry', correcting my 'za-pah-REE'—even though, being a Hungarian name, officially it should be 'SA-paa-ry'. Already this story was getting complicated.

It was clear from the exhibition that Margit Szapáry was of great importance to the local region, where she is referred to as the 'Countess of Lungau'. Her world had been completely recreated: sweet, fairytale-like, and even including a model railway. Christian Blinzer, the young philosopher who had curated the exhibition, proudly showed me around and gave me a copy of the catalogue, which I leafed through once back at my hotel.[1] The booklet was meticulously produced, and was mostly about Margit Szapáry as benefactor of the Lungau region. (Blinzer, who grew up in Lungau, would later write his Master's thesis on her, in Linz.) While browsing, I came across a section on the fate of Finstergrün's interior furnishings, which had been sold in their entirety at a Munich auction house in 1941.[2] Blinzer's investigation had revealed that the auction was held under pressure from Hermann Göring, the right-hand man of Adolf Hitler.

It was then that I realised tracing the providence of my Gucci suitcase might give me something more than a good story to tell over dinner, showing off my cocktail dresses, lace and fur collars at Dutch parties, and a pleasant sojourn in Austria. What had happened to the Szapáry family to bring this suitcase all the way to Amsterdam? And why had the contents of their castle been sold off in one fell swoop? Who was this 'Countess of Lungau' with a Hungarian name who had managed to endear herself to so many in a far-off corner of Austria? I felt as though I had opened the door of a Germanic *Wunderkammer*—a whole cabinet of curiosities.

* * *

What makes a life story meaningful? If we arrange the highlights from birth to death, it quickly gives the appearance of unity, with a logical sequence of events from cradle to grave creating the illusion of a seamless history. But if one only has fragments from which a life must be reconstructed—as I did, with Margit Szapáry—then the broader historical context soon comes creeping in. It was like taking apart old jackets, and creating a new item of clothing from the usable pieces.

My investigation began with surprise: at the apparent ease with which objects can be discarded, large or small, that must once have meant something to somebody. Flea markets, thrift stores and auctions are gold mines in this respect. The past often seems all-too-easily exchanged for modern commodities of the present. The effect can sometimes be seen in old houses filled with modern furniture—a lack of historicity equally on display whenever estate agents are advertising another soulless block of flats. In these instances, something seems to have been sacrificed that was already in such short supply: the acknowledgement of our forebears, and of the fact that we are a part of a history—the history of our homes, of the place where our homes are built, and of all those who have lived there before us. We are only here temporarily. We will disappear—but our homes remain. For the years of our lives there, homes compel us to listen to them—and then to add our history to them, remain-

SECRETS OF A SUITCASE

ing 'of our time'. The present, after all, is where we must live. And it should be possible to do so in any home, big or small, provided it was built with care.

After I bought the Gucci suitcase and discovered the albums, dresses, furs and lace collection inside, my surprise only grew when I found out that it was an aristocratic family who had cleared out like this. Because if there is one social group that cherishes its history, it's the nobility. Besides their name, their past is often all that remains of their former grandeur.[3]

Anybody who has ever cleared out the home of someone who has passed away, especially a parent or grandparent, knows how emotional it can be to have the trappings of an entire life—clothing, furniture, books—heaved into a thrift-store truck because nobody wants them. After the children and grandchildren have chosen their keepsakes, a watch or a dining set, what's left—some papers and photo albums—will fit easily into a box and collect dust in the attic. Look, that was Dad's life—or Mum's.

What did the Szapárys do with their lives? Were they 'of their time'? Or did they cling to the past? Were they victims of fate? Did they manage to remain the 'agents of their lives', or did they become 'circumstantial collaborators', as the philosopher Peter Sloterdijk put it?[4] Outside of their suitcases, what baggage of ideals had Margit and Jolanta carried with them, and how had they rearranged them time and again in new surroundings?

These were my main questions when I decided to finally take a proper look at the Sotheby's boxes in my attic.

PALATIAL HOMES

The Gucci suitcase drew me into the nineteenth-century Central European empire of the Habsburgs, with its myriad aristocratic families. These days, places like the former East Germany, Hungary, Czechia, Slovakia and Poland are no longer associated with splendour. But they are where the richest of the rich once lived: in Silesia, where a modern aristocracy ran coal mines and furnaces. They developed the region, supervised the judiciary, cared for the poor and the sick, and built schools. But today we can best feel a sense of their exceptional social status through the palatial homes they were able to build, thanks to their amassed fortunes.

My journey into the past began in one such luxurious mansion: Villa Rosalia in Abbazia, a seaside resort on the Adriatic Sea now known as Opatija. Today it lies in Croatia, but it was then part of Hungary. At the turn of the twentieth century, the European nobility would visit Abbazia to seek rest and treatment for all kinds of ailments. Abbazia is close to the port town of Fiume (now Rijeka), the Habsburgs' only open connection to the sea at that time. From there, it was a simple matter to reach Venice by boat. This was Austro-Hungarian territory, until the First World War redrew all the borders.

As the twentieth century began, however, very few yet suspected what was to come—except perhaps for the unfortunate Crown Prince Rudolf, son of Elisabeth (Sisi) and Franz Joseph I, who were both queen and king of Hungary and empress and emperor of Austria, under the Habsburg dual monarchy.[1] But in 1900, Rudolf had already been dead for ten years. Rudolf had been destined to become emperor, but his sympathy for French liberalism was seen as too dangerous by his father and his entourage. They had held him at arm's length from any real power, forcing him to resort to anonymous

SECRETS OF A SUITCASE

articles in the Viennese press. His tenuous position as heir to the throne, combined with a suspected case of advanced syphilis, led to his suicide at the age of just thirty. Before that, he had been a frequent visitor to Abbazia.[2]

There must have been a steady stream of royal dignitaries who travelled there by carriage, boat or train. Around 1900, Abbazia was at the height of its fame, and large investments were being made in the construction of new villas to accommodate the prestigious guests. Casinos, pavilions and clinics added to the wellness and entertainment options for visitors. It was in these beautiful, fragrant, warm and revitalising surroundings that our two protagonists first met: the 29-year-old Silesian Countess Margarethe Henckel von Donnersmarck, and Count Sándor Szapáry de Murazombath, Széchysziget and Szapar, aged 42. They were both very much at home in the region, with familial connections nearby. Sándor's great uncle had ruled the roost as governor in Fiume for some time, while Margarethe's grandmother owned three villas in Abbazia, including Villa Rosalia, where she stayed in the spring.

In 1900, the very rich still enjoyed the exclusive privilege of gathering on picturesque coasts with pleasant climates, where they could escape their usual, more oppressive surroundings and recover from a variety of ills or affairs of the heart. Freud had only just started his therapeutic work in Vienna, where one could lie on a sofa in his office and finally get to the bottom of all those dreams about trains racing through tunnels. Abbazia still only offered baths in hot, cold or salt water. But, after soaking, one could indulge in sweet treats, which were available from the new patisserie (*Konditorei*) recently opened by culinary artist Émile Gerbeaud. The patisserie must have been a regular haunt of Sándor Szapáry, who was addicted to chocolate. For evening excitement there was the casino, another popular form of entertainment in those days.

Precisely where the pair met is unknown. Unmarried wealthy countesses did not simply wander about unescorted in 1900. Sándor Szapáry likely either presented himself to Margarethe's family, or arranged an introduction. They probably made a deeper acquaintance later while promenading on the boulevard. Perhaps they even met Lenin, who stayed there under the alias 'Dr Jerzenkiyevits' in order

PALATIAL HOMES

to observe the habits and customs of his class enemy from close by. From an open window, the young couple perhaps heard the sounds of Mahler composing his fourth symphony over in Villa Jeanette (the final movement of which is to be performed 'very comfortably').

If they had stayed a while longer, they might even have bumped into James Joyce on one of their strolls; the writer had travelled with his beloved Nora to Trieste, on the other side of the small Istrian peninsula—the very limits of civilized Europe—to escape the confines of Dublin, only to recreate them afterwards in *Ulysses*. This version of events is rather improbable, however, in a time when strict distance was always maintained between the strata of society: one did not simply fraternise with an English teacher playing house with his girlfriend, with whom he had already sired several illegitimate children. By contrast, the main purpose of Margarethe and Sándor's connection was most likely the production of lawful heirs.

In 1900, the noble house of Henckel von Donnersmarck was many times wealthier than the Szapárys, and especially compared with the branch to which Sándor belonged. Margarethe's family tree can be traced back to the 1400s, and even, according to the literature, has roots in my own homeland, the Netherlands.[3] Early in the fifteenth century, after a flood of the river delta that would later constitute most of the country, three enterprising brothers left the town of Kalkar (in the province of Gelderland) for Hungary, where much land still lay fallow after attacks by the Mongols. The Von Kell brothers—later Hen Kell—settled in Donnersmarck, the capital of Szepes county. Their knowledge of water management, acquired in the Gelderland river region, was invaluable in their new marshy home, and in 1417 their skills and craftsmanship earned them a place among the nobility. Their motto became *Memento vivere*, 'Remember to live'. This, along with the centuries-old aristocratic adage *noblesse oblige*, set the house in good stead for a promising future.

From then on, the family's prosperity grew with each successive generation. It is amazing what sufficient food, warmth, clothing, healthcare and education can do to turn even a house of economic

13

climbers into aristocratic lords and ladies. Especially if they manage to keep a solid roof over their heads.

The first to lay such a foundation was Lazarus I Henckel von Donnersmarck, who became the Habsburg emperor Rudolf II's 'banker' in the late-sixteenth century.[4] In other words, the emperor borrowed large sums from Lazarus, and paid very little of it back. Legal action ensued, after which the family received compensation in the form of a castle, Neudeck, as well as some large forested regions in Silesia surrounding the city of Beuthen (now Bytom), including the right to mine any natural resources contained therein.

In the eighteenth century, religious disagreements caused the Henckel von Donnersmarck family to split into two branches, one Catholic and one Protestant, that were later referred to as 'Neudeck' (Lutheran Protestant) and 'Beuthen' (Catholic).[5] The Neudeck branch adopted its own powerful new motto, one it would need later on when it was threatened with a lack of heirs: *Vivit, non est mortuus* ('He lives, he is not dead'). Each of the two branches brought forth a visionary entrepreneur. On the Protestant side was Guido (1830–1916), who became highly influential in nineteenth-century Germany as a landowner, pioneering industrialist and diplomat. His wealth and business acumen allowed him to develop a positive relationship with his great-nephew Otto von Bismarck and Emperor Wilhelm I, and later with Wilhelm II.[6] On the Catholic side was Hugo I (1811–90), Margarethe's grandfather.

The surname Henckel von Donnersmarck is best known today as that of the Oscar-winning director of *Das Leben der Anderen* (*The Lives of Others*). And while movie critics often make fun of Florian Henckel von Donnersmarck's many names, they are no mere noble affectation: they indicate which branch of the family he is from. He and Margarethe share a common ancestor, Hugo I. Hugo's eldest son, Hugo II, was Margarethe's father; he had two brothers, who also produced descendants. They all continued to reap what the exceptional talents of Hugo I had sown, as one of the first enterprising aristocratic landowners in Silesia and one of the founders of the first industrial revolution in Germany.

PALATIAL HOMES

In 1832, as the only son and heir, Hugo I inherited all of his father's possessions in Beuthen. He would go on to work in agriculture, livestock breeding and heavy industry.[7] In the early 1840s, he built the first modern blast-furnace for the mines on his property, which he named Laurahütte after his wife (*Hütte* is German for 'metalworks'). It seemed quite common for this first generation of industrial nobles to name their smoke-spewing enterprises after their beloved wives, daughters or grandchildren, such as Valeska or Sophia. In 1846, on the birth of his son Hugo, he also inherited all of the older possessions of the Henckel von Donnersmarcks in Austria, including Wolfsberg Castle in Carinthia. In 1872, after the death of his first wife, he built a residential palace for his second wife (another Laura), on Vienna's Ringstrasse.

He could afford it. The previous year he had sold his blast-furnaces for a tidy speculative profit of six million Thalers (around £140 million at the time of writing)[8] to one of the first joint-stock companies in Germany, Vereinigte Königs- und Laurahütte AG.[9]

Sándor Szapáry's grandfather was not as well-off as Margarethe's. At the time of their marriage, Sándor was the commander of Emperor Franz Joseph's Hungarian horse guard. The role was predominantly ceremonial: his most important duty was to sit upright on horseback in gala uniform during imperial parades in Vienna. Each of his uniforms was more splendid than the last, adorned with golden tassels and furs, as can be seen in the few surviving photographs of him. The counts of Szapáry certainly did belong to the old Hungarian nobility, with a family tree going back even further than Margarethe's. Extensive research was carried out in the 2010s by distant relatives living in France, Spain and Australia, and many in the United States. These descendants include presidents, ministers, ambassadors, famed economists, tennis players and ski champions. In the British royal household, the controversial[10] Princess Michael of Kent is a Szapáry on her mother's side. The mother of this 'princess' shortened her own name to 'Szapar' when she opened a beauty parlour in Sydney, Australia.

With over one hundred living relations, the Szapáry name will not die out anytime soon. But the same cannot be said of the noble *house* of Szapáry—for that to remain intact, suitable marriages must be made between partners of equal standing. And it is in this respect that Sándor's branch of the family harboured some concern around the turn of the twentieth century. Sándor's father Béla had died in 1870, and his mother Gabrielle and sister Ilona were living peacefully—and piously—in Pressburg, which later became Hungarian Poszony but is now Bratislava, capital of Slovakia. His unmarried brother Péter was employed by the Viennese embassy in Paris, but spent most of his time at the horse races in Longchamp. Sándor himself lived in Vienna, where the Jockey Club was his home base, as it was for many other bachelors of high social standing. Vienna was teeming with counts, barons and princes of the Habsburg dual monarchy in search of prestigious appointments. The most sought-after post was an ambassadorship in one of the European capitals, a position for which Sándor unfortunately did not qualify.

We don't know whether Sándor danced an elegant Viennese waltz, which was the principal prerequisite for such a post. It is not a talent one immediately suspects of him, given the tall, white-fur-lined boots he wears in his engagement photograph, part of his gala uniform. One also needed money, since Austro-Hungarian ambassadors were expected to pay their own way, including the maintenance of a royal household and hosting the necessary receptions.[11] The sums required were far from trivial, and well beyond Sándor's means.

Sándor's mother, the beautiful widow Gabrielle Atzél von Borosjenö, must have been quite worried that her two sons had remained unmarried for so long. They simply did not possess the fortune for making an 'equal' match. She was overjoyed when her Sándor was engaged to Margarethe Henckel von Donnersmarck in the spring of 1900. She immediately presented herself to Margarethe as *deine Mutter* ('your mother') in her first letters to her daughter-in-law,[12] letters that she would continue to write almost every other day. She also proved to be quite a well-read correspondent, citing Rousseau in her first letter in almost pristine French: *Ce qu'il y a de meilleur dans le coeur de l'homme, n'on sait jamais* ('What is best in the hearts of men, [one] will never know'). It was an entreaty to continually look for the 'best' in the heart of her dear son.

Whatever may have been in Sándor's heart, it was certainly full of plans and ideals for Margarethe to discover, which must have piqued her enthusiasm in Abbazia enough to convince her to marry

PALATIAL HOMES

him. He will have told her about his purchase of a hunting lodge in Lungau the year before, a mediaeval castle. He had plans to rebuild it and live there for most of the year, a prospect that must have held some appeal for Margarethe.

Margarethe and Sándor's decision to choose a remote home in nature as their principal residence was unorthodox. Once married, they might easily have gone to live close to their family on some estate or other, or moved into an apartment within the Ringstrasse palace built by Margarethe's grandfather Hugo I. Moving in with family would actually have been quite unremarkable—indeed, it was the norm for almost all aristocratic couples in the Habsburg empire, unless the husband was head of a noble household.

The influx of new wealth in Vienna in 1900 also meant that there was plenty to do in the city: daily receptions in the 'best' houses, and a wide range of concerts, plays and other artistic entertainments. Before even Paris had gained its reputation as a cosmopolitan hub, Vienna was the first truly European city,[13] with many nationalities drawn there over the preceding decades. From Wittgenstein and Freud to Loos and Mahler, the Austrian capital was the home of artists, authors and intellectuals who had made far more progress than their contemporaries in the rest of Europe, in areas as diverse as economics, medicine and philosophy. In the early twentieth century, they convened in the city's many coffee houses, where they honed their wits on one another and discussed commentaries on the façade of existence by authors such as Karl Kraus or Arthur Schnitzler.

They must have been a truly romantic pair, Sándor and Margarethe, to eschew Vienna's many charms for one of Austria's most remote regions. Immediately after their wedding, held on 18 July 1900 at Margarethe's parents' estate in the Silesian town of Krowiarki, they left straight away for Finstergrün, the castle that Sándor had purchased in the Lungau. There, nestled up on the plateau with a view of the surrounding mountains, was where they were to ensure the arrival of new Szapárys.

Lungau remains a remote region to this day. It is a UNESCO heritage site, protected not only for its natural environment, but also because of the local culture, still carefully preserved by the residents. The prettiest dirndls and most elaborate lederhosen are still worn during their many celebrations; they sing beautifully, and their marching bands can be heard for many miles. But that is more or less where the entertainments end. For a chic après-ski, one must travel hundreds of kilometres westward to the Lech region, which is also far more accessible by car, train, or plane.

According to the proud websites of various tourist offices, the contemporary Lungau does seem to be very mountain bike–friendly (including the electric variety). Paragliding is another option, along with a variety of snow sports, of which there is still an abundance in winter. There is no longer a need to travel there by sled, wrapped up in a knee-length fur coat, as was the case a hundred years ago— that is, if you visited Lungau in the winter at all, being willing to endure the eleven-hour journey from Salzburg via a mountain pass. Nowadays, the unadulterated countryside and panoramic vistas can be enjoyed on the road, from the comfort of one's bicycle. Contemporary Lungauers now focus on ecotourism, using local wood supplies to build small, environmentally friendly and self-sufficient holiday homes for climate-conscious holidaymakers.

During my archival research in Salzburg in 2019, I asked my host about the region. 'Hmm, Lungau,' she said thoughtfully, momentarily distracted from her final gestures of hospitality towards the Booking.com review I would complete on the way home. 'You pass through it on your way to Italy. But otherwise it's rather out of the way, and a little backward too. Economically especially. Lately I think they've been doing a little better, since the farmers have started getting into organic products, which are becoming popular. But yeah, otherwise, what can I say? It has the highest suicide rate in all of Austria.' Such a dramatic statement seemed completely alien on the lips of this cheerful blonde Salzburger, for whom life's greatest pleasure seemed to be feeding tourists sponge cake and soft-boiled eggs. She furrowed her brow. 'Why is that?' I hastened to ask, hoping to finish quickly with the topic and to see her cheerfulness return.

'Perhaps they see their lives as pointless, stuck there in a dead-end valley behind the Tauern mountains,' she said. 'Plus there's nowhere to go. The roads, the railways, other forms of transportation and facilities, they're all way behind. I wouldn't want to live there either. Nice place to visit, sure, but I can never wait to get back to Salzburg.'

In 1900, the residents were even more isolated than they are today. Vienna was for living—Lungau was for hunting.

FINSTERGRÜN

Near Ramingstein, on the narrow road to Tamsweg that winds along the Mur river (and where, if you really put your foot to the floor, you can reach Salzburg on the motorway within ninety minutes), look to the left and you will see Finstergrün Castle perched high atop a bluff, nestled among the pine trees like a bird's nest. It promises a marvellous view across the mountains, the kind of environment that made up three-quarters of nineteenth-century Europe, from northern Italy to Finland. It is a place fit for fairy tales, and when the sun is out, the scenes would be right at home on a kitchen calendar.

But Finstergrün—which means 'dark green' in German—also carries a mysterious connotation. *Finster* does not merely mean 'dark' in a visual sense, but also imparts a sombre tone, which the tall pine trees do tend to evoke, especially during autumn rain, or when everything lies snow-covered beneath grey skies. Then the stories one imagines are not about life's appearances, but about the sinister reality behind the façade. Things are often *finster* in Lungau.

'Finstergrün' is not the kind of name one invents for one's first home. It dates back to the seventeenth century, when it was used both to rename the thirteenth-century Fort Ramingstein, and in descriptions in old documents. *Finster* could also be a reference to the gloomy cave crypts by the ruins of the old fort.[1]

Sándor bought the castle ruins in 1899, a decision that represented a turning point in his life. He wasn't just looking for hunting accommodations: rather, he seemed to want a whole new beginning for the house of Szapáry in Austria, and for himself as a knight, a title that he adopted soon after acquiring the property. He also commissioned a portrait of himself on horseback wearing a white cape and a feather in his hat, which hangs to this day in the great hall of

Finstergrün. It was time for a son, a new heir to the Szapáry name. Sándor was of the right age—now all he needed was a wife, and one of means.

Sándor was a hunter. The Hungarian nobility had been visiting Lungau for decades to hunt large game which, due to the remote location, was free to reproduce almost undisturbed. Known as *Hochjagd* (the 'high hunt'), this privilege was reserved for the aristocracy and forbidden among the common folk. If you could take down a bear and display its hide as a rug before your open fireplace, or stuff an entire family of bears (complete with cubs) as a decoration for your entrance hall, then you could call yourself a successful hunter. Up until the First World War, the hunt was an exclusive pastime comparable to the later status and benefits of golfing at 'members-only' clubs. In the 1890s, Sándor went hunting regularly with Hans Wilczek, who at the time was one of the most famous men in Austria.

With an age difference of over twenty years, the friendship between Sándor and Wilczek must have resembled a father–son relationship. Sándor, whose father had died young, probably looked up to Wilczek—and not only because he was exceptionally tall and athletic. (He seldom walked downstairs, according to his autobiography, preferring to leap out of a first-floor window.) He was the scion of an old family with an enormous Silesian fortune. But all his fame was self-earned, through his dangerous expeditions to the North Pole and the African hinterlands. Wilczek was one of the few aristocrats who made a genuine contribution to the cultural life of Austria.[2] He was a colourful figure, headstrong and, with Emperor Franz Joseph himself, an exception at the Viennese court, in that he was no antisemite.[3]

Wilczek was an explorer, a scientist and a passionate hunter. Reading through the memoirs he compiled for his grandchildren, what stands out is his boundless energy. Fully one quarter of the text is dedicated to hunting parties he took part in, and he was especially proud of the bear he once had in his sights and shot down. Bears were one of the most dangerous wild animals in Europe at that time and, by his own account, Wilczek's 'rolled like a kraut' down the snowy hillside. He had himself photographed beside it, and later hung up the hide in the old armoury of his castle as proof of his

FINSTERGRÜN

manly prowess. His memoirs wisely omit the fact that he also enjoyed hunting women, though it was common knowledge in Vienna that he had fathered several children with his mistresses.[4]

Unusually for his time, Wilczek began studying archaeology, art history and physics at a young age. He also married young, at the age of twenty-one. But from that moment on, he cannot have spent much time at home, as he travelled to Russia and Africa, served as a volunteer soldier in the Austro-Prussian War of 1866, and in 1872 took part in the first Austro-Hungarian expeditions to the North Pole, which he financed personally. This is why there is an archipelago called Frans Joseph Land to the north of Svalbard, and an island named after Wilczek himself in the northern Arctic. After his return in 1874—with a lavish reception to honour his two years of sacrifice in the icy polar regions—he became president of the Austrian Geographic Society, where he campaigned for permanent weather stations at the North Pole. From 1874 to 1906, however, his main preoccupation was the restoration and furnishing of his monumental family estate near Vienna, Kreuzenstein Castle (after which he promptly resumed his Arctic travels). The castle became an attraction for visitors from both Austria and abroad, where Wilczek often gave tours to the emperor's distinguished guests. He also arranged good marriages for his daughters, who were paired with a Kinsky, a Palffy and a Thurn und Taxis—all ancient, reliable and noble Habsburg families. He himself owned a home on Vienna's prestigious Herrengasse. He knew everybody, and everybody knew him.

As if all of that weren't enough, Wilczek was also the Lord of Moosham, a castle in Lungau situated only a few kilometres from Finstergrün. His story of how he had acquired Moosham is characteristic of the way he lived: grand. In 1886, his travels took him past the dilapidated castle. A café had been set up there by the local farmers, where he spotted a late-Gothic pinewood furniture set.[5] He immediately offered the farmers 500 Austrian guilders for it, because no matter where he was or what he was doing, his mind was constantly occupied with furnishing and decorating Kreuzenstein. The farmers, who had taken ownership of the Moosham ruins in order to make use of the arable lands, were unwilling to part with the items, attached as they were to the castle's history. But Wilczek

23

seems to have made an impression nonetheless: several months later, in Vienna, he received a letter from the farmers offering him the entire castle—albeit without the surrounding land—for the reasonable sum of 1,500 Austrian guilders (20,000 Euros at the time of writing).[6]

Wilczek had fallen for the castle's charms and, as a surprise for his family, he decided to set it up as a country home. The fact that Moosham had played host to witch trials in the past can only have added to the heavy air of mysticism surrounding the restored ruins in the minds of the family, who were otherwise living comfortably at Kreuzenstein, close to the capital. They would often visit in summer.[7]

Wilczek must have shown Moosham to Szapáry in the late 1890s, as it was then that Wilczek made note of the Hungarian's desire to own a similar property. Exactly how the two men met is unknown, but Szapáry describes Wilczek in his memoirs separately as 'my friend, who sadly died young', along with many others (including Crown Prince Rudolf), most of whom turned out to be hunting companions. Because Lungau was well-known as a hunting ground for the Hungarian nobility, they likely shared a common passion. Szapáry's decision to make his main home in the region throughout the year was also welcomed by the local peasantry, as aristocrats could bring prosperity to the area if they were based there.[8]

Wilczek may have loved hunting as a pastime, but for Hungarians like Sándor, the hunt was much more than a hobby. One of the most famous novels of Hungarian literature, *Embers* by Sándor Márai (1942), describes the hunt's potential for erotic symbolism. The protagonist, a general, suspects his friend of having seduced his wife and is about to shoot him down during a hunting party when he says: 'Hunting is a passion, as is everything associated with blood and death.' This line echoes another Hungarian, Felix Salten,[9] who never attained the same level of fame as his own hunting tale: *Bambi, a Life in the Woods*.[10] In the hands of Walt Disney, who laid down a thousand dollars for the film rights in 1939, what had started as a parable about human society became a sanitised children's story. Salten, too, had wished to convey a message about the sensuality of both humans and animals, and their shared indifference to bloodlust. He found the romanticisation of nature, which amassed many devotees in his time, to be predominantly a sign of ignorance.

FINSTERGRÜN

Perhaps Sándor had spent long enough as a bachelor enjoying the hunt. He married Margarethe at the age of forty-two, at a time when most men married in their late twenties. He likely had a mistress before that, perhaps a ballet dancer from the opera, as did almost all unmarried Viennese bachelors of some social standing.[11] Vienna was a bustling city at the time, its cafés, bars and restaurants staying open all night. The homes of the noble families were hubs of intense social activity. There was always some charitable cause or other for which a lavish *tableau vivant* or a masked ball simply had to be organised. The Habsburg nobility did not work hard; mostly they played hard, entertaining themselves and each other. Via an extended network of family relations, they were part of a large-scale European aristocracy, sharing more common background with its members in other kingdoms than with their own countrymen. Customarily they did not have real jobs, only honorary military or diplomatic posts. And though these positions did require entrance examinations, they could easily be circumvented by the Habsburg nobles, many of whom had received poor educations from private tutors. This is often seen as one explanation for the lack of political insight that led Austria-Hungary into the First World War, and the rapid collapse of the empire after its defeat.[12] The Habsburg aristocracy were more preoccupied—when they were occupied at all—with agriculture on their own estates. And with their pastimes, such as hunting.

Hunting was also part of the fixed social calendar, the cycle of which entailed certain rituals that determined one's place within the elite. Around four or five large hunts took place per year (depending on the season, and whether the hunt was for partridge, pheasant, deer, hare, large game or birds of prey). These required long advance preparations by beaters, to ensure enough game for a large company to shoot at. There had to be adequate food and drink available throughout, as well as sufficient opportunity to discuss state matters and business affairs in private. The hunt was also a suitable time to arrange marriages for children, relatives and acquaintances. In short, hunting parties were a hive of social activity, with a little target practice thrown in for good measure. They could easily occupy a third of one's year. Exceptional personal qualities (such as discipline) were necesssary to achieve political or business success alongside them. The upper echelons of the Habsburg monarchy may have lacked education, but they certainly had no shortage of social diversions.[13]

Wilczek's memoirs reveal that he and Szapáry had already inspected mediaeval castle ruins in the Lungau region in 1898. The advent of a privately financed train line in 1894—the Murtalbahn, which ran from Stiermarken, with a connection to Vienna[14]—undoubtedly increased the castle's appeal. Making the regular journey to Lungau by horse and carriage would have been quite arduous.

According to his memoirs, it was also Wilczek who told Szapáry about Finstergrün, though accessibility and habitability were an issue, and some extensions would be necessary to make the castle a pleasant home. That required money, and Wilczek implies that he aided Szapáry a little with the initial purchase of the ruin.[15] Thankfully, the wealthy Margarethe Henckel von Donnersmarck crossed Szapáry's path in 1900, after which the renovations were 'no longer a problem', as Wilczek dryly notes. It seems that Wilczek was eager to have some nice neighbours.

On the day of their marriage, 18 July 1900, Margarethe and Sándor posed for a photograph with their entire family in front of Krowiarki Palace, Margarethe's parents' estate in Silesia. Wilczek, who was Sándor's witness, towers above all the other guests. There can be no doubt as to the affluence of the assembled party: the wedding banquet featured turbot, lobster and even pineapples, accompanied by glasses of Montrachet, an expensive white French Bourgogne from 1881. As a wedding gift, the estate's miners presented Margarethe with an opulent photo book of the palace where she'd grown up in Siemianowicz, located much nearer to her grandfather's mines and blast-furnaces. The album includes not only photographs of the palace, but also of an enormous, heated greenhouse. That explains the pineapples.[16]

Margarethe and Sándor Szapáry left for Lungau almost immediately. They travelled south-west from Krowiarki via Pressburg, Vienna and the Henckel von Donnersmarcks' old family home in Carinthia, Wolfsberg Castle. Their itinerary can be reconstructed by the postcards and letters Margarethe sent back to her mother. It would seem that she hadn't seen Finstergrün at all between her engagement in May and her marriage in July, so she had a surprise in store. Sándor had wasted no time after the engagement, and had made a start on the restorations straight away.

She writes excitedly about the journey. Wilczek's name is mentioned frequently, and it is clear that he travelled with them on and off. They also paid several family visits en route. After arriving at Finstergrün, Margarethe notes in a letter to her mother only that the work is progressing 'diligently'.[17] She makes no further mention of the castle where she was to live for so long, but writes at length about the magnificent landscape. She was enraptured by a walk they took through the mountains, but even more so by Moosham, where Wilczek gave her a tour. His castle was already fully furnished, and during the renovations at Finstergrün she would often stay at her 'dear' Moosham, as she calls it in the letters to her mother.

Margarethe and Sándor's journey to Lungau hardly seems like the typical honeymoon undertaken by wealthy couples in that period, who would travel to Venice, Rome or—more exotically—Egypt. But Sándor and Margit limited themselves to hotels close to Finstergrün, in Bad Ischl and Salzburg. In early September, when autumn set in, they travelled to Pressburg, where they stayed in a 'winter house' on the exclusive Franziskanerplatz. Margarethe asked her mother to send letters to that address, but by late September they were already back in Lungau, according to her correspondence, as it was almost time for the deer hunt, and the renovations at Finstergrün were still in full swing.

There was much to be done. First of all, an adequate road was needed to facilitate delivery of construction materials. A water supply was also indispensable. Sándor's vision was to build a brand-new, but otherwise authentic, mediaeval castle beside the ruins of the old fort. In practical terms, this meant no new-fangled facilities such as gas or electric lights, despite the fact that the arrival of electricity had been enthusiastically proclaimed by Crown Prince Rudolf himself twenty years earlier, at the Third International Electrical Exhibition in Vienna (1883). Prince Rudolf had promised the captive audience a 'sea of light' in Vienna, which was interpreted as the dawn of a new age. Many found it *too* revolutionary (in Berlin, Kaiser Wilhelm I and his chancellor Bismarck were so suspicious that they started viewing the liberally minded Prince Rudolf as a threat to their own ambitions in Central Europe). As for Sándor, he had no intention of introducing such comforts to Finstergrün. The castle was to be illuminated with candles and oil lamps, and heated by wood stoves. It was a bold choice for a man whose wife had grown up surrounded by coal mines.

Wilczek invited the newlyweds to stay at Moosham for an extended period, so that they could oversee the construction at Finstergrün from close by.

Since the job was effectively to design a new castle, the couple engaged the services of a well-known architect. Money, after all, was no longer a problem. They chose Ludwig Simon, who was awarded various high-profile jobs around the turn of the century by Franz Ferdinand, the nephew of Franz Joseph I, who had become the new crown prince after Rudolf's suicide in 1889. Simon would work on both Arstetten, Franz Ferdinand's private residence, and the restoration of Schloss Blühnbach, the crown prince's hunting lodge near Werfen (south of Salzburg).

Simon certainly took on no trivial assignments, so it is worthwhile taking a closer look at this other castle restoration project. Originally built by the archbishop of Salzburg,[18] for most of the nineteenth century Schloss Blühnbach was leased out to a noble hunting association. In the early twentieth century, with Simon's help, Franz Ferdinand converted it into a private hunting lodge, which involved hermetically sealing off the surrounding 14,000 hectares of alpine meadows and forest, arousing great discontent among the local population. At that time, Franz Ferdinand was known as one of the most skilful hunters of the European aristocracy, and he shot down over 300,000 animals during his lifetime.[19] Sometimes, much to the disgust of passionate hunters such as *Bambi* author Felix Salten, he had them rounded up and corralled for him, so that he could pick them off as though at a fairground attraction.[20] His eventual death—shot dead in Sarajevo, the shot that triggered the start of the First World War—was a rather fitting end to his life.

Now Ludwig Simon, the great architect of Blühnbach, had the honour of overseeing the (re)construction of nearby Finstergrün, at the behest of the newlyweds. Although the job certainly promised drudgery, he may have been inspired (or even encouraged?) by the imposing figure of Wilczek. For would an elite architect have accepted such a minor commission from an unimpressive count, even one who had just married an incredibly rich heiress, if he had not been persuaded to do so by an influential personage such as Wilczek? There are unfortunately no records to this effect, nor would any such arrangement have been documented if it did exist: it would have been discussed in passing, as was the custom, over a glass of champagne and a well-cooked steak—a repast to which Wilczek was quite partial, before, during and after his hunting parties. Wilczek may have introduced Sándor into his network; and who knows, he may even have had a hand in helping him obtain such a wealthy bride, which would have been cause for even greater discretion.

It is altogether possible that Wilczek had long since caught wind of the rich but unmarried Margarethe Henckel von Donnersmarck, during one of his hunting parties. He will certainly have known of the family, if only because of the annual horse race held in Vienna in honour of Margarethe's grandfather, who had owned a famous stud farm. The Count Hugo Henckel Memorial race was organised each year by the Vienna Jockey Club, of which both Wilczek and Sándor were members.[21] But even if there were back-room dealings, does it really matter? Margarethe Henckel von Donnersmarck can only have been happy with a Szapáry, a member of a respectable Hungarian family who wooed her in the spring of 1900 with his glorious plans. No woman approaching her thirties would otherwise have decided within two months to marry a man who intended to build a 'mediaeval' fort in a far-off corner of Austria.

As construction of Finstergrün progressed, Sándor and Margarethe travelled in search of unique furnishings for the castle interior. They stayed at Moosham with Wilczek; in their Pressburg city villa close to Sándor's family; near Margarethe's family in Silesia; and in Vienna with Margarethe's grandmother. In his memoirs, Wilczek notes with surprise how quickly, 'for such a young woman', Margarethe acquired the knowledge of art history necessary to appraise the value of antique furniture: 'I have never seen a woman who, despite minimal preparation, has demonstrated such great aptitude in matters of art and architecture. Everything passed through her hands, and she, who during her upbringing had understandably not concerned herself with matters of style or art history, quickly became a seasoned connoisseur.'[22]

Really, had not concerned herself? Wilczek's summation shows that he knew less about Margarethe's background than he thought, for the granddaughter of Hugo I Henckel von Donnersmarck was practically forced to learn about remarkable antique furniture while playing in her grandfather's stately homes. Some decades prior, Hugo I had carried out a spectacular Neo-Gothic renovation and refurbishment of Wolfsberg Castle in southern Austria.[23] The ins and outs of palace restoration were therefore not so alien to Margarethe. She was also the daughter of Hugo II, whose greatest social contribution seems to have been spending the fortune amassed by his father on the restoration and refurbishment of not one, but two estates within a ten-year period: Krowiarki and Brynek. These were no mere mediaeval ruins near remote Austrian villages, but small towns in and of themselves, right in the middle of prosperous Upper Silesia.

Hugo II was still preoccupied with the acquisition of Brynek when Margarethe married Sándor. He may have passed his enthusiasm on to his new son-in-law, who was busy building a castle of his own. Finstergrün may not have been as grandiose as Krowiarki or Brynek—all that remained standing when Sándor bought it was the old tower. But with assistance from the great Viennese architect Simon, and some tasteful interior design and decoration, it had the potential to become quite a gem.

The place remained a construction site for many years. But when Margarethe proudly wrote her mother a letter from 'Finstergrün' for the first time, on 23 February 1904, she must have felt as though she had finally arrived at her destination.

One month later, she was a widow.

A GOOD GIRL

At the Henckel von Donnersmarcks' Siemianowicz estate, the menu on Sunday 13 March 1887 was generous and hearty: potato soup, venison roast, spinach in a cream sauce with egg croquettes, the well-known Silesian specialty *Heringskartoffeln*—herring with cheese and oven-baked potatoes—and, for dessert, *Baba chaud aux abricots*, a warm cake marinated in rum and served with apricots. Margarethe Henckel von Donnersmarck, then seventeen years old, had written out the menu for her family in her finest handwriting. The most striking feature on the page was not the lettering, however, but the illustration framing it: a wild, rampant green vine, with leaves that seem to be reaching out towards the food like voracious tongues, and large, orchid-like flowers blossoming voluptuously in light blue and pink. Such vegetation was not to be found growing wild any-where in the gardens of Siemianowicz. Thankfully, there was a greenhouse—the one pictured in Margarethe's wedding album.

This menu, carefully preserved beside several others, forms the opening page to the *Memories of my Daughter Margarethe* by Wanda Henckel von Donnersmarck née von Gaschin von und zu Rosenberg (1837–1908). The four black, leather-bound volumes are conscien-tiously stored in the Salzburg Provincial Archive, along with several other important documents pertaining to the life of Margit Szapáry and her castle, Finstergrün. Within several minutes of submitting my request, these tomes were slowly trundling towards me on archival carts.

In the black-bound albums, Margarethe's mother Wanda had arranged cards and letters from her daughter that she kept from Margit's childhood until her own death in 1908. But the collection is certainly not complete, and it would seem that when, at the end of her life, she collated the four books (all at once, judging by the identical bindings and gold lettering), the dedicated mother care-

SECRETS OF A SUITCASE

fully curated their contents. Occasionally entire years are missing, and there are barely any records of some of the most important events in the life of a young woman, such as the dance cards from balls, or holiday souvenirs. Photographs, likewise, are absent. Most of the entries are mere correspondence, the kinds of messages that modern mothers and daughters exchange through messaging apps, along the lines: 'How are things with you? Everything fine here.' But it is striking to see them here carefully written out, and often with a kind of stiff mother–daughter formality.

Margarethe consistently writes the phrases 'My dear, kind mother' and 'your Margarethe' and, often, 'forgive me if this letter disturbs you'. Wanda must have been a dominant woman and Margit a submissive daughter, going by the evidently well-known Silesian saying about the 'golden finger' of Wanda Henckel von Donnersmarck, who had lost her right ring finger when a hunting rifle exploded in her hand: 'When Countess Henckel taps the table with her finger, all Silesia trembles.' The cards also reveal much fondness, however, and a great mutual concern for one another's health.

Margarethe regularly sent open postal cards, which at the time were a rather modern means of communication, not yet in wide use. These she alternated with ordinary letters. After her marriage, she would occasionally add a picture postcard, containing photographic images of the cities she visited. That, too, was a new method of correspondence. At the ages of thirteen and fourteen, she had kept her mother painfully up-to-date on the state of her health ('Madame influenza came to visit again') and about her excursions with her French governess. She constantly expressed her good wishes for her mother's health.

Usually, the letters came from Siemianowicz, where Margarethe grew up and received her private tuition. Exactly where her mother was during those times is not always clear, but because much of their correspondence dates from the months of July and August, she had most likely fled the inland Silesian heat for cooler climes. Several of the cards were sent to a hotel in Oostende (Belgium). Wanda went regularly in search of treatment for minor physical 'complaints' that her daughter mentions, without ever naming them explicitly.

Aside from the elaborate Sunday menu, Wanda's 'Memories' include nothing from the years 1884–93, which may have to do with the early death of Margarethe's elder sister, who passed away in 1884

A GOOD GIRL

at age twenty. The letters resume in 1893, when Margarethe was twenty-three—this time, written from the renovated Krowiarki, Wanda's own ancestral estate. In her mother's absence, Margarethe kept her informed of any invitations and telegrams received, and whether there had been any guests. Essentially, she was managing her mother's personal correspondence. In the late 1890s, she herself visited a resort in the Harz region with her younger sister Irmgard, during which time she kept her mother up-to-date by sending girlish cards and letters, decorated with flowers. These were still written exclusively in German; only after she was married would she occasionally write to her mother in French or English.

The most striking aspect of this dutiful correspondence is what does *not* appear in writing. Margarethe never sends greetings to her father, her brothers Edgar and Hugo (the future Hugo III), or anyone else in her mother's company. She nearly always mentions her older, unmarried sister Sara, and occasionally her grandmother. Nor is there any reference to religious activities, which seems odd for somebody who was said to have become so pious later in life. There is also some doubt as to whether Margarethe was 'out' in society, as young women of her standing generally were, following their début. There are no descriptions of balls in her letters, let alone of any dancing in Vienna or, failing that, even at the old court capital of Breslau. Margarethe's engagement to Sándor must therefore have come as a bolt from the blue—at least, that is the impression given by the letter her brother Hugo wrote, in response to the telegram from Krowiarki breaking the news. Alongside a few brotherly quips ('you're to marry a man from Hungary, where they dance the Csardas...'), he wonders what is to be done about Margit's domestic responsibilities in Krowiarki, such as maintaining supplies, supervising the laundry, and her position in the women's circle. He also expresses some cynical concerns about the priest to officiate at the wedding, who will need to rehearse some banal formalities and wash and starch his white collar, and mentions 'our stoic ways'. To the rest of the family, the news of the betrothal was communicated summarily, again by telegram.

Margarethe Henckel von Donnersmarck married late by nineteenth-century standards, at twenty-nine. Based on the descriptions of her behaviour and appearance, she must have been a decisive and robust woman. In her wedding photograph, she stands half a head taller than her husband. She was most likely no gracious dancing partner or submissive young wife. She was, however, a dedicated daughter with a gift for bookkeeping, and shouldered much of the administration of her elderly mother's Silesian estates, unusual for a daughter in those times.

Financially, she herself was kept on a short leash, as was customary in rich families of the empire, in order to teach children the value of money. An 1890s ledger from the Salzburg archives shows that her allowance was indeed extremely small for an adult woman in the upper echelons of society. She recorded a sum of 20 marks per month (increasing to 25 marks in 1895), with which she bought herself slippers and simple toiletries such as honey balm. Otherwise, she spent most of her allowance on art supplies like methylated spirits and turpentine, because she enjoyed drawing and painting. These expenses were meticulously noted in columns labelled *Soll* (debit) and *Haben* (credit).[1] The cards sent to her mother show that she did make some art trips to Reims and Munich. So it wouldn't have been so strange for her to accompany her older sister Sara, who had a bad knee, to their grandmother's house in restorative Abbazia.[2] But did she have to get engaged once she got there?

The more we learn about the Henckel von Donnersmarck family, the more puzzling it seems that Margarethe met this Hungarian count with an illustrious name, a famous friend and a virtually empty bank account, and then decided to tie her fate to his. The question arises: how did nineteenth-century aristocratic German and Austrian women truly live? And how can we distance ourselves from the nostalgic depictions on British page and screen of the good, rich and noble life? Thankfully there is recent research on the subject. Monika Kubrova's study *On the Good Life* and Martina Winkelhofer's *The Lives of Noblewomen*, both in German,[3] give sufficient reason to suppose that things might have turned out very differently for Margarethe.

Kubrova's research draws on scores of memoirs by noblewomen, predominantly from Germany and Austria, to argue that German women in particular were more free than their counterparts in other lands of Europe's infamous, strictly gender-segregated

A GOOD GIRL

'spheres' of living. These Germanic 'ladies of the manor', or *Gutsherrin*, combined the roles of wife, mother, mistress of a household or estate, and roles as members of their community—which may have been the court, or else fulfilling a social role by caring for the local poor and sick. In Germany, which at that time was divided into countless smaller principalities, there was much for them to do. All noblewomen were prepared for such a life—firstly through childlike play, and later more seriously. 'Having family' was not merely a privilege, but also a responsibility. The status of every aristocratic woman obliged her not only to be active in these four spheres, but to excel in them, in the names of the families into which they were born and married. It was a way for them to garner greater prestige for the noble house, and thereby also for themselves and their children. In this system, for example, the wife of a diplomat would act in concert with her husband to make a success of 'their' embassy.

There were a few prerequisites: a woman was to have been successfully introduced into 'the world', she was to marry according to her station, and then, preferably, produce a male heir. This carefully constructed path to social success would be instantly ruined, however, if she were to divorce later. Divorce was only justified if 'the world' believed that a husband had acted extremely shamefully. Such was the case in the trials of the allegedly homosexual Liebenberg Circle, also known as the Eulenburg Affair, which implicated Kaiser Wilhelm II himself and others of his entourage—the 1907–9 courtmartials and civil trials of these leading men were set in motion by a betrayed wife.[4]

Being widowed, on the other hand, was perfectly honourable. A widow could remain active both as a hostess and in society, while also maintaining her position in the various large and small aristocratic circles in the towns and cities of Central Europe, contributing to the happiness of those around her. Of course, not all widows were so lucky, but the unlucky ones were mostly either rebellious or very talented women who were actively thwarted. A sad fate also awaited other women who found themselves in difficulty and lost their status due to poverty, their husbands' gambling debts or some other circumstance. But, by and large, Germany's structure of many principalities offered noblewomen far more opportunities to develop themselves and their talents than most women from lower classes, and even compared to many aristocratic women in the rest of Europe.

Margarethe had such talents, and must have been a precocious child. She received tuition at home, as was customary for children of the nobility at that time. But her education was not limited to languages and practical handicrafts, which was considered adequate for high-born girls well into the twentieth century. She received lessons in German grammar, French, English, mathematics, optics, physics, history, art history, mathematical geography, and drawing. Her arithmetic was outstanding, and she showed a particular interest in art history. The reports by her teachers were full of superlatives. Her talent for art can be seen not only in her floral illustrations, but also in the landscaping and interior design sketches she produced in and around Finstergrün immediately after her marriage, which served as templates for the tradespeople working on her home.

Aside from the tangible documentation of her education, Margarethe left no diaries or memoirs behind describing her early life in Siemianowicz or Krowiarki, just as she wrote little about her life after that time. One possibility is that a lot of material has been lost. Over the course of the twentieth century, much evidence in Central Europe disappeared due to the need for people to abandon their homes in great haste—homes that were then thoroughly ransacked and set alight. Thankfully, her ledgers tell us enough. For one thing, it is remarkable that she kept them herself.[5] In the nineteenth-century Habsburg empire, it was certainly not customary for women to take care of the finances.

We might employ cinematic techniques to reconstruct a life such as hers: we can zoom in, zoom out, include wide shots of the landscape, make 'travelling shots' alongside or through the house, and examine the lives of women with a comparable class status. And continue to ask questions, such as: how should we interpret Margarethe's social position at the time of her engagement? She seems never to have been presented officially to society, which was a commonplace ritual for children of the high nobility at the time. Mothers could enhance their own reputations through the 'coming out' of their daughters, putting their parenting skills on display.

Margarethe came from a very wealthy family, she was healthy, and had a good head on her shoulders. Yet nothing is known about any previous proposals of marriage that she had rejected. She must have travelled to Abbazia on her own initiative—with her ailing elder sister Sara in tow—to stay with their grandmother, and perhaps to see what would happen.

Resorts and spa towns often served as marriage markets in those days. Margarethe and Sara were able to lodge in one of their family's luxury villas, which offered ideal circumstances for meeting potential suitors. And that is precisely what happened for Margit, finally, at twenty-nine. Her own mother had married at nineteen, and her grandmother at twenty-three.[6] Why did Margarethe get engaged so late? Was it her sturdy, towering physique? To secure a good marriage, wives needed to satisfy a number of nineteenth-century beauty ideals, such as an hourglass figure and a narrow face. Or was she perhaps too headstrong, another quality that was looked down upon in the marriage market? Was her mother Wanda too overbearing? Did she not want Margarethe to marry at all, since she was using her as secretary and manager of the estate? Did she want to keep her daughter close to her, after the death of Margit's elder sister Eleonore? Or was Margit just not particularly fond of men?

Around 1899, Margarethe was photographed for an official portrait, wearing a ball gown and numerous family and other jewels, including a diamond tiara—a rather uncommon accessory for an unmarried woman.[7] It's interesting that this photograph resembles portraits from preceding centuries, in which candidates for betrothal were painted in a favourable light in order to impress other marriageable parties. Was this her own idea? Looking at the photo, she doesn't seem particularly happy about it. We cannot know. But what she most likely wanted was the full package: to be wife, mother, mistress and *Gutsherrin*; otherwise, her decision would not have been made so quickly after meeting Sándor in Abbazia in 1900. Her dowry alone will have made her at least somewhat attractive to suitors, though evidently there were none to be found in the vicinity of Krowiarki in Silesia, despite her family's sizeable fortune and noble pedigree.

One potential explanation is especially intriguing: that the Henckel von Donnersmarcks had a reputation problem. Not one of

SECRETS OF A SUITCASE

their own making, but one that had its source around 50 kilometres from Siemianowicz, near Tarnowskie Góry. More specifically, in a Versailles-like castle called Neues Neudeck.

A GOOD NAME

'Give my regards to uncle Guido,' wrote the fourteen-year-old Margarethe to her 'dear, kind mama'. The greeting was in fine handwriting, on one of her daily postal cards from the summer of 1884. It was sent from her grandparents' palace in Siemianowicz, where she was under the supervision of her governess and private tutors.[1] According to the address on the card, Margit's mother was residing in Neudeck at the time, with the other, better-known branch of the family—the Protestant Henckel von Donnersmarcks. 'Uncle Guido' Henckel von Donnersmarck (1830–1916), after the untimely drowning of his oldest brother in the river Oder, became the sole heir on the Lutheran side of the family. He had run the business empire with vigour from the age of eighteen, and lived elsewhere for many months of the year. In the mid-nineteenth century, his other home was Paris; from the late 1880s onwards, it would be Berlin. But several years before Margarethe wrote to her mother, he had retreated to Neues Neudeck, a palace built beside the far older, original Neudeck Castle.

This new Neudeck was a striking edifice nestled among the equally sizeable estates of the other Silesian magnates. It was designed by Hector Lefuel, an architect also responsible at that time for building the extensions to the Louvre in Paris. This new Neudeck was particularly opulent and befitted Guido Henckel von Donnersmarck: at the start of the twentieth century, he would become the fourth-richest person in Germany, beaten only by King Ludwig III of Bavaria; Bertha Krupp von Bohlen und Halbach, heiress to the German steel manufacturer of the same name; and Prince Albert of Thurn und Taxis, who had earned his fortune through a monopoly on German post offices and correspondence services.

While the wealth of Margarethe's Catholic side of the family depleted towards the end of the nineteenth century, the opposite was true of the Lutheran branch. Evidently, the two families were not business partners, despite living in such close proximity and maintaining clearly cordial, if occasional, relations. Each was busy developing the Silesian mining and steel industries in their own way. The Lutheran branch was far more involved with the application of chemical processes to improve the quality of cast iron and steel. Uncle Guido was interested in the newest advances in chemistry with importance for the industry, and would later be dubbed the 'phosphate king' of Europe. (Phosphate is a by-product of the steel industry, and a major component of synthetic fertilizer.) The nineteenth-century developments in chemistry also enabled the extraction of cellulose from wood as a resource for paper, celluloid and rayon. Guido briefly held the patent on acetate, which was used in the burgeoning film industry, but sold it shortly before his death, as he saw little value in it.[2]

The sudden death of his brother had meant that Guido was unable even to complete grammar school (*Gymnasium*). Through self-study, however, he succeeded in acquiring an honorary doctorate in chemistry. He was an acolyte of the doctor and physiologist Jacob Moleschott, known for the phrase: 'There are no thoughts without phosphorus.' To Moleschott, the human body was a chemical factory, and he was also one of the first to concern himself with the chemical composition of food in relation to health. Independent minds such as his held an enormous attraction for Guido, and for the rest of his life he would carefully monitor his diet.[3] Uncle Guido had absolutely no intention of living life as a layabout, and used his own resources to grow into a highly successful entrepreneur. He was a free thinker, and in many ways an exceptional individual.

In the summer of 1884, when Margarethe's mother Wanda was staying at Neudeck, Guido was rounding off a turbulent period in his life. His wife had died on 21 January of that year, he himself had turned fifty, and it was time for him to start thinking about a new marriage and—finally—an heir. But his recent bereavement meant that he was still not ready to face that reality. Guido's first wife had been a personality with a lifestyle as emancipated as his. Pauline Thérèse (Esther Blanche) Lachmann was a woman with a past. In the mid-nineteenth century she was known as La Païva, the most famous courtesan in Paris. Before marrying her in 1871, Guido had already been her devoted lover for nearly twenty years.

A GOOD NAME

La Païva was eleven years Guido's senior, and when he had first met her in Paris—in 1853, when he was just twenty-four—business was not his only reason for visiting the city. Paris may have been a financial and economic European hub, but it was also a breeding ground for liberalism. The democratic movement was being monitored keenly by the Prussians and Austrians, for if it were to infiltrate their own territories, it might easily erode their own royal power. Guido therefore also fulfilled a diplomatic role for his second cousin Otto von Bismarck, who had been the Prussian emissary in Paris for several years. Guido's status as an entrepreneur and his free-thinking sympathy for liberalism must have influenced his diplomatic activities. But in Paris, he was preoccupied with another matter. He had become enchanted by La Païva, who ran a very popular 'salon', where politics was often discussed. In 1857 he bought her a castle, Pontchartrain, not far from Versailles, and he enabled her to build her own city mansion on the Champs Élysées. After many years of construction, Hotel Païva was finally completed in 1865. According to one of the many rumours in circulation about the house, the oriental bathroom contained a bath of bronze encased in a sculptured block of onyx, with three taps: one for hot water, one for cold water, and the third for champagne. Another rumour concerned Guido's gift of yellow diamonds (still referred to by auction houses as the Donnersmarck Diamonds, and recently resold for several million); they were supposed to be the same colour as the marble staircase in her palace.

The international press regularly reported on Guido's activities. This scrutiny of his private life, fairly intense for the day, was the price he paid for his wealth. Articles about his liaison with, and subsequent marriage to, the Parisian 'priestess of Venus' were even published in special editions of various provincial newspapers, alongside details of the interior decoration of Hotel Païva, with its ceiling murals and mantelpiece ornaments in the shape of half-naked men and women. American newspapers such as *The Washington Post* and *The Chicago Daily Tribune* went a step further, claiming that Guido's ancestors had Jewish blood in their veins, which accounted for both the family's current wealth and his own partiality to Esther Lachmann—birth name of the originally Russian La Païva.[4] The Parisian commentary by author Alexandre Dumas Junior on the

41

SECRETS OF A SUITCASE

mansion's extravagant luxury and La Païva's audacious lifestyle was cited gleefully by all: 'The palace is almost finished—all it needs is a sidewalk.'

What these reports neglect to mention is the fact that La Païva must also have been an intelligent conversationalist for the men known to have lived with her. The first was the French-Austrian composer Henri Herz; the second, English politician Edward Stanley, Fourteenth Earl of Derby; the third, Portuguese merchant Albino Francisco de Araújo de Paiva; and lastly the Silesian industrialist Guido Henckel von Donnersmarck. She was able to hold her own opposite him for nearly thirty years—no mean feat with a man of his character. He remained faithful to her, accepted the ostracism that resulted from their marriage (Wilhelm I and Bismarck refused to receive her at the court in Berlin), and bitterly mourned her death in 1884. The story goes that he even buried an empty coffin at her funeral, so that he could preserve her body in spirits in a secret chamber at Neudeck, where— even after he remarried—he would lock himself up for hours to stare at Blanche's body in graceful suspension.[5]

It is doubtful whether Margarethe's mother Wanda was able to offer him any consolation that summer in 1884. Guido was likely preoccupied with the distribution of his capital and businesses which, without an heir, would fall to the Catholic Henckel von Donnersmarcks. It is quite possible—a hypothesis supported by his biographer Rasch[6]—that his remarriage three years later was a desperate attempt to prevent the 'loss' of his assets to Wanda's side of the family. Though amicable, familial relations were not *that* generous. His next wife was the stunningly beautiful, and most importantly youthful, Russian widow Katharina von Slepzow. She bore him two sons: Guidotto—a combination of Guido and Otto (for Bismarck)—and Kraft. At dinners and other occasions, Katharina most likely wore the famous Donnersmarck Diamonds originally made for La Païva; no doubt she will have raised quite a few eyebrows. The jewellery collection of Guido's wives must have been more valuable than even the British Crown Jewels at that time.

With his new bride—who *was* socially acceptable at court— Guido could move to Blücher Palace on Berlin's Pariser Platz.

Neudeck once again became a country retreat. His Berlin neighbours were part of the new German upper-middle class, and included bankers, entrepreneurs, department-store owners and publishers.[7] The wives of the high bourgeoisie, such as Aniela Fürstenberg, Hedwig Fischer and Milly Friedländer-Fuld, organised lavish dinners and other social gatherings almost daily, with a limitless supply of champagne and French wines. Their apartments must have been the size of country estates,[8] with tennis courts, equestrian grounds and auditoria. Other members of the nouveau riche established themselves in equally palatial villas near Tiergarten or in Grünewald.

During this period of cultural flourishing in the Prussian capital, a house where guests could be received in private was the most sought-after status symbol among the new elite. A good example had been set by prominent Parisian women with their own salons, such as La Païva, and several well-known aristocrats in Vienna. By this time, however, the role of the salons had already been partially replaced by private gentlemen's clubs, such as the Jockey Club or Travellers Club, where not only your family name but also your earnings were important.[9] The energetic wives of new wealthy entrepreneurs saw their opportunity, and leapt in to fill the gap created in society life. This was a response to the Kaiser's compartmentalised court culture, which was only accessible to the nobility.

The Silesian land magnates noticed little of this social shift, for most lived outside Berlin. The Kaiser did visit them every autumn for some hunting in the convivial Silesian atmosphere, where he would shoot with his friends from the Liebenberg Circle. They were Guido's regular guests at Neudeck.[10] After being elevated to the title of prince (*Fürst*) by Wilhelm II, Guido was also officially admitted to the imperial hunting party. The other Silesian magnates stifled their envy, and continued leading their withdrawn estate lives, far from the cultural and political goings-on in Berlin and Vienna. Their fortunes continued to grow, and to be spent on renovating their palaces, since labour was still inexpensive. They also hoped that the Kaiser might come by to visit them for a day of hunting. But Wilhelm preferred to consort with members of the Protestant elite like Guido, who bred pheasants specially for the Kaiser at Neudeck, so that he could shoot four hundred in a single day. The animosity among Guido's peers towards this preferential treatment, and the

SECRETS OF A SUITCASE

social exclusion provoked by his life choices, meant that at his funeral, on 23 December 1916, Guido was buried at Neudeck by an exceedingly small company. It did no justice to his major contributions to the prosperity of his country, and was no reflection of his enormous estate. The conservative Silesian nobility proved themselves just as unbending as the cast iron produced in their factories.

While Guido was working in Paris as an entrepreneur and diplomat, and developing more and more international interests, Margarethe's grandfather Hugo I was primarily focused on mining in Silesia. His only great extravagance—besides his stud farm—was the palace on Vienna's Ringstrasse, built for his second wife. But he also continued to develop new enterprises, such as setting up a paper mill (which still exists today, as Mondi) along with the modern steel and railway company Voestalpine, for which he also laid the foundations in Austria. Hugo I's sons and grandsons found even his enterprising spirit difficult to match, let alone the extravagances of Guido. The eldest son, Hugo II—Margarethe's father—made not the slightest attempt to compete. Along with his two brothers Artur and Lazarus, he managed the estates and businesses and collected the dividends—the new way of getting rich at the time.[11] As we know, Hugo II's other passion was renovating palaces, of which he took on three: Siemianowicz, Krowiarki and Brynek. Krowiarki came into his possession in 1877, via his wife Wanda. A fantastically decorated mansion surrounded by an English garden, he moved in with his family after the refurbishments. In 1890, he also inherited from his father his grandfather's palace in Siemianowicz, where he and Wanda started their own family and where Margarethe grew up, right in the heart of the mining region's sights and smells, so pivotal to the growing wealth of the Henckel von Donnersmarcks.

The third palace was Brynek, which he did not acquire until 1904, but which would become his greatest passion. Brynek was to be his own personal residence, situated north of Siemianowicz in a picturesque setting free from the smoke, soot and industry of the surrounding furnaces and steel factories. Hugo would not rest until it was his. He ultimately swindled an eight-year-old heiress out of it, and had renovation blueprints drawn up and a model built in 1900, before he had even made the purchase.

A GOOD NAME

Brynek's gardens and estates cover 36 hectares, including an English-style landscaped garden with special plants whose colours match the new stones used to rebuild the palace.[12] The collection of old trees remains famous to this day, and includes oaks that are now 300 years old. After taking possession of Brynek in 1904, Hugo's renovation and reconstruction works commenced the following year. He first demolished 90 percent of the old building, and effectively built a new palace in its place. It was wider, taller, and with a neo-Baroque chapel accessible via a glass passageway. As icing on the cake, each corner boasted two towers with onion domes, completing the palace's eclectic appearance.[13] The construction cost the Henckel von Donnersmarcks about £50 million in today's money.

In 1900, when Margarethe had found a suitor she liked among the appropriate elite nobility, Brynek was still only in the planning stages. Marriage was not a pressing concern in the way it had been for Uncle Guido on the other side: the Henckel von Donnersmarcks already had an heir and future head of the household. (The future Hugo III, Margarethe's eldest brother, only had a daughter, but had transferred his title as lord of their branch to his brother Edgar, who already had a son). The family's assets also seemed inexhaustible, and so in a certain sense Margarethe was free to do as she pleased, within the constrained expectations of her sex and social class. Maybe there were other reasons for taking the train with her sister Sara from Breslau to Abbazia, where she just so happened to find a husband?

While Margarethe was growing up in Siemianowicz, her Uncle Guido and Aunt Blanche (the former La Païva) were busy settling down at Neudeck. The Polish edition of a Guido biography does not mince words, starting with its title: *A Scandalous Life*. Margarethe was ten years old when Guido returned to Silesia for good. Although the couple had withdrawn to the New Palace at Neudeck, La Païva was hardly the type to put her feet up. She quickly transformed Neues Neudeck into a 'party palace', and organised hunting there for her Parisian acquaintances.

45

SECRETS OF A SUITCASE

Shortly after Blanche's death in 1884, Guido's interest in women landed him in yet another scandal when he brought an illegitimate son into the world. Thankfully this was far away in New York, but it did happen exactly when the time would have been ripe for Margarethe's début into society. Guido had sorely tested the flexibility of those closest to him, and most likely somewhat tarnished the Henckel von Donnersmarck name with his unbridled admiration of sensual women. Understanding the subtleties of Margit's family tree—in which Guido was only a distant uncle, and a Lutheran besides—was perhaps asking too much of Vienna's high-born coterie, which had made an art form of sarcasm and malicious gossip. Most had probably never even visited the distant mining region of Silesia. To this day, many still conflate the two family branches, much to the frustration of the Catholic side.[14]

Suppose that Guido's pious seventeen-year-old niece, dressed in a white gown, had remained a wallflower at her first ball in Vienna? The embarrassment would have been extreme, not only for her, but for the whole family. Kubrova and Winkelhofer cite enough examples of this type of situation. And if she had not managed to secure an engagement within a year, her chances of a suitable marriage would have practically evaporated. Margarethe had had little choice but to wait, and concentrate on doing good in her immediate surroundings: helping her mother manage the large household estates, taking the occasional trip with her family, and listening to her father talk about his plans to acquire and renovate Brynek. Money cannot buy everything, and certainly not a reputation. In a situation such as hers, a poor, slightly ageing Hungarian hussar might easily have seemed like a knight in shining armour.

In 1900, people such as Sándor and Margarethe could not simply marry whomever they liked—they could not act as independent individuals. Men and women of the aristocratic elite needed permission from the head of their family. Prior to marriage, even men were limited in the ways in which they could manifest as free individuals—and women were subject to even tighter constraints. Until they married, they remained on their parents' estate and travelled little, mostly visiting family when they did.[15]

46

A GOOD NAME

Even once married, women's conduct was still governed by strict rules. Leaving aside their poor legal status, they also had their heritage, nationality, religion and traditions to contend with. Living freely and emancipated took great resolve, as well as considerable financial independence. Around 1900, not a single unmarried woman was in such a position. Many nineteenth-century novels describe conflicts between emotion and reason via the love lives of women. These were inspired by what must have transpired in and around European estates. However, these tales are of women who behaved differently due to being impoverished, orphaned, or rebellious. Access to one's own money is frequently an important theme in such novels.

Though Margarethe may have conducted herself in a traditional manner, she still belonged to a more modern brand of aristocracy, as her grandfather Hugo I had earned his fortune in Silesia through hard work. He did not squander his time or money on hunting grounds, at racecourses, in bordellos or casinos. As a young lady on the eastern edge of the Habsburg empire, part of former and future Poland, Margarethe enjoyed slightly more freedom, and received more education, than women in the Austrian heartland.

Might the proximity of Cracow, a Polish university town, have made a difference? Or perhaps Breslau, another centre of scholarship? In any case, Poland was certainly ahead of other nations when it came to women's education, one of its best-known daughters being Marie Sklodowska Curie (1867–1934). Curie was a contemporary of Margarethe and the recipient of two Nobel Prizes (for physics in 1903, and chemistry in 1911). One catalyst for women's education that benefited Marie Curie was the Polish uprising in 1860. Women had played a major part in the rebellion, and enjoyed a level of freedom that later translated into improved provision for female learning, including Warsaw's (illegal) 'Flying University'.

Warsaw and Siemianowicz were separated by a border, however. Though close to the Polish lands, Silesia was not Polish—in fact, it was not German either. It was Silesian. The inhabitants were even more patriotic than their neighbours, the region having been caught in an eternal tug-of-war between Prussia, led by the Hohenzollerns, and Austria, ruled by the Habsburgs. In other words, between Protestants and Catholics. The region's strictest borders therefore

SECRETS OF A SUITCASE

separated these two faiths, and the same applied to the Henckel von Donnersmarcks. German did remain a common language, however, which created a sense of unity. French was only ever employed to keep secrets from the servants, as was the practice in all elite European households at that time. Some of the common folk spoke Polish, or Russian, as many Russian Jews had fled west from pogroms and settled in Silesia. The poverty of these refugees was matched only by that of the 'water Poles', the downtrodden half-Polish Silesians who lived near the river Oder. Their predicament will not have left a deep impression on the young countess, who was living high and dry in the palace, surrounded by expansive grounds and protected from a host of dangers such as crime and infectious disease. There she lived in a world that had its own specific rules both for the instruction of young women, and for the conduct of the 'high-born' in general.

WHERE IT WAS

There are few studies available on the day-to-day life of the Silesian aristocracy in the nineteenth century. Was this because, before the fall of the Iron Curtain, researching the lifestyles of any Silesians was not only difficult, but also a matter of some sensitivity? The barbarism of the Nazis in the 1930s and 40s is always lurking in the background, after all. Is this why the British nobility seems to hold Europe's monopoly on romanticised screen representations of life on country estates? Or is that simply because Britain's castles and estates have never found themselves in the crosshairs of heavy artillery?

As with all questions that arise when trying to describe a life like Margarethe Henckel von Donnersmarck's, there are few answers to be found. The task can be compared to slowly colouring in the figures of an extremely blurry photograph, while the background remains greyed out—like watching an old film. But now that we have met a few key figures, it is time to try and fill in the scenery of the country itself: Silesia, or Śląsk, as the current 'voivodeship' (province) is called, an 'inkblot on the map'.

* * *

In Germanic collective consciousness, 'Silesia' is now little more than a half-forgotten dream, a bit of nostalgia perhaps, recalling its near-homophone, 'Elysia'. Probing the origins of this persistent nostalgia for a lost land, author Hans Dieter Rutsch calls Silesia the 'Prussian Arcadia'. By way of illustration, the cover of his book boasts a well-known romantic painting by Caspar David Friedrich, *Wanderer above the Sea of Fog* (1817), depicting a man perched on a mountain summit surrounded by mist and ice as he surveys the landscape, evoking a sublime natural experience.[1] The painting was supposedly inspired by a journey through the Giant Mountains forming the boundary between Silesia and Bohemia, which feature recurrently in the work of Friedrich and other German Romantics, whether artists or writers. Around the turn of the eighteenth century, the likes of Goethe and Theodor Fontane (author of the naturalist novel *Effi Briest*) also regularly visited Silesia, and were captivated by its natural grandeur. The regional atmosphere was what inspired the Breslau-based German scholar Hoffmann von Fallersleben to write his song lyrics *Die Gedanken sind Frei* ('Thoughts Are Free'), which remain popular to this day. Silesia was once synonymous with Germany's glorious future. But *das war einmal*, as the Germans say—all in the past.

* * *

The beautiful scenery was not all that Silesia was famous for. The area was also rich in natural resources, buried deep beneath its surface. The only problem was finding them and, after that, knowing what to do with them. These are problems that do not solve themselves: the region's extraordinary economic boom was the result of several crucial decisions made by bold individuals, and the toil of thousands of labourers.

Silesia once belonged to the great Habsburg empire. Between 1742 and 1763, however, Frederick the Great of Prussia waged three wars to conquer it. This impetuous king, who was a friend of Voltaire, was well known partly as the ruler who forced his subjects to eat South American potatoes (and, because potatoes can be used to make vodka, they were unfortunately also responsible for widespread alcoholism among his people).[2] A lesser-known fact, however, is that Frederick the Great was the one to initiate mining activities in earnest.[3]

After conquering Silesia, he planned to begin with geological surveys, but lacked the necessary manpower. The land was sparsely populated, and there had already been conflicts between the Protestants and Catholics (resulting in the latter being driven out). Frederick therefore sourced labourers from Harz, introducing a number of rather progressive social welfare programmes to make the work more appealing, including paid sick leave.[4] He appointed

WHERE IT WAS

a young, energetic director who had amassed considerable expertise through both study and fact-finding missions to Britain and elsewhere: Friedrich Freiherr von Reden. Von Reden solved mining's greatest problem in Silesia, which was the flooding of the mine shafts.

Shortly before his death, Frederick the Great allocated funds to purchase a steam engine from Britain, which was transported at great cost over land and sea and ultimately arrived in Tarnowitz in 1788. This 'fire machine', which worked at ten horsepower to extract sixty cubic feet of water per minute from the shaft (a quantity that would later increase tenfold), finally made safe operation possible. Even Goethe came to view the mines, and in 1790 wrote in the guest book: 'Far from educated people, at the ends of the kingdom, who is helping you to find buried treasures and happily bring them to the light? Only intelligence and honesty can help; both keys lead to that richness guarded by the Earth.'[5] Poetically expressed, although the Silesians somewhat resented the phrase 'far from educated people'.

The arrival of the steam engine allowed von Reden to introduce yet more far-reaching modernisations to mining and the production of high-grade cast iron. Instead of using charcoal, which was plentiful in Silesia due to its many forests, he stoked the furnaces with coke, improving the quality of the iron. Though the coal required to make the coke was available in abundance, it was buried scores of metres below the surface, in strata difficult to access. Von Reden needed to make multiple trips to Britain to master the necessary techniques, but in 1796 continental Europe's first coke furnace finally became operational in Gleiwitz, Silesia. Its coal was supplied from the Queen Luisa mine (named after Frederick Wilhelm III's popular wife), while the neighbouring smelting plant produced iron and steel products. This was the beginning of Silesia's transformation into the most significant industrial centre in early nineteenth-century Germany.

Once it became clear that coal was the new black gold, it was fervently sought in all of the existing mines using new methods and machines. Here, too, improvements to the production processes in full swing throughout early capitalist Europe ensured the most efficient solutions.

Exploration of a mine called 'Prince Carl Zu Hessen' revealed thick layers of coal, and was slated for expansion. In 1800 it was officially reopened as Königsgrube ('King's Mine'), and ultimately gave rise to the adjunct blast-furnace and steel manufacturing complex Königshütte ('King's Metalworks'),[6] which was opened with great ceremony in 1802. Von Reden wrote: 'From nothing, a plant has arisen here that puts fifty thousand Thalers into circulation yearly, revitalises an uncultivated region, and supplies the distant Royal Provinces with essential quantities of raw iron, furnace slag, and granulated iron.' It was the jewel in the crown of Frederick's original plans. In the decades to follow, trains—the mode of transportation that ushered the nineteenth century into the modern world—facilitated the sale and delivery of iron and steel. The railways forged a connection between remote Silesia and the rest of the world, although not all Silesians can have been happy with the region's new nickname as 'Prussian England'.[7]

In the nineteenth century, the value of coal and iron ore was recognised in various parts of Europe, including Belgium, Sweden, France and even far-off Ukraine. British mining engineers were welcomed everywhere as advisers. The cast iron and steel were used to build trains for the ever-expanding railway network, as well as for weapons to fuel the various wars between European countries.

Drilling deep into the earth and using a blast furnace to melt iron ore and produce high-quality iron and steel requires significant investment and considerable technical ingenuity. But before that, initiative and a measure of courage are needed. At first, aristocratic landowners preferred to lease their land to the early venture capitalists, as they had done previously with the zinc and calamine mines on their extensive estates.[8] They were hesitant to become industrialists themselves. To win them over, the Prussian government led by example, launching the enterprise that ultimately produced the Königshütte smelting plants. But to be sustainable and successful, Königshütte needed more than a single enterprising king, who was always plagued by vacillating ministers, fussy administrators and the whims of bureaucracy. Seasoned industrialists were better-suited to facing the challenge of fierce capitalist competition that broke out in early nineteenth-century Europe, when the continent was flooded by cheaper British iron due to the abolition of import tariffs and the ideological pivot towards free markets.

WHERE IT WAS

With a progressive attitude and enormous capital in Silesia, the Henckel von Donnersmarck family showed the boldest initiative. Aided by British engineers, Margarethe's grandfather Hugo I had already built the Laurahütte plant in the 1830s, with a large blast furnace and steel-rolling mill that he ran successfully from its inception. Siemianowicz, where Hugo I built Laurahütte, is not far from Königshütte. And while the latter faced many challenges (mostly slow-moving bureaucracy), enterprising landowners such as the Henckel von Donnersmarcks successfully capitalised on the enormous demand for iron and steel. They rectified the persistent labour shortage by building 'auxiliary prisons' for the government on their land, essentially securing free labour for themselves. Use of women and children as workers was also widespread.[9]

The state-run Königshütte began to buckle, and it became ever more apparent that its continued survival would depend on privatisation. In 1870, the entire complex was ultimately sold to Hugo Henckel von Donnersmarck for a million Thalers. He knew what to do to render the public enterprise profitable once more, and did so within the year. But that was not all—he immediately merged its production with his own Laurahütte and created a single public limited company, a new business structure for the time. He then sold both of the works (Königshütte and Laurahütte) to this new company, for six times the purchase price. It was a masterstroke.

Hugo I and his nephew Guido were among the first Silesian industrialists to establish a limited liability company of this type, yet another bold initiative. Both searched for stakeholders in France and Belgium. They eventually came upon the founder of the French bank Société Générale, the Comte de Morny, and the Belgian Mosselman family. Alfred Mosselman was a contemporary of Guido, and had a similar reputation: for years he lived publicly with Apollonie Sabatier, another well-known 'priestess of Venus'.

With their limited companies and contacts in Paris—Europe's principal commercial centre at that time—the Silesians secured a reliable source of international information and *savoir faire*, obtained through regular mandatory shareholder meetings and their common interests.

SECRETS OF A SUITCASE

Hugo I acted at the right time in 1870, shielding his family from money troubles for decades to come. His shrewdness was rivalled only by that of his nephew Guido, who made particular use of the tensions between France and a unifying Germany in the late nineteenth century, and of the vast network he had built up since his time as a young diplomat and entrepreneur in Paris. Guido was also judicious in the purchase of patents, and benefited—as he would later generously acknowledge—from the business acumen of his first wife Blanche: La Païva.

Both uncle and nephew were individually and jointly responsible for seizing these new opportunities, aided by the advances that led to the first and second industrial revolutions. But they had a weakness: they loved their land too much, deciding to build their palatial estate homes in Silesia, and doggedly maintaining that this was the only place where such riches could be earned. Guido—the more cosmopolitan of the two, who had lived for years in Paris and Berlin—even put this in writing to his two young sons shortly before his death in 1916.[10] Their intransigence would ultimately come at a great cost. But who at that time could have predicted two world wars, or that the borders of Europe would soon be completely redrawn?

In the early twentieth century, the expanding mining industry must have made Upper Silesia a rather drab and unappealing place. In his childhood memoirs, German-Silesian author Horst Bienek wrote that housewives living near the mines could not hang their white laundry outdoors, as it would instantly turn black from the soot in the air. But the dirty and dangerous work did give many labourers opportunities, such as a dependable salary, healthcare, and education for their children. This applied even to Jews, whose numbers rose significantly in Silesia at the end of the nineteenth century due to ongoing pogroms in Russia and Ukraine. The Jews fled en masse to the West, where they faced an uncertain future as *Ostjuden*, or 'eastern Jews'. They were confronted with many forms of exclusion, leaving them no choice but to turn to traditionally permitted Jewish occupations and become innkeepers, lawyers, landlords or bankers. In the Silesian mining industry, they could also become firemen, which—considering the flammability of the material of most houses. and the heavily forested surroundings—was certainly no luxury. This was an opportunity accepted with mixed feelings.

WHERE IT WAS

On the unification of Germany in 1871, Silesia was no longer a Prussian territory, but became part of the new German Empire. Forty years later, the 1910 'Martin list'—one of the first-ever rankings of Germany's richest—still boasted four Silesians. This privileged position would change dramatically after the First World War, when the Treaty of Versailles saw a considerable portion of Silesia ceded to the newly reconstituted Poland. The eastern region of Upper Silesia, where much of the lucrative mining industry was located, thus fell under Polish rule in 1922. Germany lost 95 per cent of its iron ore, 80 per cent of its zinc and 70 per cent of its coal, which just shows how dependent on this region the highly capitalist German economy had become.[11] The Nazi invasion of Poland in 1939 returned the area to Germany until 1945, when four million Germans were driven out of Silesia by the Soviets marching on Berlin. Poland then became Poland once more, and Silesia became Śląsk. Germany was forced to pay for the acts committed in the name of its people during the Second World War. Silesia also became the new home of displaced Poles, who in turn were driven out by Soviet war refugees from Russia and Ukraine.

After the Second World War, the 'expellees' often hailed Silesia as a paradise lost. At that time, the understandable grief at the loss of their homeland and the leaving behind of all they held dear was compounded by a sense of rancour directed at communists. Conservative groups in particular took advantage of this sentiment, and the commotion over issues like Silesia lasted well into the 1980s, under Germany's measures of dealing with the dark past known as *Vergangenheitsbewältigung*. This is another reason for the lack of accounts describing 'normal' life in the region in the nineteenth and early twentieth centuries. In a speech on 8 May 1985, forty years after the end of the Second World War, President Richard von Weizsäcker achieved some acceptance of the fate of Silesia by pointing out rather firmly that Germany itself had been responsible for the war and for the deaths of six million Jews.

In light of this history, it remains difficult to take a dispassionate view of Silesia, whose borders and peoples have been displaced with such regularity. The region was the site of much forced labour during the Second World War, due to the large railway network which had been constructed during the nineteenth century to aid the industrial activity. The Nazis' choice of Upper Silesia, with its rich Jewish history and flourishing trade cities, as the location for the Final Solution's largest extermination camp has further blighted the region's place in history. Auschwitz has ensured that Silesia remains a 'guilty land', the scene of the greatest crime against humanity ever committed.[12] The Polish name change to Oświęcim has done nothing to alter that fact.

WILL AND FATE

Today, the inner courtyard at Finstergrün contains a large vertical board of Margarethe and Sándor's wedding photo. There are two large holes where their faces are supposed to be, which you can poke your head through if you stand on a small rise at the back. Most visitors find this opportunity to be photographed as the castle's original residents a source of great hilarity—unlike Margit and Sándor, to whom marriage and posing for photographs were both very serious matters, reflected by their expressions in the original shot. Sándor is dressed in a ceremonial uniform of the Royal and Imperial Hussars, blue with black-and-gold tassels; Margit wears a long white veil, and the kind of white wedding dress that became popular in elite circles during Middle Europe's nineteenth-century Biedermeier age. Her waist is cinched by a corset, giving her the then-fashionable S-bend silhouette, and making her sturdy figure appear a little top-heavy.

Though the photograph shows two people conforming to the conventions of their day, their castle tells a different story, having been built in 'mediaeval' style. Its plain austerity is utterly distinct from the eclectic architecture and decoration of the Henckel von Donnersmarcks' Silesian palaces, and the couple's decision to eschew such extravagance for their own home, even in its dilapidated state, can almost be viewed as an act of rebellion. Alfred Döblin, who visited the Silesian palaces in the 1920s and documented his experiences in *Journey to Poland*, writes despondently: 'A few speculations and they were immensely wealthy ... and because they had money, they could think of nothing better to do than order the same furniture for their villas as [Emperor] Franz Joseph had.'[1] Sándor and Margarethe Szapáry did the opposite: their castle was a mediaeval fort, and furnished in an appropriately frugal manner.

One of the postcards that Margit sent to her mother early in her marriage shows Finstergrün as little more than a large, square tower. Thankfully Margit and Sándor could stay with Wilczek at Moosham, an edifice that also partially served as a model for their renovations. Otherwise, they travelled about: to Vienna, where Margit's grandmother still lived in her Ringstrasse residence; to Wolfsberg, Hugo I's castle in southern Austria; to Krowiarki in Silesia; and to Pressburg, where their city villa awaited. All their movements were precisely documented as 'travel expenses' in Margit's first household ledgers, which she kept to show that she was a capable housewife. We might wonder what Sándor, so long a bachelor, thought of the fact that she even wrote entries for his cigars and chocolate.

At first, the nomadic couple maintained close contact with the local tradespeople in Finstergrün's nearest village, Ramingstein, who were to bring Ludwig Simon's costly plans to fruition. (Simon charged the princely sum of 50,000 crowns per year for his services, equal to around £300,000 today.) For some time, then, the Szaparys served as an important employer for the Ramingstein area. They also quickly produced two children—a son, Béla, in 1901, and a daughter, Jolanta, in 1902—both born at Krowiarki, Margit's family estate in Upper Silesia, rather than in Finstergrün's 'birthing room' (which had not yet been completed). Margit evidently trusted in her mother's experience, and sought out the protection of her childhood home to give birth, a process never without its dangers, especially in those times.[2] She only visited the Viennese doctors (who were actually quite highly regarded) for checkups, of which she sent brief reports to Wanda in French.

Sándor was regularly away hunting, and at these times Margit remained alone at Moosham. From there she supervised the building works at Finstergrün, and took responsibility for quite a few matters. When there were floods in April 1903 and landslides blocked the roads and railways, she wrote to her mother (in English, so that the servants could not read it): 'Please do not mention it to my husband.'[3] Sándor was supposedly hunting in Silesia at the time, and was not to be disturbed by such unsettling news. This—and the fact that she indulged his slightest wish—hints that Margit must have been in awe of her husband.

Their daughter Jolanta's memoirs recall that Margit was often asked to send chocolate to Sándor while he was out hunting—not a

WILL AND FATE

fact that a two-year-old would actively remember, of course, so she must have found out about her father's chocolate addiction later.[4] According to one of her mother's ledgers from that time, his sweet tastes accounted for around 18 crowns per month, equal to a labourer's weekly wage. Jolanta informs us that his nickname in the family was Tiger, due to his enormous appetite.[5] It also seems to have been his undoing in the end, as he died of 'indigestion' after a brief illness in March 1904. As a 46-year-old man, a trained hunter and a military officer, he must have eaten an awful lot for this truly to have killed him. We might conclude that an additional illness must have been at play, one that caused the fever mentioned by Margit in the heart-rending telegrams sent to Wanda in the final weeks of March 1904.[6] Sándor also seemed to be having trouble with an infected tooth, which led to sepsis.[7]

It was a tragic death for somebody who had aimed to make a fresh start in Finstergrün by adding a new branch to the Szapáry family tree. It was not meant to be. Margarethe's ageing mother sped to her side, and was with her when she buried her dear Sándor. Margit sent a proper thank-you telegram when Wanda was en route home to Silesia. One month later, Margit was back in Abbazia with her grandmother, most likely taking solace. What was she to do?

The young widow, who had already broken with convention by travelling to Abbazia so soon after her husband's death,[8] decided to return to Lungau with her two small children. She and Sándor had not built Finstergrün for nothing, after all. The castle's structure had only just been finished, and much work was still needed to complete the furnishings as planned. She was 33 years old.

The marriage contract that her father had negotiated with Sándor in April 1900 must have stipulated that, in the event of his death, she would have access to the considerable dowry she had brought to the union, as well as any supplementary assets from her family. Virtually all children of Silesian magnates came with one million (gold) Marks when they wed (almost £7 million today).[9] They also received a quarterly 'apanage', an allowance issued by the head of a noble family to other members for their maintenance. In Margit's case, this came to 6,000 crowns (around £36,000). One recorded apanage from Pest in Hungary, which will have been Sándor's contribution to the household, amounted to 1,500 crowns, which

59

immediately illustrates the financial discrepancy in the marriage. Margit's financial position was thus exceptional for an Austro-Hungarian lady, explicable only by the fact that she was part of a noble Silesian house made up of modern industrialists. In addition to their centuries-old assets (that were often recorded—right down to the teaspoons in the kitchen—in a *Fideikomiss*, a kind of mandatory financial trust managed by the head of a noble household that governed the entirety of the family's possessions), they also had 'new' money, an income that grew markedly year after year due to their lucrative mining and steel-manufacturing ventures.

This income was completely disposable. It allowed Margit to remain at Finstergrün, which had been built using her dowry—granting her independence from the wishes of the Szapáry family after Sándor's death.[10] She could afford to pay for staff to raise her children, to run her household, and to complete work on the castle itself. So, she didn't return to her parents in Silesia. Instead, there in the flickering candlelight of her makeshift fortress, she must have concluded that a new purpose awaited her in that isolated region of Austria.

At the time, Austria was hardly known for its modern conveniences. Principally an agricultural nation, its share in European industry was only six percent.[11] Outside of Vienna, one encountered a combination of 'misery, ignorance, and chronic epidemics of the plague and cholera.'[12] Whole areas of the country still had no roads. The average life expectancy was 40 years, and one third of the population was illiterate.

Margit Szápary's fortune allowed her to care for the poor and infirm in her local area, which was the traditional role allocated to noblewomen. Her family had already done so on a large scale in Silesia, providing education and medical care to the mineworkers and their families.[13] With Hugo I's millions as a foundation, even his granddaughter retained enough to become the patroness of a tiny Austrian mountain village. Her castle became the symbol of her new status as the widow Szapáry. As diminutive as 'Finstergrün House' may have been, with its few farms and water source purchased separately, she founded her own empire—as the Countess of Lungau.

* * *

At the turn of the nineteenth century, most noblewomen had no creative hand in the homes they lived in. They were furnished with family heirlooms that required dedicated care and preservation. Respect for family history meant that these items could not simply be put in storage,[14] and so the interiors of grand palaces were filled with these keepsakes, creating a rather similar ambience wherever one went and inhibiting virtually all aristocrats—even the heads of house—from developing any kind of personal style. But Margarethe Szapáry did, and that is what makes Finstergrün so special. Neither the interior nor the exterior of the castle bore the slightest resemblance to any home she had lived in before her marriage. We can see this from surviving photographs of Krowiarki and Brynek.

The original interiors have disappeared wholly or partially on the now dilapidated estates; but, thankfully, much can be seen on YouTube, in the 3D simulations made by Polish hobbyists in recent years, which are based on old photographs and floorplans. All of this visual material presents a mixture of the historic architectural and decorative styles that were considered tasteful in the nineteenth century. Individual pieces of furniture can still be found in their original condition at auctions, in museums, or in paintings by Adolph von Wenzel or Anton von Werner. Often they were Louis XV or Empire pieces, interspersed with simpler styles from Biedermeier Germany, Sweden, the Netherlands and Georgian Britain. The architecture of the palaces themselves shows a blend of English influences, such as the Tudor style, and the French style, Versailles being the shining example.

These European residences were a hodgepodge of everything that had proven either impressive or imposing in the past. The patchwork of styles can be seen not only on the country estates, but also in the centres of expanding cities like Vienna, where construction of large government buildings was exploding. In *The Age of Capital*, economic historian E.J. Hobsbawm suggests that this 'orgy' of late nineteenth-century development is 'more likely to stimulate apologia … than universal admiration.'[15]

In any event, the key aspiration for these homes and buildings was a quality of 'grandeur', best achieved through allusions to a glorious past. The Renaissance—which had seen Europe's very first burgeoning of aristocratic entrepreneurs—appealed most to the new business magnates of the industrial revolution, closely followed by the opulent Parisian style from the era of Napoleon III (1848–52). But, truthfully, the construction boom had little to do with art or architecture, and more to do with self-assurance among the nouveau riche. The design elements that were truly innovative and a product of their time—such as lifts, and enormous glass bay windows or greenhouses made possible by a solid iron frame—were not prominently visible. Examples include the greenhouse at Siemianowicz, or the covered glass walkways connecting the various parts of Brynek.

The restoration of mediaeval church and castle ruins in the late nineteenth century had spread 'like an contagious disease' (Hobsbawm),[16] especially among the nouveau riche who had succeeded in acquiring such an old 'family asset'. Interest in the Middle Ages was further fuelled by the popularity of historical novels set in that era. Many artists also painted and drew mediaeval ruins, as the German Caspar David Friedrich had already been doing for some time, and Zingg and Reinhold before him. Germany had also seen a revival of interest in northern German myths and legends, in which a key role was played by castles and their long, often mysterious histories. The late nineteenth century had also seen the advent of spiritism and séances, where a castle's former residents would be summoned as spirits from beyond the grave.[17]

So, Margit and Sándor's Finstergrün project was perhaps not as original as it might first appear; but they remained true to form once they had set their minds to it. The castle itself was to be Central European in style,[18] without the slightest hint of anything French or British, and with some innovative elements. But, as old as Finstergrün may have appeared, it was also contrarian, an aspect that would not become apparent until Margit herself got to work—on the interior.

In the years following Sándor's death, in 1904–8, Margit's focus lay primarily on the completion of her castle, for which she undertook frequent travel. The aristocracy's presence was expected at festive gatherings in the capital, such as the sixtieth anniversary of the reign of Franz Joseph in 1908, and as a monarchist she will most certainly have attended.[19] But she was often absent: her name can be found only sporadically in the society columns of major Austrian newspapers, which always precisely documented the comings and goings of the nobility. In the meantime, she transformed Finstergrün into a small museum of the valuable items she purchased during her travels. The contrast with her surroundings, where poor farmers eked out a meagre living through agriculture, livestock farming and woodworking, must have been stark indeed. In Ramingstein, the biggest employer was a paper factory that made packaging for tea and tobacco products, and exported teabags to China. In 1900, the village had around 1,200 inhabitants, and had made a remarkable recovery from a major forest fire that had burned the entire region to ashes in 1841. There was a police station, a small school with two classes, a post office, and a forestry agency for the estate of the Schwarzenberg family, with whom Margit became friends.

During these early years, Margit provided assistance after minor emergencies in the area. When the village of Lessacher Oberdorf burned almost completely to the ground in 1908, leaving 200 residents homeless and dispossessed, she organised accommodation for the children at the Franciscan abbey in nearby Tamsweg, which had a hospital, a kindergarten and a housekeeping school. For the months of the children's stay, Margit paid for their board and living expenses. Between 1908, the year when both of her parents died in close succession, and the outbreak of the First World War in 1914, she made large investments in the improvement of infrastructure in and around Ramingstein. One such venture was the provision of a security deposit to support the construction of a local telephone network, which was completed in 1911. She never got her deposit back. Even greater, however, was her contribution to the construction of what was then a modern school in Ramingstein. She was closely involved and, on its completion in 1911, the school was equipped with central heating (unlike Finstergrün), proper sanitation, a gymnasium, and a garden where the children learned to grow vegetables.

For her assistance with building the school and other contributions, Margit was awarded the Order of Elizabeth by the emperor, which was cause for great celebrations in Ramingstein. She had expedited the award herself a little, by keeping a very detailed account of all of her good works since her arrival in the region (the use of 'I' in the multi-page typed summary of great deeds betrays its author).[20] Clearly, Margit very much wanted to be a part of the prestigious Habsburg order, which would give her national standing. Money for the construction and decoration of chapels and churches was also plentiful, and she supported the initiative to establish a Capuchin order in Lungau. The local clergy also had no hesitation in reaching out to her whenever they needed a new crucifix, or when a church roof was in need of repair.

MODERN WOMEN

Rummaging through one of the boxes in the Salzburg Provincial Archive, a small piece of brown leather tumbles out. Turning it over reveals a passport photograph bearing the name 'Countess Margit Szapáry', in her own handwriting. The edge is torn, and the leather resembles a cover used to protect identification papers. The photo shows a woman staring undaunted into the camera, with a white cap on her head. She seems so unlike the woman I have come to know, dressed completely differently from her engagement and wedding pictures, or the woman photographed later in life, when she was rather more full-figured, and walked hunched with a walking stick after an accident in the 1920s. In this passport photo, she seems nothing at all like a widow in mourning, or the frail older woman in white-collared black from the 1930s.

A little later, I come across a 1911 brochure for Finstergrün with another photo of Margit, with the same confident mien, but this time beneath a simple straw hat and even the beginnings of a small smile. She is dressed in a dark sailor's shirt, and the picture seems to date from the same period as the one with the white cap. Both shots are reminiscent of the portraits taken of early twentieth-century female intellectuals and artists who liked to retreat into nature, as did many members of the Bloomsbury Group in Sussex, England, or the writer-psychiatrist Frederik van Eeden's circle in the Netherlands. They opted for austere home furnishings and led decidedly non-urban lives, despite most having originally been city-dwellers.

Standing on her own two feet, and almost certainly influenced by the unpretentious farming women around her (rather than the trussed-up ladies in Vienna), in the years after Sándor's death Margit adopted an unmistakably modern look during her self-imposed isolation in Lungau, for herself and her home. It was a castle, certainly, and one that conformed with the recent trend of renovating medi-aeval ruins. But it was not a castle built to hold enemies at bay—for that it was far too open. It was built to accommodate views, not defences. The windows may have been relatively small, but they are also quite numerous. Simon had designed Finstergrün in accordance with Sándor's ideas, after the couple's travels through Austria, Slovenia and Hungary in search of inspiration; still, Margit exerted a considerable influence, especially through the later finishing and interior decoration. It became a home for an independent woman.

It is in this creation of a 'room of one's own', that we see one coun-tess Henckel von Donnersmarck (Margarethe Szapáry) echoing another: forty years earlier, Uncle Guido's wife Blanche had also worked tirelessly to build palatial homes, making use of the very same inexhaustible supply of Silesian capital that now fuelled Mar-git's designs. Blanche, too, was revolutionary. Hotel Païva and Fin-stergrün defy comparison in many respects, but in this common foundation—the iron and coal wealth of Silesia, extracted in Si-emianowicz, Gleiwitz and Tarnowitz—we can see how two women built a home. So: what had La Païva done with the millions Guido threw in her lap?

Blanche instructed the then still relatively unknown architect Pierre Manguin to build her a city residence on the Champs Élysées.[1] Her intention was to create a cultural salon of even greater renown than the predominantly musical salons she had started with in the 1840s in the home of her first lover, the piano manufacturer, com-poser and pianist Henri Herz. To that salon she had lured Richard Wagner, who wasn't yet popular in France, and the more famous Franz Liszt, both of them bringing journalists and authors in their wake. Herz himself set about popularising and publishing simplified operas and other musical works, primarily as intimate piano duets for gentlemen and ladies.[2] But when Herz slipped away to the United States to seek his fortune (and to escape his spendthrift mis-tress), she was forced to close her musical salon. When Herz's fam-ily realised that he was not coming back, they threw the woman who had become known as 'Madame Blanche Herz' onto the street, which can only have aggravated her thirst for vengeance against moral crusaders.

66

MODERN WOMEN

In the revolutionary year of 1848, she crossed the Channel, with suitcases containing several fashionable gowns she had managed to borrow from up-and-coming Parisian designers. Once in London, she used them to draw the eye of Edward Stanley, fourteenth earl of Derby and a Conservative MP who would serve as prime minister three times between 1852 and 1868. He became the longest sitting leader of the Conservative party on record, and he earned some of his fame supporting the abolition of slavery in parliament. His estate near Liverpool is still in the hands of his family, now with several additions including a safari park. Stanley was immensely wealthy, and showered Blanche with gifts. After a few years, she was financially independent, and returned to Paris. It was time for a respectable husband whose title would finally grant her official access to the upper echelons of society. In the German resort town of Baden-Baden, she found the impoverished but charming Albino de Païva, son of a merchant from the Portuguese colony of Macau (now a city in China). Though she was wealthy enough to provide for him, she wisely had him sign acknowledgements of his debts to her, which she later used to coerce him into marriage, in 1851. Now she had a title fit for a calling card: la Marquise de Païva e Araujo.

Blanche opened a salon at Place St Georges, a locale that further bolstered her status. There she hosted opulent dinners and other extravagant gatherings, draped in resplendent veils and adorned with glittering diamonds. Invitations were in hot demand: her friend and author Théophile Gautier was a regular guest, along with a battalion of journalists and writers such as Sainte-Beuve, Flaubert, Taine, Dumas and the acerbic Goncourt brothers. They found Blanche cold, 'a kind of monster from a Scandinavian saga'. The artist Delacroix, who also attended on occasion, found her love of luxury 'frightening'.[3] Still, like a sphinx, she must have had many men under her spell, as there was an unending stream of callers. She left Albino Francisco de Païva e Araujo shortly afterwards: his purpose had been served, and he returned to his wealthy mother in Portugal, where he committed suicide in 1872 as a ruined man. From 1853 onwards, Blanche was very well kept by the young count Guido Henckel von Donnersmarck, who allowed her to continue amassing both jewels and fascinating dinner guests—and to build her own house.

67

SECRETS OF A SUITCASE

If La Päiva had 'frightening' taste, she did not express it in the external design for the house: Hotel Païva was designed by Manguin in the eclectic style common at the time. Its façade is Neo-Classical, with Venetian influences discernible at the rear, as with so many houses in that era. Several years before construction began, Guido had purchased Blanche a small renovated palace near Versailles, called Château de Pontchartrain. So, the feeling of a home exuding aristocratic affluence was already familiar to her. When it came to Hotel Païva, the location was the crucial factor: on the Champs Élysées, close to the Rond-Point and the Tuileries Palace, the epicentre of French power. The view was inconsequential; more important was that people down on the street could catch sight of the illuminated windows, and know that she was entertaining.

There were no gardens. For that she had Pontchartrain, where exotic fruits and vegetables were grown in greenhouses to impress her dinner guests on the Champs-Élysées. Here, a formal terrace— an extension of the patio beside the dining room—would suffice, opening on to a small winter garden. Having a park behind the house was less important than having an inner courtyard, with stables and room for carriages to turn around; Blanche's select group of invitees valued their privacy. Otherwise, the interior layout was standard for the day: a kitchen in the basement, and rooms for receiving guests on the ground floor. There was—of course—a salon, in addition to a dining room, a music room and a smoking lounge. The private quarters were on the first floor, including a master bedroom with double doors that opened onto the Champs-Élysées; beside it was the bathroom, with the library at the rear. The servants' quarters were located on the second floor. There were no guest rooms, not even for Blanche's two surviving children: a son from her first marriage, which had allowed her to escape her family in Moscow and move to Paris, and a daughter from her time with Herz.

The essence of Hotel Païva, and Blanche's unconventional intentions for her home, can be seen in the design of the private rooms on the first floor. The master bedroom's dimensions and aspect— looking out onto the Champs-Élysées, at the front of the house— are a striking, deliberate and very unorthodox choice. The floorplan also accommodates two people who spend much time together, yet sometimes wish to be alone. The smaller bedchamber for 'Monsieur le Comte' adjacent to the master bedroom, and his small bathroom with access to the library, suggest how the couple wished to live: independently, and yet close to one another, with a small dining room at the rear of the house that was accessible from both sides.

For the materials, Blanche opted not for natural masonry, white-plastered walls or dark oak beams, as Margit would. Simplicity was not La Païva's style. Instead she decided on marble, wood inlay, enamel, murals by famous artists, tapestries commissioned from Smyrna, and solid-silver chandeliers. The mansion's staircase, which rapidly garnered fame, was sculpted in situ from Algerian marble, better known as yellow onyx. No effort or expense was spared, and the ostentatious interior décor was entirely comparable to that of the banker James de Rothschild (1792–1868). He too had built his own palace to spite the Parisian aristocracy, who had refused to admit his Jewish wife to court.

Anybody seeking Gothic statues of the Madonna or other saints at Hotel Païva will be disappointed. Without exception, the women depicted in the paintings and the statuettes set in architraves or on mantelpieces—the Aphrodites, Dianas and Nymphs—are naked, with voluptuous proportions, modelled on specimens from classical antiquity. The painted and sculpted men are either representations of classic Italian authors such as Virgil, Dante and Petrarch, or hunters depicted in all their masculine glory, with rippling shoulders and thighs à la Hercules or Apollo (or Guido, though that may be mere power of suggestion). Cherubim, or other plump, naked, childlike figures, frolic among them. At Blanche and Guido's request, Manguin had designed an entire world specially for them, inspired by the age of French glory in the seventeenth century and based on the private chambers of Anna of Austria, wife of Louis XIII. Their private rooms contained depictions of the most famous female figures from Greek and Roman antiquity, with whom La Païva herself blended seamlessly.

Unlike Margit, Blanche did not travel around to find furniture and other interior pieces. Instead, she had them designed and built according to her wishes by young artists and craftspeople, some of whom will have been freed from financial worry for years after the commission. She ordered an oval mahogany bed in the shape of a clamshell, for example, with red satin upholstery and a mermaid at the head of the bed, accompanied by two swans swimming alongside her. But it seems Blanche found it a tad gaudy after all, as she sent the bed back, after which it was given a place in the most luxurious bordello of nineteenth-century Paris, La Fleur Blanche on rue des Moulins. In 2017 it sold at Sotheby's for nearly one million Euros as part of the *Erotic: Passion and Desire* auction series.

The list of artists and craftspeople who worked on Hotel Païva seems almost endless. Although there are barely any photographs and no surviving portraits of Blanche—she herself stated that she wished to remain mysterious, though others claim she was simply aware that she was no classical beauty—she did have her likeness on show in her home. She is clearly recognisable, from head to toe, as the goddess of the night in a ceiling mural in her salon, painted by Paul Baudry.[4] He had made a name for himself in 1862 with a nude painting, *La Perle et La Vague* (The Pearl and the Wave), which he claimed to portray a Persian fable. After his mural for La Païva, he received the commission for which he became best known: the ceiling of the grand foyer in Paris's new opera house, the Palais Garnier.

Blanche makes several artistic cameos in her own house. Her face is lent to the image of Amphitrite, wife of Poseidon and goddess of the sea, in a central 'medallion' positioned before the stairhead. The most striking decorative feature of the external façade is the head stationed above the master bedroom's central window: a woman with half-closed eyes and a tiara on her head. No further identification is needed.

Hotel Païva was the home of a woman finally getting what she wanted, after a long and hard road—from the Jewish neighbourhood in Moscow where she was born into the family of a fabric merchant all the way to the Champs Elysées, where she lived with Count Guido Henckel von Donnersmarck. The intertwined Gs and Bs dotted throughout the premises clearly show that the mansion was a declaration of love: to Blanche from Guido as the property's financer, and to Guido from Blanche, whose ideas had given it shape. The glorified nudes visible all through the house presage the realism that would come to influence visual art over the latter half of the

MODERN WOMEN

nineteenth century, the portrayal of naked bodies no longer requiring a mythological or biblical pretext. After Baudry made his *Perle et Vague*, and before he started working for Blanche, Édouard Manet caused a scandal in 1863 with his *Déjeuner sur l'herbe* (*The Luncheon on the Grass*), which portrays two clothed men picnicking with a naked lady in the forest. The woman looks unashamedly toward the viewer. She shows not only her breasts, buttocks and thighs, but also a large pair of bare feet, in a time when small, dainty feet constituted the feminine ideal. This is a proud woman, modelled by a friend of Manet, Victorine Meurent.

This unabashed adoration of the human body is the dominant theme throughout Hotel Païva. It is a temple of love, and glorifies sensuality without recognition of sin. It is an answer to the denigrating term '*grandes horizontales*' often used to describe women such as Blanche. Her house shows that she is a woman of her time. It also makes one other thing perfectly clear: La Païva is no longer a lover to one and all, despite the baseless allegations levelled to this effect by the Goncourts. She now lived exclusively with and under the protection of Guido, who was becoming ever more powerful as an international businessman, trying to deal with the Franco-German hostilities. Their marriage in 1871 made Blanche more socially acceptable, which in turn would also help Guido. During the Franco-Prussian War (1870–1), he was appointed city commander of Metz by Kaiser Wilhelm I, and he participated with Bismarck in the peace negotiations, becoming one of the architects of the 5-billion-franc 'reparations' payment imposed on France. Later on, he would express regrets, as he came to consider the indemnity a factor contributing to the First World War.[5] Nevertheless, as a reward for his service in the war with France, Wilhelm I made him governor of Lorraine, which had been conquered along with Alsace.

Guido's aspirations had already become noticeable at Hotel Païva. After losing the war, the French became much more hostile in their attitude towards Germans. More politicians were now at Guido and Blanche's table, where the dinners had got smaller and more intimate.[6] What might they have talked about? Art, certainly, but once most of the guests had left, politics would have been on the agenda, especially with the republican politician Léon Gambetta, who dined at the house weekly. Neither Guido nor Blanche were fervent nationalists—Blanche far from it, in fact, with her Russian-Jewish descent, her formative years in London, her Portuguese ex-husband, and her years in the company of the free-thinking Guido. And if the count himself was any kind of patriot, then he was Silesian, not Prussian. He was always conceiving and creating opportunities for new enterprises, both in Germany and abroad. Blanche, hostess extraordinaire, provided him with support and advice, and he didn't scruple to take advantage of the tensions between France and Germany whenever it proved fruitful. His aim was to operate close to the centre of activity, without ever stepping too near the maelstrom of power. When Bismarck asked him to become minister of finance in the newly unified German state, he politely declined. He likewise showed no interest in supervising Wilhelm II's planned construction of a direct Berlin–Baghdad railway in service of Germany's colonial aspirations, which were a potential nightmare for the British.[7] No, Guido had his own plans.

For over ten years, Guido and Blanche enjoyed the social hub that had become their Paris home. Meanwhile, in far-off Silesia, work on Neues Neudeck had been completed in accordance with Blanche's wishes. The architect Lefuel had fashioned a copy of his Louvre extensions, though the Silesians quickly took to calling the New Palace 'Little Versailles'. An English garden had been added by the Irishman John Fox. Construction must have been laborious, as the lack of a train station near Neudeck meant that all of the materials had to be transported by horse and cart. Guido and Blanche were proud of the palace. Unfortunately, most of the neighbours refused to attend the grand opening in 1876, dropping the invitation with thumb and forefinger back on the silver platter and turning away in derision. Guido and Blanche paid them no heed and instead invited their business acquaintances, as the rising post-war tensions between France and Germany had prompted them to spend more and more time in Silesia.

Blanche would continue to miss her Paris home once she and Guido withdrew completely to Neudeck, after she suffered a minor stroke. In 1884, she died there at the age of sixty-five. She had achieved her life's goal: she had married Guido. Due to a lack of heirs (Blanche's two children had passed away), Guido re-inherited everything he had ever given her. He did not sell Hotel Païva until nine years after her death in 1893; it was clearly difficult for him to give up the place.

Forty years after La Païva created her radical home, Margit Szapáry built Finstergrün. But this was no home for entertaining guests or hosting soirées.

Her architect, Simon, was no innovator either. First of all, he was charged with the upkeep of St Stephen's Cathedral in Vienna, an important maintenance post. Conservation and preservation were his priorities, and he did what his employers told him to do. This is why his name is not mentioned among Vienna's great visionary architects of the day, such as Otto Wagner, or Adolf Loos, famous for his condemnation of ornament.[8] But a closer look at Finstergrün does reveal some details that are common to Wagner, Berlage and others, and which unmistakably herald a new era, despite Finstergrün's intended 'mediaeval' appearance. A castle structure, after all, would inspire the first blocks of social housing erected in the early twentieth century, the most famous British example being the Rowton Houses. One of them, the Grade II–listed Arlington House in Camden, London, still serves today as a hostel for homeless, vulnerable and low-income tenants, complete with its corner towers and octagonal turrets.[9]

The emphasis on the vistas to be enjoyed from the castle's many vantage points is another original design point. Right from the start, Finstergrün incorporated small openings into its thick stone walls, offering ever-changing views of the impressive mountain landscape from different angles. These, in turn, required internal passageways and bridges to connect the various spaces—a technical challenge due to the use of heavy beams and natural stone, but local builders ensured that the plans were carried out precisely.[10] The use of modest materials such as wrought iron and wood is another striking aspect, along with the almost total lack of any ornamentation, either on walls or ceilings or in the interior decoration (with the exception of locks and hinges, and antlers of various sizes). Nowhere are there any vases, statues, paintings, side tables with photographs, mirrors, crystal lamps, chandeliers, or planters of sub-tropical flowers, all from different time periods and styles, which is what make fin-de-siècle interiors so oppressive and stifling. Unlike most noblewomen of the empire who married into old families, Margit—whose husband had hailed from an impoverished branch of the Szaparys, and who was not living on the ancestral estate—had no cartloads of family heirlooms that she was obliged to take care of. Starting right from the beds, chairs and tables, she was free to furnish her home entirely as she wished.

Finstergrün's furniture was made principally from sturdy oak, which lent itself to beautiful craftsmanship, and pine, which was ubiquitous in the area. The pieces were largely fifteenth- and sixteenth-century in style, and Central-European Gothic. Niches in the castle were occupied by simple inbuilt tables and benches, made by local craftspeople and modelled after mediaeval examples, many of which could often still be seen standing around in farmhouses in the Tamsweg area. A standard reference work on German furniture reports that, in the fifteenth century, Tamsweg was even a minor centre for high-quality furniture-making, simply because a few excellent cabinetmakers happened to live there.[11] The hydropower available from mountain rivers such as the Mur encouraged the construction of sawmills, and the refinement of technology enabled the production of ever-thinner boards, which in turn opened possibilities for wooden ornamentation incorporating exuberant influences from nearby Italy. This centuries-old local expertise is evident not only at Finstergrün, but in the churches in and around Tamsweg. Wilczek, a connoisseur of old interiors, knew exactly where to look, and had already obtained a sacristy cabinet for his own Kreuzenstein castle.

Despite all the cabinets and chests, Finstergrün never had a cluttered appearance. This was because plenty of openings had been designed indoors, allowing for different perspectives of the spaces, viewed from various angles. The only concessions made to comfort were the luxury soft furnishings, such as Persian carpets, wall tapestries and cushions, whose geometric designs represent a stylised interpretation of nature. This was in keeping with trends emphasising the 'universal oneness between humankind and nature', which also influenced the work of Viennese artists early in the twentieth century. Many of Finstergrün's fabrics were woven by women and, just like much of the furniture, anonymous hands; they are often astonishing products of old agrarian culture.

74

They were used to upholster sofas and decorate walls, and are reminiscent of the artists' studios from the turn of the previous century, or Freud's consultation room in Vienna. Conceptually they are in line with the 'Asian' design language used in upholstery patterns by Otto Wagner and Berlage. Their often-vivid colour palette is not, of course, visible in the surviving black-and-white photographs, but can still be seen in the soft but lively watercolours which Margit painted of several rooms. They imbue the interiors with a warmth of which the castle itself was likely bereft, due to the minimal heating available. There were many such spaces, serving at once as sitting rooms, bedrooms or studies. Nowhere does the label of 'salon' apply, which in itself was new for the time.

The Austrian historian and writer Nora Watteck, who grew up in Lungau, published an article in the late 1970s describing Margit's bedroom as it must have appeared in the 1920s.[12] The white of the walls is dominant, along with the green of the felted floor coverings. The bedspread had brown hues, woven in a geometric Florentine motif (known as *point de Hongrie* or 'Hungarian Point'). The room also contained a sixteenth-century wardrobe and a chest for blankets topped with three statues of saints, which stood at an incredible one-and-a-half metres tall. Otherwise, there was a Central European, and more specifically South Tyrolean, four-poster bed— and that was all. The room's most striking feature was not a piece of furniture, but the view through a large window onto the mountains and trees, all exactly the same hues of green and brown as the room's furnishings. There were no mirrors or reflective ornaments suggesting the bedchamber of a woman who liked to look at herself. 'You either liked it or found it strange, there was no in-between', wrote Watteck.

At the nearby Premhaus, a building on Ramingstein's Burgstrasse where Margit would later spend the winters and accommodate her guests, the interior was even more spartan. It, too, had whitewashed walls. Plain, light-coloured wooden farmhouse furniture stood on the light, sand-strewn floor. The walls were decorated with a Gothic cross, a few dried-out insect skins and some decorative woodcuts. Vases contained bunches of wildflowers. In its day, such an austere interior will have been considered 'sensational', though now it is the norm in any modern home decorated in Scandinavian style.

SECRETS OF A SUITCASE

Walking around Finstergrün today, mentally filling in the empty spaces based on the available photos and watercolours, one notices the modernity of its consistent austerity, a radical departure from the exuberant eclecticism that surrounded Margit during her childhood. The castle's greatest stylistic aberrations are its murals, which were suggested by Wilczek, who had had the same done at Kreuzenstein. They were made by the Munich artist Max Mann von Tiechler, and modelled after fourteenth-century frescoes that can still be seen at Sabbionara Castle in northern Italy. For Margit, Mann painted a great mediaeval tournament, with knights in full regalia on horseback, and courtly women observing from a royal box. The contrast with the ceilings of Hotel Païva could not be starker. Mann did not hide the fact that he had copied Sabbionara: 'Why should I design something myself if this copy is a far better depiction of what I wish to express in Finstergrün?' he wrote to Margit in a defiant tone, saying also that he was 'happy to sacrifice his person' for this 'magnificent' example of mediaeval art.[13]

The commanding painting of Sándor as the Knight of Finstergrün also makes quite an impact in the large dining room, or great hall, where several mediaeval suits of armour and weapons were on display. Why was there no portrait of Margit as lady of the manor? It was she, after all, who financed and decorated the castle. But no: the lack of mirrors, even in her bedroom, is a sign that she was no vain woman—or at least that she did not enjoy looking at herself. What the house did accrue over the years, however, besides an abundance of candleholders and oil lamps were more and more religious objects—baptismal fonts, altars, crucifixes, icons, statues of the Virgin Mary, and even a costly painted altarpiece from the fifteenth century. In some ways, the house must have seemed more like a church; or rather, a private cloister into which the widow Szapáry had withdrawn. Conspicuous in the surviving photos of the interior, and of the placement of furniture especially, is the intimacy of all those 'nooks', with desks and benches placed in front of tall windows, which were partially formed of round stained glass, further adding to the 'medieval', churchly ambience. Finstergrün could be either open or closed, depending on the mistress's mood.

Margit would not remain a modern woman, partly due to the rise in conservatism among the aristocracy of the early twentieth cen-

76

MODERN WOMEN

tury, as their position became threatened by democratic movements and the proletariat's growing rage at the unfair distribution of wealth. This anger was most notably found among adherents of Lenin. There was also discontent regarding civil marriage, general education, and public healthcare. The Church's influence waned as a result, and the nobility's solution was to double down on the aristocratic ideals associated with religion. Congresses and other gatherings were organised to this effect,[14] and Margit seems to have become far more devout in the second half of her life, which is reflected in the interior of her home.

A second possible explanation is that the ever-dominant Wilczek likely insisted on helping with the renovation and furnishing of Finstergrün. Wilczek, after all, had already extended his passion for hunting animals to hunting 'Gothic' treasures and old construction materials, such as gates, cornerstones and doors, which he purchased throughout Europe by taking shrewd advantage of country-dwelling, impoverished village pastors. His hoarding tendencies intensified as he got older, and as extended hunting parties began to tax even his considerable athletic qualities. We might imagine that, after Sándor's sudden passing in 1904, he presented himself as Margit's mentor. I read as much in a 1911 brochure on Finstergrün,[15] in which the deferential writer credits Wilczek with the honour of having brought Finstergrün back to life by alerting Sándor to 'the Gothic and Romanesque art epochs', of which the Hungarian then became an 'impassioned friend'. This brochure also claims that Wilczek assisted with the construction and furnishing of the chapel at Finstergrün—a necessary feature of any 'mediaeval' fort, and a convenient storehouse for artistic treasures besides—and with the commissioning of a mural.

Wilczek was hardly the type to hide his qualities beneath a sheen of modesty; he won't have denied his involvement. But the records of the construction nuance this claim somewhat. The correspondence with Mann, the fresco artist, was handled by Margit for several years, and the questions from the foreman, Holzinger, were all answered by her in her characteristic hand. These were no minor decisions, but concerned the shape of the roof and the positioning of doors and windows, as well as an important remembrance of Sándor: the stairway between her bedroom and the stables, which

SECRETS OF A SUITCASE

she decided to keep. This was the route he would have taken when leaving for a hunt in the early morning, either alone or with her, as she also enjoyed the sport.

A competent artist, Margit made detailed sketches down to the smallest elements, including the locks and hinges, to serve as models for ornamental blacksmiths like the Italian Clonfero. These items have survived the decades, and can still be admired at Finstergrün today. Although it was conceived as a mediaeval castle, and specifically one in a Central European style, still room was made for a few exceptions, some of which might be called quasi-Renaissance. The covered galleries on the first and second floors, for example, with their ornate arched windows, are elements that would seem more at home in a Venetian palazzo. They guarantee a view looking out, and as much light as possible in some spaces, while still keeping the inside secluded. The most important room is the great hall, which still serves as a summer dining room for guests today; its high ceiling boasts the Sabbionara frescoes. The four surrounding storeys, connected via a spiral staircase in each corner, contain larger rooms with vague designations (most records and drawings simply state *Zimmer*, or 'room'), with the exception of a cloakroom, a bedroom, a bathroom and two children's rooms—though the relevant blueprint dates from May 1904. There is also a spacious stable, surrounded by servants' quarters. Nearly all the castle's walls are whitewashed.

Though these white walls are certainly 'authentic' and 'mediaeval', they also herald a modern age in which light and colour play a key role in design. In these newer spaces, the mediaeval sobriety of dark, whittled oak is exchanged for sleek, economical wooden furniture made of much lighter-hued woods, such as beech and birch. Likewise, the stupendous views of the surrounding greenery were certainly a modern inclusion, and represented the radical inverse of what a house was traditionally supposed to be: the status symbol of a rich aristocrat or industrialist, designed to impress itself upon visitors or passers-by from a distance, the grand scale of the property further accentuated by a circular driveway and rows of trees. This potent architectural style is missing at Finstergrün, however rugged the castle may appear perched atop the rocks. It seems more impregnable than imposing.

The absence of an authoritarian architectural style is common to buildings created in the early twentieth century by experimental

78

architects and their—often female—commissioners. They are designed more 'from the inside out', prioritising the view from indoors.[16] This is a salient feature of the St Hubertus hunting lodge, for instance, built between 1914 and 1920 by Mrs Kröller-Müller, whose husband would be sensible enough, in 1919, to multiply his assets by purchasing a share of the recently deceased Guido's businesses (the Eisenwerk Kraft smelting plant).[17] Or take the Edith Farnsworth House (1950), the female physician's single-room glass retreat, built in the woods near Chicago by the Bauhaus architect Mies van der Rohe. In such alternative houses, women dared to make a break with tradition, and use their own resources to build and furnish residences where views were paramount. Finstergrün was not quite so experimental, having too classical a form and a more museum-like interior. But it was unique, having been built for personal use by a single mother of two children, who chose to live an independent life amid breathtaking natural beauty.

* * *

Hotel Païva is the most impressive and best-preserved remnant of the Henckel von Donnersmarcks' material wealth, Finstergrün's interior having changed beyond recognition. But both houses appeal to the imagination, each in their own way. From the outset, Hotel Païva was the manifestation of a successfully ambitious common-born woman, her unapologetic *mise-en-scène* for a profound sensual affinity. Finstergrün is the opposite: a monument to the bond between a young widow and the ideals of her bold Hungarian husband, with his fantasy of 'starting again'.

In August 1907, building supervisor Holzinger drew up a detailed progress report on construction at Finstergrün, for the tax authorities.[18] His report stated that the entire premises already counted 126 different rooms—from pantries to stables—only twenty-three of which were still awaiting completion. The presence of only a single bathroom is striking, while the toilets are not even listed as such. John Ruskin once made the important observation that 'a good sewer is a far nobler and a far holier thing … than the most admired Madonna ever painted'.[19] Margit will no doubt have made appropriate arrangements, but the lack of modern conveniences is conspicuous in this report as construction nears its end, and is especially noteworthy for a woman who had grown up in relative luxury on the fruits of the industrial revolution.

The castle took on considerable proportions, and was far larger than Hotel Païva. It is quite easy to get lost inside, and much of it will have gone unused by Margit's small family, who rarely welcomed guests in any large numbers. As we know, it was also difficult to heat, with many of the rooms connected via open passageways. At an elevation of one thousand metres in the Tauern mountains, heating was quite a challenge, which Margit would later come to realise. But she was stubborn and refused to admit defeat, not even after 1905, when her grandmother's death ruled out retreats to the warmth of Abbazia, as her family villas became the property of Kaiser Wilhelm II. Trips to Silesia were also off the table once both of her parents died, one after the other in 1908, and her brother Edgar moved into Brynek with his family. Margit's inheritance from her parents was uncertain, as a large portion of the family capital had been invested in Brynek's reconstruction and renovation. But there must have been something left over for her.

A CRUMBLING EMPIRE

Early in her Lungau life, when Margit was still wealthy, she probably hardly noticed the considerable sums she was spending on Finstergrün, acquiring unique furniture items and paying tradespeople to decorate her fortress. But for someone like her, interior design was not an occupation to which she could dedicate her entire life.

To categorise Margit as a feminist would be going too far, contrary to the beliefs of today's Lungauer. But in her new life, from around 1908, she did develop an interest in social issues and in the ways that women could contribute. That year she joined the Salzburg chapter of the Catholic Women's Organisation (CWO),[1] the successor to the Austrian Empire Women's Organisation, which was itself a reaction to socialist women's associations campaigning for the right to vote. The CWO's motto, *Gut Österreichisch, Deutsch und Christlich*, can be somewhat freely translated as 'True to Austrian, German and Christian Values', forging a striking connection between religion and, here, dual nationalism. The organization was also openly antisemitic, advising Catholic housewives not to patronise Jewish businesses. Margit was not especially active in the association to begin with, spending most of her first few years building a road to the castle as well as a private storehouse at Ramingstein station—otherwise her home would never have been finished. Also in 1908, she joined the Red Cross, in which many upper-class women were socially active.

Raising her two children was not easy. In a letter to her mother, Margit complains that her nanny is unable to control them.[2] Good staff were likely scarce in remote Lungau, so it was probably a relief of sorts when her young son Béla left for Pressburg in Hungary, to be raised under the wing of his Szapáry grandmother, Gabrielle. On Béla's departure, aged six, his mother presented him with five pages of typed instructions for his teachers.[3] Supposedly, it had been

SECRETS OF A SUITCASE

Sándor's last wish that his son grow up as a Hungarian—an odd legacy from a father who had himself planned to start afresh in Lungau as the Knight of Finstergrün, with no particular patriotic aspirations of his own. The castle also lacks any suggestion of nationalistic leanings, so these must have developed quickly within a few years of his marriage if this really was his dying wish.

Pressburg was the administrative centre of Hungary at the time, and a bastion of nationalism. One disadvantage for Béla was the fact that he would be raised by two women, without any close male family members to shepherd his growth into a stout-hearted Hungarian—a requirement that one might have expected, under the circumstances. His grandmother was mainly active on the religious front, as was his aunt Ilona, a gifted pianist who often appeared at the Viennese court. His uncle Péter had died childless in Paris in 1906. Where was Margit sending her son? She herself had no desire to be Hungarian, and barely spoke three words of the language in her entire life.[4]

At that time, being 'Hungarian' represented a desire to separate oneself from the Habsburg empire, the grand dual monarchy of Austria and Hungary. But such a desire was at odds with Margit's own aspirations, eager as she was to belong to the Austria of Emperor Franz Joseph I. She demonstrated as much several years later when she accepted the Order of Elisabeth, named after Sisi, the famous empress. It's clear from the order's rules that it made significant patriotic demands on members. Keeping Béla at Finstergrün, especially in his younger years, would have made much more sense. But instead, Margit opted to fulfil her late husband's last wishes, paying a price for her choice to remain in far-off Lungau. The decision to say goodbye to Béla did give her the freedom to fill her life with charitable activities that had no direct connection to motherhood, let alone Hungarian nationalism. Still, her decision to send her first-born and only son on a one-way trip to Pressburg is one of the more puzzling mysteries in her life. It can only be explained by a sense of *noblesse oblige*, which always puts the duties of motherhood below the interests of 'the house'.[5]

What kind of country was Hungary at that time, around 1900? Today it is known—not without reason—for being conservative and xenophobic. The Hungarians often complain that Europe shows little understanding for them, and blame this attitude on historical

82

A CRUMBLING EMPIRE

ignorance. They are not entirely wrong. For centuries, Hungary, like Poland, was overlooked by the major European kingdoms, when it wasn't being exploited and trampled on. Although Hungary has existed in various shapes and sizes for over a thousand years, for a long time it was partially occupied by the Islamic empire of the Ottomans, bringing Turkish influence into the Hungarian language. Of all the peoples of Hungary, which has comprised no fewer than fifteen nationalities since the nineteenth century, it is now the Roma who suffer the greatest persecution whenever there is need of a European scapegoat. That's as far as knowledge of Hungary goes in Western Europe; at best, some know that Hungary is the land of *puszta*, horses, bell peppers and goulash. The situation was little different in 1900, as we saw in Margit's brother's missive reacting to her engagement.

For centuries, the Western powers had had enough of their own problems to deal with. As the Hungarian historian Dalos remarked, in addition to the Europe of 'libraries, universities and painting', there was also the Europe of 'the dead, the infirm, refugees, natural disasters, the plague, cholera, livestock disease, starvation, pyres, galleys, pogroms and witch trials'.[6] The main history of Hungary, long considered primarily a mining district of the Habsburg empire, revolved around its border with Austria right up to the fall of the Berlin Wall in 1989. The kingdom was left to its own devices, and took care of itself as best it could. Uprisings were mercilessly crushed by the Habsburgs, enduring only as a recurring thread running through the scarce early Hungarian literature.

The great Hungarian noble families, such as the Esterhazys and Palffys, along with their Bohemian counterparts—the Schwarzenbergs and the Kinskys—were persuaded to send their sons to the Habsburg court in Vienna, where they stood a chance of becoming officers in the imperial army. Most, however, withdrew to their estates and led peaceful lives punctuated by hunting parties (important social events, as we know). The lesser nobility, condescendingly referred to by the Viennese as the 'owners of seven plum trees', were appeased with *Landtagen*, state-parliamentary meetings held with fluctuating regularity in Pressburg.

The situation changed rapidly in the mid-nineteenth century, when the previously subjugated Hungarian aristocracy began acting like engaged citizens. The first Hungarian dictionary and grammar was published in 1845. It was a good start, and the newly founded Academy of Sciences aided Hungary in its ongoing development. A railway network was built, and Pest—which later merged with Buda—replaced Pressburg as an unofficial new capital. The dual monarchy emerged out of Austria's weakened position following yet another conflict with Prussia: the defeat at Königgrätz in 1866 put paid to Habsburg aspirations of establishing a great 'Republic of the Danube' joining the Austrians with the Prussians, and was viewed as a fatal missed opportunity for bringing about an early united Europe.[7] Bismarck, the Prussian chancellor, saw no need for such a trajectory, instead steering Germany's path to a united federation, secured in 1871 after victory in the Franco-Prussian War. It was as a consolation prize that the Austrian Emperor Franz Joseph I crowned himself king of Hungary in 1867, along with Elisabeth, who became his queen. This dual monarchy would be the last of the Habsburg empire. Under it, Hungary remained as it always had been: the orchard and granary of Austria, bereft of any administrative or economic power.

This was particularly irksome to the Hungarian nobility, whose sense of nationalism was growing stronger in the wake of developments sweeping Europe in the second half of the nineteenth century, particularly Germany and Italy. During this period of relative prosperity, Budapest came to be known as 'little Paris'. It boasted the continent's first underground metro, a well-designed layout of boulevards, streets and squares, a luxury department store modelled after Paris's La Samaritaine,[8] and—not unimportantly, given the constant threat of cholera—an effective sewerage system. One member of the Szapáry family played an important role in the Hungarian Municipal Public Works Department, which was responsible for the sewers.

In 1896, the country celebrated its 1,000-year anniversary. Despite the ongoing repression of democratic and liberal movements, Hungary had by now developed into a modern nation, most notably in an economic sense. It had a lively intelligentsia and a rich cultural life in the early twentieth century, with composers such as Bartók and Kodály garnering fame throughout Europe. The predominantly liberal political climate manifested in the battles for legally recognised civil

A CRUMBLING EMPIRE

marriage and women's rights. Through positive discrimination towards Jews, some were admitted to the nobility. However, the flipside of this economic growth was the exploitation of the working class, whose members rose up in protest. Only six percent of the population had the right to vote, and they elected a parliament that exhausted itself in squabbles about which language should be spoken and when. Mass emigration to the United States ensued: over a million farmers and impoverished Jews fled via Fiume in Croatia, fed up with the major landowners' exploitation. The debate surrounding the kingdom's ethnic plurality remained heated and volatile.

The Hungarian occupation of Bosnia-Herzegovina in 1878 fuelled both nationalist sentiment in general, and one fantasy in particular: that Hungary might reassert dominance in the Balkans as it had in the Middle Ages, forming a buffer against the Turks. But the Hungarian nationalists were impotent in the sphere of power formed by the surrounding major nations. First of all there was Austria, which also wished to strengthen its position in the Balkans, especially now that a unified, nationalist Italy was laying claim to all regions containing ethnic-Italian minorities, such as the Adriatic coast. But all these dreams need not have led to war in 1914, not even the attack on the Habsburg heir Franz Ferdinand in Sarajevo. The archduke was despised in Hungary for his desire to abolish the dual monarchy, which enshrined equality between Austria and Hungary. He did not even wish to be crowned as the Hungarian king.

After Franz Ferdinand's murder, Austria sent Serbia an ultimatum, demanding that the independent kingdom take responsibility for the assassination and welcome Austrian police officers to investigate the attack. As war ultimatums go, the Habsburgs were hardly in the strongest position; it was already clear that the Serbian government had had nothing to do with it. In Russia, the Austrian ambassador—a Szapáry—was summoned and told: 'This is a provocation to war.'

There are various theories about the cause of the First World War. Some of these involve Britain, and its fear of Germany's increasing industrial and economic power. This, in turn, was partly due to the excellent education offered by German universities, which were threatening to overshadow Oxford and Cambridge.[9] But whether Europe was sleepwalking into the war (according to

Christopher Clark) or triggered it intentionally, Germany did seem to be the country that would benefit most from the ultimatum sent to Serbia. Wilhelm II wanted war; he wanted more land and colonies especially, with his desire for 'a place under the sun'. And that is what he got—the war, that is.

Margit had family spread throughout Central Europe. Through her trips to Silesia and Vienna and her visits to Béla in Pressburg, she will have kept abreast of these developments. She also read the newspapers, though the *Tauern Post*, the local Lungau paper that began circulating daily in 1908, contained mostly propaganda. In 1914 the German and Austrian public were being prepared for a brief but intense war, of which the Germanic allies would be the obvious victors—a kind of triumphalism also evident on the cover of Jolanta's postcard album. In 1915, the *Tauern Post* wrote:

> Though we must have confidence in our army, only when the bells of peace peal far and wide will we become aware of the purifying power of war. Only then will the great cleansing truly become apparent to us. But even now, let us come together as one people, and together bear this heaviest of burdens. Each of us will then feel that we cannot be defeated, that instead, a grand, free and new resurrection awaits us.[10]

There is no evidence that Margit expressed any scepticism about the notion that the Austrians were destined to win 'through the glorious unity of the people'. She was not the type of person to climb the barricades, or to join the first women-led freedom movement that came along. That initiative had already been taken in Vienna by Baroness Bertha von Suttner, born Countess Kinsky, originally from Bohemia. As early as 1889, she wrote a novel titled *Die Waffen nieder!* (Lay Down Your Arms!), which was translated into twelve languages and reprinted thirty-seven times. The novel outlines her experiences in the bloody Russo-Turkish War of 1877–8, when she lived in the Caucasus region. The Russians had the Bosporus in their sights, with hopes of creating an open pathway to the Mediterranean Sea. Bertha describes what the war meant for women and children, and her account could not have been more at odds with the Habsburg empire's glorified militarism. She was ridiculed, but she also earned worldwide fame.

A CRUMBLING EMPIRE

Bertha was invited to give lectures far and wide. She organised peace conferences, where she made her case for an international court to arbitrate conflicts between nations. She considered the first of the peace conferences at The Hague, an 1899 initiative of the Russian Tsar Nicholas II, her crowning achievement. But because she was a woman and, astonishingly, barred from participating herself, she organised a concurrent 'salon' for international pacifists in the nearby Kurhaus hotel. It was during that very conference that the Permanent Court of Arbitration was founded, for which the Palace of Peace was later built. The Hague's status as a centre for international humanitarian law is thanks to Bertha von Suttner's efforts.

She had many admirers, such as the steel magnate Andrew Carnegie, and Alfred Nobel. It was Bertha who prompted the Swedish dynamite manufacturer to institute the Nobel Prize, and who inspired Carnegie to finance the construction of the Palace of Peace. He did so, on the condition that it also contain a library. (Carnegie, who was otherwise a dyed-in-the-wool businessman, spent almost his entire fortune on libraries, in the belief that knowledge was the only thing that could help people rise up out of misery.) The Palace of Peace was opened in 1913, in the presence of Bertha and the young Dutch Queen Wilhelmina.

All of these sensational initiatives by a rebellious Austrian woman, and a noblewoman to boot, cannot have gone unnoticed by Margit. Although she lived far from Vienna and the Habsburg court, there is no cause to doubt Margit's heartfelt support for Emperor Franz Joseph in the autumn of his life, with all of his displays of dual-monarchical power, such as hussars in full regalia. She was immune to the vicious satire in which Vienna's early twentieth-century elite excelled, writings by the likes of Karl Kraus, author and publisher of *Die Fackel* ('The Torch'), who gleefully dissected fin-de-siècle politics. Nor would Margit have enjoyed the work of doctor and author Arthur Schnitzler, who exposed the amoral and erotic animus of Viennese from all walks of life. One wouldn't have found these works, nor any studies by other contemporaries such as Freud, on the shelves of Finstergrün's small library, which only contained books by the likes of Goethe. Such literature would only have caused the castle's mistress to lie awake at night in her beautiful four-poster bed.

SECRETS OF A SUITCASE

While Wilczek sacrificed the large copper bell from his Kreuzenstein castle so that it could be recast as a military cannon,[11] at the start of the war Margit invested large sums in war bonds, as did most members of the Habsburg aristocracy. The country was being led by an emperor who had been on the throne for decades, and was at the end of his strength after the suicide of his son Rudolf in 1889, the murder of his wife Sisi by an anarchist in 1898, and the Sarajevo assassination of his nephew Franz Ferdinand in 1914. He died two years into the war, after which the Habsburgs' 50 million subjects, or at least the non-Austrians, saw their chance. These Poles, Hungarians, Romanians, Czechs, Croatians and Italians made up around two-thirds of the empire's total population. At the close of hostilities, they deserted en masse from the Habsburg army, which was led by despised, arrogant Austrian officers, to fight instead for their 'own' countries. Nationalism, the sentiment so openly capitalised on by the populist German and Austrian media of the time to keep people motivated in the ranks and on the home front, took on a new form, as the struggle began for independence among oppressed groups. (There was a ban on their own languages in schools, for example.) And so it was that the Habsburg empire fell apart, before there was even time to sound the last post.

The new nationalism carried a sinister undertone, however. The rising tide was based on identification of a common enemy, but this enemy was not another, external nation, such as the French. Instead, a segment of the empire's own population was designated alien and threatening, on the basis of various racist characterisations: the Jews. The Viennese mayor Lueger—who governed the city from 1897 until his death in 1910, after the ageing Franz Joseph had successfully delayed his appointment for two years— was even wont to use bacteriological terminology to describe the danger supposedly inherent among the Jewish people. Lueger was an early inspiration for the young Austrian art academy student Adolf Hitler, who had just arrived in Vienna from his home in Linz. After the First World War was over, Hitler turned out to have had a very different perception of the conflict than the French or Germans. Like many other Austrians, he saw the war as a necessary cleansing process, leaving behind only 'pure' countries free of foreign influence or weak elements.

88

A CRUMBLING EMPIRE

Contrary to expectations, the war had proven to be a matter not of months, but of four long years. In Hungary a shadow government was formed 'as a precautionary measure'. When Franz Joseph died in 1916, he was succeeded by his great-nephew Karl I. Karl made some paltry peace proposals in 1917, which were not accepted. The First World War only concluded with the inglorious demise of the once-mighty Habsburg empire, which had risen to grandeur not through battle, but by securing peaceful marriages: since the sixteenth century, the Austrians' motto had been *Bella gerant alii, tu felix Austria nube* ('Others wage war, but you, happy Austria, marry'), and the marriage bed was the means by which they had absorbed parts of Hungary and Bohemia. Now, Austria became a 'remnant', in the words of the then French Prime Minister Georges Clemenceau: a tiny country with an engorged capital, Vienna. What had once been central became peripheral.

After an attempt to merge with Germany, Austria became a federal republic in 1919. The social democrats governed for a time, followed by Christian-social governments from 1920 to 1934. The dethroned Karl I withdrew to Switzerland, the nobility's influence having been excised from national government. The Hungarians looked on with amazement as their equally nationalistic neighbours—Poland, Romania, Czechoslovakia and Yugoslavia—reduced their country to a third of its former size, a development endorsed by France, Britain and Russia under the Treaty of Versailles. Karl, who even renounced the Viennese imperial crown in 1918, did attempt to reinstate himself as king of Hungary in 1921, but was exiled by the republican government. He died of pneumonia in Madeira in 1922, a lonely and ruined man. That same month, his widow, Zita of Bourbon-Parma, received a letter from a countess in Lungau who had always remained loyal to the Habsburg monarchy, and who deeply regretted that she could not pass on her condolences in person, due to the great distance separating her from the widow in exile. Margit Szapáry seemed to have been lost forever as a champion of the Hungarian cause.

DOUBLE-ENTRY BOOKKEEPING

Austrian historian Nora Watteck recalls Margit as 'A large woman, with bright-blue eyes and a metallic, masculine voice, dressed in hunting attire. There are whispers that she wore Lederhosen beneath her long skirts, which would have come in useful during the hunt.'[1]

Margit had reinvented herself. The girl who had painted water-colour flowers, the splendid bride in her tightly corseted wedding gown, the woman in a sailor's shirt and white cap—these characters were no more. An unexpected contender had entered the arena, one who stood her ground. She'd had no choice: the First World War had turned Margit Szapáry into a managing director.

In the early twentieth century, Margit was a wealthy widow, but no 'salon aristocrat' of the ubiquitous type.[2] She had more important things to do. While other noblewomen in her life, including her mother- and sister-in-law, were whiling away their hours in committees, deciding whether to erect a statue to Franz Ferdinand or how to add sparkle to some church anniversary or other, Margit went out in search of matters more pressing. She conducted herself in a manner befitting the 'lady of the manor', a true *Gutsherrin*. People could come to her if money was needed to solve a problem or to support a worthy cause in her adopted region. This trait, like the funds to finance it, was yet another legacy of her upbringing. In the years before the war, Margit had donated the prizes for the best horse-breeder in Tamsweg, supported the local volunteer fire brigade, purchased gold-embroidered pennants for associations, and personally attended festive markets. It was as though Austrian crowns had suddenly started growing on Finstergrün's pine trees. And, although the First World War would bring a premature end to these halcyon days, the conflict would awaken new qualities within her.

At the start of the war, which broke out in late July 1914, Austria quickly noticed that the country was actually being governed in rather amateurish fashion. Until then, for example, it had been taken for granted that hospitals, and emergency departments especially, could only be run by women of noble birth. And if there was only one such woman in the vicinity, and she was prepared to fulfil the role, she may have had no choice than to shoulder the title of 'Countess of the Lungau'. This was a role that one did not simply ignore in the face of tragedy, with the first war widows and orphans appearing on one's doorstep. As early as September, just two months after the fighting began, the Austrians were utterly defeated in Galicia by the Russians.

This was a war of 'industrialised mass slaughter [where] human flesh stood against killing machines'.[3] The soldiers had hardly any protective armour (such as steel helmets), resulting in large numbers of wounded and infirm soldiers requiring care. Their number had not been anticipated, and so no measures taken. Margit sprang to meet the need with her influence, her money, her level-headedness and her knowledge of double-entry accounting. She held meetings and planned for the future. She transformed the Szaparys' residence in Pressburg, the former Hungarian capital, into a sixteen-bed emergency hospital, and arranged for Russian and Italian prisoners of war to take the place of Austrian conscripts in the Lungau fields. And she worked tirelessly to organize military service exemptions for as many boys and men as she could.

In 1916, as the war was raging, as soldiers on the front line were dying from mustard gas and as the first tanks were deployed against the fragile bodies of young men, Margit wrote a six-page brochure on healthy nutrition. Major food shortages were threatening starvation on the home front, and the brochure was distributed widely in the Lungau region. In it, she advised housewives to start using cornmeal instead of wheat flour, since wheat was needed for the soldiers. She also organised cooking demonstrations in Finstergrün's large kitchen, and suggested seeking out other substitute grains and growing as many of one's own vegetables as possible. She concludes her brochure:

> And you, housewives and mothers, cook delicious food, and prepare every meal with great care. Do not believe that the time you spend in the kitchen is wasted, for by doing so you are serving the

DOUBLE-ENTRY BOOKKEEPING

> Fatherland more than ever, and your ladles are just as important as any soldiers' armaments.[4]

Though well-meant, this advice did come from somebody whom we might doubt had ever stood ladle in hand preparing food, let alone someone who had ever sown and harvested her own vegetables. Many of Margit's readers would certainly have done so, and would already have known how to prepare appetising food as economically as possible. This was just how some noblewomen approached the notion of 'good works'. Her advice seems motivated above all by a need to support the government, and to impress upon readers the importance of maintaining both trust in their leaders and hope for victory.

During the war, Margit and her daughter Jolanta went to live on the Premhaus farmstead not far from Finstergrün. It was easier to heat, which was important, since all of the male servants had been conscripted, leaving nobody to chop wood. Finstergrün required a large household staff: it took three men alone to keep all of the stoves burning, and another two for the oil lamps.

When Jolanta left to attend a Viennese boarding school in 1916, Margit was left living alone until several years after the end of the fighting. But with her wartime activities, she was anything but lonely. She became the driving force behind an initiative more praiseworthy than anything she had done until that point, an inventive enterprise that went beyond just handing out cheques. Her goal was to bolster agriculture in the struggling region, not only because of the food shortages, but also—with great foresight—to ensure that the returning servicemen would be able to provide for themselves once the war was over. The fact that Lungau is still renowned for its (now organic and ecological) agriculture is thanks to the foundations laid by Margit's decisive action during the First World War.

When Salzburg's municipal government started buying up neglected estates to grow food for the hungry population, an initiative known in German as the *Gemüsebauaktion* or 'vegetable campaign', Margit was charged with its general management. She set up six farms, taking meticulous note of their inventories and designating the land for useful purposes. She purchased seeds, seed potatoes,

SECRETS OF A SUITCASE

tools, and synthetic fertiliser, which was new to Lungau, but not to her. The production of phosphate and potassium as a byproduct of the Silesian steel industry was a Henckel von Donnersmarck side-line.[5] She ordered the fertiliser from Fulda personally, and distributed it across the six farms. She oversaw the financials and appointed competent people like Holzinger, Finstergrün's construction supervisor, to keep the entire project running smoothly.

Margit supplied Salzburg with fresh vegetables and potatoes, sending 2,000 kilograms of cauliflower as early as 1916. She herself calculated the maximum yield of cauliflower from seed, as well as the amount of land required. She was rather headstrong, however, and also personally organised the transport to Salzburg, which entailed a considerable detour around the Tauern mountains by train. When it arrived, the cauliflower was quite mouldy, reducing her takings markedly and eliciting some stern letters from Salzburg. Margit was the one in control on many fronts,[6] which brought both advantages and disadvantages. But the alternative solution here—transporting the cauliflower by horse and cart through a mountain pass—would also have been out of the question, since the strong young men required for the job were all off fighting in the war. Lorries were still a rarity.

Margit remained undaunted by such setbacks, and by 1918 her enterprise had yielded 130,000 kilograms of shelf-stable vegetables (white cabbage, leek, kohlrabi and beets); 4,500 kilos of rye, barley and wheat; and nearly 600 train cars of potatoes. True, she was financing everything herself, which made matters much easier. But such a complex enterprise cannot succeed without a solid administrative backbone, which she developed quite naturally, learning as she went. She also inspired others around her to contribute to local food supplies—her neighbour Hans Wilczek even became a bee-keeper, adding a layer of sweetness to their dry slices of bread.

All of these activities contributed to a growing level of respect for Margit. Her cornmeal recipes and her organisation of a berry and mushroom hunt in 1917 may have been a drop in the bucket when it came to supplementing the meagre fare available in Lungau, but did nothing to detract from her rising esteem. As often seems to be the case with busy people, she even found extra time to help those who came knocking at her door. She became involved in prisoner exchanges, since, as a member of the Red Cross, she had access to the lists of prisoners and victims of war. She scoured the lists for the names of men from Lungau, and took steps to have them exchanged for Russians or Italians. She was also involved with compiling and sending care packages of food and clothing to Lungau soldiers fighting on the front in Carpathia, where the Austrian army had to hold back the Russians in the winter of 1915. No fewer than 800,000 soldiers were lost through capture, defeat, cold and illness. This was a significant number, given that just 1.3 million Austrian soldiers had originally gone to fight in the war.[7]

Even Ramingstein's schoolgirls were enlisted, led by their handicrafts teacher Anna Jud in knitting warm socks and undershirts for men on the ice-cold front. Margit purchased the wool and had the packages sent via Salzburg; miraculously, they reached their destination,[8] which eased somewhat the suffering of the rank and file, who felt they were living more like animals than people.

These activities were, of course, a kind of propaganda, conceived to unite the (female) home front with the brave (male) soldiers, keeping morale and patriotism intact—and ensuring the recruitment of new soldiers.[9] But this only partly explains the energy and resources Margit invested in her efforts. She had clearly realised that she was capable, that her talents lay in organisation, administration and lobbying those in high places. She leveraged her name and status without hesitation whenever necessary. And that was often, as the devastating conflict rolled on for four long years.

Margit was forty-seven at the end of the war. She had demonstrated her strengths, and her readiness to roll her sleeves up and get to work—provided she was the one in charge. Another helpful factor was her ongoing wealth. She lost some assets in 1918 when it transpired that she had backed the losing side, her war bonds rendered worthless, but some of her grandfather Hugo I's fortune still remained, even though the family lost much Silesian territory—and therefore industry—in the peace negotiations, which redrew the Polish border after 1922. The devaluation of the nation's currency also had a big impact.

Thankfully, Margit's Catholic branch of the family had invested some capital in an English business in London.[10] And in any case, she was still expecting—and would receive—money from her Silesian inheritance. What did increasingly cause problems was her health. In 1916 she became so ill that she was admitted to a hospital in Vienna for several months. That was the year her daughter Jolanta left for the Sacré Coeur boarding school in the rich town of Pressbaum near the capital, after which Margit increasingly developed heart and stomach problems. They were caused by what we would now call 'stress', of which there were ample sources in Margit's life, foreshadowed by Franz Joseph's death in 1916.

Noblewomen belonging to the Catholic Order of the Starry Cross (the Sternkreuz-Orden) automatically commanded a measure of social status and authority in the Habsburg empire. Margit was awarded this distinction upon her marriage and settlement in Lungau, and, as we know, was also decorated with the empire's far more illustrious Order of Elisabeth. But, of course, the awarding empire imploded in 1918. During high mass in St Stephen's Cathedral on 11 November that year, most of the packed cathedral bewailed what had been lost. Karl I had stepped down, writing in his abdication announcement: 'Only inner peace can heal the wounds of this war'—cold comfort for the now 'headless' nobility.[11] As for the old Hungarian aristocracy, they had nothing more to gain, unless their Hungarian, Czech or Slovak roots could play a role in Hungarian, Czech or Slovak nationalism and the formation of their new nation-states. This predicament will have been even less evident in Lungau than in Vienna, but the realisation that the old certainties were gone must have been felt in even the most remote areas of the former empire. Among the lower classes especially, Austria's defeat damaged respect for the aristocracy and the Church, who had blatantly lied to the population for so long about a glorious victory. On 3 April 1919, the people's discontent led the new republic to abolish the nobility's administrative authority, effectively banishing the heads of houses from positions in government.

Margit was certainly no supporter of the Hungarian cause but, as a monarchist and the widow of a Hungarian royal-and-imperial Hussar, she must have felt some insecurity about her position. She sought refuge in hard work, having been confronted with the terrors of the war, and all the suffering it had caused among the population. Defeat had greatly impacted Lungau, the region she had made her

96

DOUBLE-ENTRY BOOKKEEPING

home. Margit was in the thick of it, completely alone and without children. Jolanta, after her schooling at the Sacré Coeur institute, had enrolled in a nursing programme at the Viennese Rudolfinerhaus, a private hospital founded by Wilczek and the late Crown Prince Rudolf.[12] Béla had studied at an agricultural academy in the Hungarian town of Magyaróvár, which produced the farming machinery that had automated ploughing, sowing and harvesting for hardworking farmers since the nineteenth century. He then left to be a gentleman farmer in Canada, where he would remain until 1930.[13]

Margit's immediate family lived in far-off Silesia, and were in danger of losing property to claims by the Polish. There were increasingly serious uprisings by farmers and labourers, emboldened by the 1917 Bolshevik Revolution in Russia. All who belonged to the propertied classes felt that great changes were imminent, that an entire society was remoulding itself into an as-yet unknown form. The women demanded, and would secure, a major part in this new world, particularly those who had demonstrated their ability to take initiative.

Margit's initial response was a practical one. She did what any sensible person in her position would do, and ensured that her own backyard was in good order. Lungau's 292 injured servicemen and their families could count on her for support. She bought prostheses for them but more importantly, as we have seen, she bought up abandoned and neglected farms in the region, fitted them out, and gave them to the veterans' families so that they could build up a life once again. She solved the legal problems associated with the purchase of farmland, such as the details of possession and succession, by seeking direct contact with the owners and the new government in Vienna. She did what she could, alone in her fort with eight servants, four horses and a donkey, and a considerable dent in her finances. Her generosity in these early post-war years alone cost her more than 200,000 Austrian crowns.

* * *

However helpful and charitable, there was also a problematic side to this particular brand of large-scale philanthropy undertaken by noblemen and -women since the nineteenth century. They had been brought up to believe in it, it was expected of them, and they were decorated as a result. But it could also lead to arbitrary clemency, especially if the Church became involved. Philanthropy of this kind does offer several advantages that are now provided by governments in modern welfare states, funded through the tax system. The anonymous nature of taxation means that the welfare provided escapes the money-giver's individual bias, which might sometimes lead to a rather questionable form of personal glorification. This was certainly the case with Margit, who seemed not to have a problem with it whatsoever. Moreover, she was not being generous with her own hard-won earnings, but was instead drawing on her family's capital, and thus the Silesian coal and steel industry propped up by an army of labourers. What she benefited from most were the business instincts of her grandfather, Hugo I, who had multiplied his fortune first by speculating with large sums and assets in 1871, and later with the income from his various enterprises.

Margit's actions came from her upbringing and the conventions of her social class. She did break the mould in one way, by investing in solutions that eliminated dependence of the sick and infirm on alms, enabling them instead to regain self-respect and become self-sufficient by working the land. She also put her rising status to good use, petitioning dignitaries on behalf of those who were less able to do so themselves.

Still, she did also continue with almsgiving—which, as was common in those days, often went hand-in-hand with religious ambitions. One example was her commission of a wooden sculpture for Lungau that people could pay to hammer nails into, with the proceeds going to needy wives and children of soldiers, a status interpreted generously to include unmarried partners and illegitimate children. Margit and her friend Baroness Marianne von Buddenbrock, a student of art history, found a sculptor-priest to produce the statue, which was erected in front of Tamsweg's town hall in 1915, once it was clear to all that the war would drag on for some time yet. It was a statue of Samson, the gargantuan biblical figure, who had featured in Lungau processions for centuries as a symbol of Lungauer strength and fortitude. Hammering a nail into the statue was considered an act of love, religious devotion and national pride, and was to be accompanied by a charitable donation in hard cash.

DOUBLE-ENTRY BOOKKEEPING

Although the wartime combination of Catholic and patriotic fervour more often served as a poisoned chalice than an elixir, all contributions were welcome. The countess and baroness each paid several thousand crowns to hammer their nails into Samson, readily followed by the local doctor, the notary and all the other townsfolk who had a little extra to spare. All contributions were carefully published in the *Tauern Post*, making it painfully clear not only how much each person had donated, but also who had chosen not to, or given too little. And so the beginnings of a fund were set up for the victims of the war.

More interesting were Margit's initiatives to promote agriculture in Lungau—not only because they were less common than general acts of charity, but also because she was a woman. She behaved like an entrepreneur, of which there were still very few at that time. Her goal was to ease the suffering of the region's ordinary farming families, since their predicament was hardly resolved by the armistice in 1918. Only then did the real scope of the slaughter become known, and likewise its effects on the soldiers who had been sent to fight for Austria and Germany without helmets or even decent uniforms— not to mention the preponderance of diabolical weapons that had been engineered all too eagerly by men unburdened by moral scruples. Whether these issues of guilt were raised in Lungau is unknown; they may have been set aside in the face of more pressing matters, such as the food shortages. The lack of essential knowledge and manpower led to failed harvests, and the distribution of cereals and other foodstuffs across the country was poorly organised. Hungary also preferred to feed its grain to its own livestock, rather than send it to Austria. The increasingly nationalistic Hungarians wanted little more to do with the old Habsburg system; in 1922, Margit's own son Béla became Hungarian at his own request.[14]

Lungau was left to fend for itself, and the commoners resorted to what had always been mere sport for the rich: hunting large game in their own local woods. Margit, who knew a thing or two about hunting, led the party, along with several beaters. During the first winter after the war, twenty-seven animals were shot. They stilled the people's hunger slightly, and the enterprise set a good example for other noble landowners with hunting grounds in the region. They, too, opened up their lands.[15]

One such nobleman was Hermann Epenstein Ritter von Mauternburg, a German-Austrian doctor who had been knighted by Franz Joseph I in 1908. As a sign of gratitude, he'd chosen to naturalise as an Austrian. In 1894 he had moved into Mauterndorf Castle, the third-largest mediaeval castle in Lungau after Finstergrün and Wilczek's Moosham. Epenstein had a godson, the child of his married mistress. The boy adored his godfather, who had raised him as though he were his own. This godson was a regular guest at Mauterndorf. His name was Hermann Göring.

PART TWO

THE ROARING TWENTIES

Hermann Göring's father was governor-general of Namibia,[1] where he worked to lay the foundations for a well-managed colonial state. Bismarck was not overly satisfied with the local German democracy put in place by Göring Senior, who was transferred and spent several years on the rather inhospitable island of Haiti. It was his final diplomatic posting before retirement. When his second wife Fanny fell pregnant with her fourth child, she returned to Munich alone in 1893, where she gave birth to Hermann. She named him after Hermann Epenstein, her doctor in Munich—a medical officer in the Prussian army who had become good friends with her husband in Namibia.

Not long after giving birth, Fanny Göring returned to her husband and older children in Haiti, leaving the new baby behind to grow up with a foster family for his first few years. When his parents returned to Germany in 1896, he responded aggressively. As Göring Senior's pension was modest, the family moved to an apartment in the small, densely populated area of Berlin-Friedenau. There, the young Hermann received much attention from the wealthy bachelor Dr Epenstein, who often came to visit, and continued to do so even after returning to Germany for good in 1898, following a long period of international travel. To assure himself of a fixed and official residence, Epenstein had purchased Mauterndorf Castle four years before. This address enabled him to ask Franz Joseph to dub him a knight of Mauterndorf, thus granting him access to the aristocratic elite—a dangerous manoeuvre, as Epenstein was half-Jewish. But titles, too, can be bought, and from then on he was known formally as Epenstein Ritter von Mauternburg. He furnished his castle the same way his neighbour Hans Wilczek had done so triumphantly at Moosham and Kreuzenstein: with gothic furniture, woodcuts, paintings and suits of armour, along with

SECRETS OF A SUITCASE

some personal souvenirs from his distant travels, such as African spears and hunting trophies.

In 1898, Epenstein purchased a second, smaller castle near Nuremberg: Veldenstein, built on the remains of an old eleventh-century fort. The castle was decorated in a similar fashion, and it was Veldenstein that Epenstein offered to the Görings as a permanent residence in 1898, when it became evident that life outside the city was preferable for the ailing 5-year-old Hermann. The castle also had more space to offer than the family's small Berlin apartment. Above all, it proved convenient, as Epenstein had become the lover of young Hermann's mother, Fanny. Their rather public affair led to an awkward arrangement, whereby her older (and now also alcoholic) husband was asked to sleep elsewhere in the castle whenever Sir Hermann was present. At Mauterndorf, where they spent their holidays, Göring Senior even had to stay with the children in a separate residence next to the castle whenever Epenstein was home. At such times, Fanny played the role of charming hostess for the many musical soirées organised by Epenstein, with musicians from Berlin and Vienna coming to perform.

It was an arrangement that would not have gone unnoticed in conservative, Catholic Lungau. Göring Junior thus came to hold his biological father in contempt, and to worship Epenstein. When asked to write an essay at school about the man he most admired, he produced a glowing appraisal of his godfather. He was punished as a result, for even at school they knew that Epenstein was half-Jewish, and had only been baptized as a Catholic to become eligible for a noble title. But young Göring took no notice. (Later, in a comparable situation, he is supposed to have retorted: 'I will determine who is Jewish'—though this quote has been attributed to various national socialists).[2] Both his father and Epenstein facilitated his admission to the cadet school in Karlsruhe at the age of twelve, and, when he was sixteen, to the Military Academy in Lichterfelde, Berlin. He enjoyed the flashy uniforms and the cultivated association with a history reaching back to feudal times. It was there that Göring met the brothers Philipp and Christoph von Hessen-Kassel, and cultivated many other aristocratic friendships that would serve him well later in life.

The year 1913 saw the end of the Görings' open marriage. Epenstein asked the Görings to vacate his residences, as he had

104

THE ROARING TWENTIES

(finally) married a much younger woman from Vienna, Lilli Schandrovich. From then on, the Görings lived much more modestly, in an apartment in Munich. Göring Senior died shortly thereafter, and Göring Junior threw himself into his military career with even greater fervour. When the First World War broke out in 1914, Göring was twenty-one and ready to 'give his life for the fatherland', as were so many of his classmates from Lichterfelde.

In 1916, Göring became a pilot in the newly established German air force and, after a mere three months, flew to the western front. There, overconfident and full of bravura, he performed dangerous stunts and succeeded in taking crystal-clear photographs from his open cockpit of the French and the British, using a large camera. He even mounted a machine gun to the cockpit, a novelty in the German air force at the time. When he tried to attack the British during one such flight and was shot himself, he was forced to make an emergency landing and only just made it back to German territory. It took some time for him to recover from his wounds. And where did he do this? In Lungau, at Epenstein's castle.

Once healed, he reported back to the army and received a high distinction for courage displayed: the *Pour le Mérite* first instituted by Frederick the Great. He would always wear it when in uniform, which would open many doors for him later on. Towards the end of the war, he was even appointed commander of the squadron led by the most successful German fighter pilot of the day, the 'Red Baron' himself, Manfred von Richthofen. Göring would remain commander until the Baron's death in April 1918.

Despite Germany's defeat, Göring was revered as a war hero, and made friends in the uppermost echelons of society. It didn't hurt that he was also quite handsome back then. To continue earning an adventurous living during peacetime, in 1919 Göring became a stunt pilot for the Dutch aeroplane manufacturer Anthony Fokker. He received a Fokker F7 on loan, which he used to attract potential customers, giving the impression that his aeroplane had belonged to the Red Baron himself. He made many successful flights in Denmark, where he took on some early daredevils as paying passengers. Göring must have been very popular with the ladies, as an excess of dalliances forced him to leave for Sweden, where he again provided entertainment at air shows, this time for Svenska Lufttraffik. Once, during a snowstorm, he flew home the adventurous Swedish Count von Rosen, who was 'eager to be back before dark'.

What happened next turned out to be a pivotal moment in Göring's life, retold with great weight by all of his biographers: the first encounter with his later wife, Carin. One account describes how Göring 'only just managed' to land his aircraft on the frozen lake in front of von Rosen's gothic castle; another concentrates on the enormous open fire where he warmed himself afterwards. He admired the mediaeval furnishings, including a stuffed bear—one of von Rosen's own hunting trophies—as well as the iron grating in front of the fire, decorated with old runes, and the swastika symbolising the rising sun on the Swedish island of Gotland. But whatever version of the story is told, a 'noble figure with rustling skirts' always descends the staircase: von Rosen's sister-in-law, the then-married Baroness Carin von Kantzow, who happened to be staying when Göring came to visit.

The account of this meeting can be traced back to the sentimental book *Carin Göring* (1936) written by Carin's equally infatuated sister, Fanny.[3] Carin was married to the wealthy but, according to her biographer, dull army officer Nils von Kantzow. She also had a young son, Thomas. But these formed no obstacle to a stormy romance between the former fighter pilot and the besotted Carin. She was a pale beauty with a frail constitution, and a member of the Edelweiss Society, an exclusive Swedish women's association inspired by the Middle Ages. It was a spiritualistic circle within the Theosophical community, populated largely by aristocratic artistes. One of the group's founders was Carin's Irish grandmother, who had introduced the late nineteenth-century trend for Celtic mysticism into her daughter's home in Stockholm, where she even built a private chapel in the garden for spiritual gatherings.

Von Rosen's snow-covered mediaeval castle, where Göring beheld his future wife for the first time, and the equally unique Edelweiss chapel both left a deep impression on him. Carin was quickly willing to follow him to the ends of the earth, and for a long time they were both maligned in the Stockholm community for the scandal of their affair, and Carin's subsequent divorce.

Carin and Herman Göring married on 3 January 1923 in Munich, and went to live in a hunting lodge in the Bavarian alps. Their newlywed bliss did not last long, however, for in the winter of 1922,

THE ROARING TWENTIES

Göring had met Adolf Hitler during a demonstration against the Treaty of Versailles. The two men took a liking to one another, and not long afterward Hitler made him commander of the SA, a paramilitary group of national socialists that would ultimately grow into his private army and, in the 1920s and '30s, terrorise the streets, deploying violence against communists and Jews.

The newlyweds descended from the mountains and relocated to a suburb of Munich, where their home quickly became a meeting point for Hitler and his growing movement. In the SA, Göring was joined by former army captain Ernst Röhm. Along with Rudolf Hess, a fellow ex-pilot, they formed a trio that could often be found *chez* Göring, where the delicate Swedish baroness welcomed them warmly as friends of her husband. The clash of cultures manifested itself in jibes on the part of Hermann's new companions. When Carin was out of earshot, for example, Hitler himself mocked the way she called her husband *Schatz* (treasure) and *Liebling* (darling). But it was quite clear that these rough Bavarians and the elite Swedish-Berliner couple still needed one another, and tensions never escalated beyond such harmless jokes.

Of all the Nazi leaders besides Hitler himself, most has been written about Hermann Göring, probably due to his theatrical personality and his high-flying marriage. But because his own account was exaggerated and inconsistent regarding the details of his career, the biographies do show significant discrepancies. His youth, his service in the First World War, the period immediately following in which he met his first wife Carin, his role in the Beer Hall Putsch, his subsequent sojourn in Mussolini's Italy—all present special challenges in distinguishing fact from fiction. What the biographers agree on, however, is the fact that Göring's godfather, whose castle was in the immediate vicinity of Wilczek's Moosham and Margit's Finstergrün, exerted a major influence on him.

In terms of Lungau, there is at least one respect in which accounts of this period differ. Though it may seem trivial, varying dates have been given for Epenstein's purchase of Mauterndorf. Whereas local records give 1894,[4] most of Göring's biographers say 1898; that is, the same year he acquired Veldenstein Castle in Nuremberg where Göring would grow up.

The local records are more likely to be correct, as Mauterndorf was in poor condition when it was sold and would undergo major renovations for a period of several years.[5] In 1898, Epenstein was appointed an honorary citizen of Mauterndorf, which probably coincided with the completion of work on the castle. For many years after 1898, Epenstein would also be busy restoring Veldenstein. Meanwhile, Mauterndorf was used as a holiday residence by both him and the Görings. Precisely because Mauterndorf was 'finished', it perhaps made the most lasting early impression on Göring. He would return regularly to the Lungau residence later in life, and even spent his final nights there before being arrested by the Americans in 1945.

During all of those years, he must have got to know the neighbours, whose castles were just as imaginative as Epenstein's. After the First World War, however, the other residents will have become decidedly less interested in the Middle Ages and womanising stunt pilots, with all of their attention occupied by matters closer to home. This certainly applied to Margit Szapáry, who was in the process of becoming the 'Countess of Lungau'.

* * *

Having demonstrated her capabilities during the First World War, Margit was assigned an important role afterwards, in the care for injured veterans and the social reintegration of returned servicemen, two tasks that would occupy the lives of many European women for years to come. A total of eight million incapacitated soldiers had returned home across the continent, many of whom had lost either limbs or their eyesight. Then there were the veterans who still experienced daily nightmares about being ordered over the top to try and bayonet the enemy. It was abundantly clear that these insomniac and depressed soldiers were in no state to return immediately to their old lives as hardworking sons, husbands or fathers. These former heroes, who had been cheered off to the front with garlands and celebrations in 1914, now joined the growing ranks of the unemployed.

In the cities, some were still able to eke out a living by selling matches, souvenirs or newspapers. In the country, returning sol-

THE ROARING TWENTIES

diers had no choice but to rely on their families, the government, the Church, and charity. But everybody had troubles of their own. Many were fighting hunger and illness, such as the deadly influenza pandemic of 1918–20, which claimed 20,000 victims in Austria alone. In the autumn of 1918, Margit was asked to join a provincial committee charged with organising both the soldier rehabilitation centres and the strategy to combat tuberculosis, another contagious disease, which had broken out quickly amid the food shortages. She created sets of instructions outlining the treatment for injured veterans, including any potential (re)training or schooling. Margit was so effective in her role that she became the one woman admitted to the council charged with caring for disabled veterans in and around Salzburg.

Although she performed useful work in her region and set an example for other powerful people, the provincial meetings were still laborious, exhausting, and not always effective. Political differences between certain members became increasingly apparent, and the question of who was to bear the cost was often a stumbling block. There were many legal and political hurdles before solutions such as veterans' housing could be realised. There was also disagreement regarding authorisations (who was allowed to make which decisions), exacerbated by the fact that older institutions were largely unavailable in the new and still relatively formless Austrian republic. Margit could not simply leave other council members to their squabbling and pay for everything herself, as she no longer had the finances available. Instead, she looked on helplessly as government funds were sometimes siphoned off to efforts generating only short-term gains, such as holidays for war orphans.

These years, however, also brought her continued pleasure in her membership of the Catholic Women's Organisation, which she had joined in 1908. She was now the president of the Lungau chapter and, as such, was also on the Salzburg district board. Just after the war, she was involved in setting up CWO subdivisions in Ramingstein and Tamsweg, where she herself became president in both cases. The women continued doing what they had done in an improvised fashion during the war—helping those in need—with the addition of occasional religious festivities, such as processions, Christmas celebrations, and communion parties.

The CWO operated in an area that was almost exclusively Catholic. The church square was a social hub, where everybody met on service and feast days, and one of the few public places in the sparsely populated Lungau where distant farming families saw one another regularly. Various societies for boys, girls, men and women strengthened the sense of community, with a focus on the dissemination of Catholic morals and ideals. The pastor gave catechism lessons in the home (for servants) or at Sunday school (for boys). Children received the most attention, including up to four additional hours of religious instruction per week in primary school. The teachers were obliged to participate in church services, and religious inspectors regularly came by to evaluate the quality of the religious education.

The woman's place in the home, where she was to care for her husband and children, was taken for granted as the natural and divine order, and remained uncontested by most Lungauers. Margit seemed to justify her postwar activities—which were diametrically opposed to this doctrine—through the application of an alternative framework of virtue: the obligations of a noblewoman towards the common people in her local community. Not until the 1930s, when she was over sixty, would she openly advocate for the participation of all women in society, lauding it as the 'enrichment of their personalities'. Until then, she simply continued to do what she would eventually campaign for, and to no public objection whatsoever. Margit Szapáry was in a category all her own, even to those in her own social circle, who had begun to worship her almost like a saint. She was subject to a different set of rules, and she comported herself accordingly.

This fact became noticeable when she started cooperating with politicians. In 1918, Austrian women were finally granted the right to vote, as was the case in many other countries after the First World War. Women had become active in the peace movements, and positive action was expected from them through their new voting rights. In Austria, as in most other countries, women's suffrage was the result of a protracted and occasionally fierce battle waged by the women themselves, who tried to win supporters wherever they could. The Dutch doctor and suffragette Alette Jacobs travelled to Vienna and Budapest as early as 1906 to give lectures on the subject. At private afternoon teas, she and her American friend, fellow advocate and president of the World Alliance Carrie Chapman Catt, offered representation 'for women who were not fond of meetings'. By this, of course, they meant women from the upper classes and others who fell under a prohibition against attending meetings of a political nature, as was the case in the Austro-Hungarian capitals.

All of these activities were in preparation for the first International Women's Congress, held in the Netherlands in July 1908. At that time, Margit was still busy finishing her castle. Besides, she already enjoyed a privileged position in Austria, and with it a different view of obedience: her allegiance was to an emperor and to a social structure that automatically allocated her an influential position. Her status as a widow did the same, as widows were no longer subordinate to their husband's views. But all of this changed in 1918, when Margit's duty to her people required a higher degree of political engagement.

At this historic juncture, there were two major parties in Austria, each of which came with a strong class and faith identity: the Christian Socialists (CSP) on the one hand, and the Social Democrats (SD) on the other. The Christian Socialists were monarchist, with a worldview closely aligned to that of the Catholic Church. The Social Democrats were in support of the new republic. Beyond royalists, the CSP was supported by middle-class groups and the lower bourgeoisie, who feared that a republic would threaten their status. The party believed that the nuclear family was the bedrock of society; advocated for the protection of 'unborn life'; recognised only religious marriages as legally valid; and promoted the sexual 'protection' of women. It relied heavily on various organisations and associations in Catholic civil society, such as Margit's CWO.

Even after the introduction of women's suffrage, the CSP did not actively encourage women to participate in party politics, by running for positions on local councils, for example. It argued that there were 'plenty of opportunities' for women to be socially engaged, and that these might also be called 'political'.[6] But politics is always linked to power, and to who has the ability to set budgets, earmark funds and take legal decisions impacting society. It is precisely this kind of power that was denied women whose activities were limited to participation in their own organisations. Nor did it

111

help that the CSP was poorly organised. In Tamsweg and Ramingstein, the party was not allocated an office until 1926; before this, it wasn't possible to integrate the activities of Margit and other leading women of the local CWO branches into municipal or national politics.

Through Bertha von Suttner, Austria had taken the lead in Europe's peace movement. It is hard to imagine Margit having been a fan, if her support for Austria during the war can be interpreted as a form of patriotism. But where suffrage was concerned—and by extension, political influence for women—she was absolutely open to mobilisation. The problem was that this was not a possibility via the CWO, which in 1920 had been expressly warned by the (male) Christian Socialist politicians not to involve itself in politics.[7]

At first, there was no need for Margit to pay the CSP any heed. If she wished to get something done, she simply circumvented the establishment and used her status, writing a letter or paying a visit. These strategies were only available to the elite, however—the high-born and well-connected, or those with a cheque book. And there is no reason to suppose that Margit lacked any sense of elitism. She did much more than simply practise Christian charity for children and the poor, needy and elderly, which the Salzburg CWO set as its official priorities for 1918. Though honourable, these aims were a little too narrow for one such as Margit. She integrated them into a sort of personal 'party platform', which included several further objectives. The specific goals of the CWO in the 1920s—all aimed at promoting the position of 'respectable women': education for girls, prohibition of contraceptives, obstructing divorce law reform, prosecuting prostitution and depriving sex workers of voting rights—were not the kind of policies to awaken a militant advocate within her. That inspiration would come with a completely new role, in the battle against Bolshevism—a later goal of the CWO. It is easy to understand why, as this cause touched at the very core of her being: her property. And that had become her weakness.

Margit's capital was melting away, due to the Treaty of Versailles and the consequent loss of Silesian family assets suddenly located over the border in Polish territory. Add to this her lost war bonds and the general devaluation of currency, and she was starting to glimpse the bottoms of her coffers. She could no longer extricate

THE ROARING TWENTIES

herself from the social changes happening around her, and would need to maintain a position close to the centres of power for as long as their objectives could be reconciled with her own interests.

Immediately after the war, she had concentrated mainly on the purchase of land, homes, equipment and insurance for the often-disabled veterans and their families. Next, she focused on ensuring that the income was spent properly. Despite her dwindling fortune, in the years after 1918 she still bore the annual financial shortfalls of this project herself. Several years later, when the war victims were in a position to purchase their holdings for themselves, she helped to draw up the necessary sales contracts, in which she placed clauses preventing their profitable resale. The farmers were carefully monitored to ensure that they were genuinely running farming businesses, and not letting their enterprise run to seed. One disabled blade-sharpener who was not industrious enough simply had the motors of his whetstones sold out from under him (though he could continue to rent his home at a reduced rate). Needless to say, Margit will have made both friends and enemies during this period.

The simple fact of her involvement gave her bargaining power, both in Lungau and elsewhere. When the construction of a power plant in the nearby Murtal region was delayed—a project of vital importance to the development of Lungau-based industry—she generated momentum by speaking to the Salzburg provincial council directly. She had important blueprints copied at an early stage, so that the relevant officials had no excuse to delay matters further. Of course, she did not act alone, and must have endured many hours' worth of council meetings with a wide range of local and national representatives.[8] This process did, however, provide her with many fruitful contacts, people who would later occupy key roles in Vienna. These included Rudolf Ramek and Johann Lackner, who worked on establishing the first parliament of the Austrian republic in 1919. Ramek would become federal president in 1924.

Ramek and Lackner, who were Christian Socialist MPs, drew up a bill aimed at decentralising the assistance provided to injured veterans. It stipulated that the local agencies would take charge of the veterans themselves and grant them a government stipend. Margit's private initiative might thus have been transformed into a government responsibility. Alas, the bill disappeared into a drawer somewhere, but still it represented the beginnings of a movement that was gaining ground throughout Europe at the time, wherever parliaments became increasingly populated by members from all social classes. It ensured that those who had difficulty keeping their heads above water in a tough society were no longer at the mercy of the Church, or of a local noble philanthropist.

Even without the bill becoming law, Margit gradually shifted her focus. It will have been with some sadness that she bid farewell to her charitable activities, which had made her so beloved and which she had carried out with such generosity in Lungau. She had occasionally been disappointed by a lack of gratitude, however. In 1924, in broad daylight, one poor servant whom she had given a job at Finstergrün stole all the valuable jewels of her niece, the Countess Nuisella Ditfurth, who had been staying with her in the Premhaus building. To add insult to injury, he also stole Margit's revolver and used it to set fire to a nearby house as a diversion. He received a lengthy prison sentence.[9]

Over the course of the 1920s, Margit was in touch with several artists, such as the painters Maximilian Reinitz, a Cubist related to Kokoschka, and Joseph Schulz. Both her reduced financial capacity and the CWO's limited scope for action meant that her social contributions were not as groundbreaking as they had once been. Her movements also became restricted in a literal sense in 1926, when she was attacked in an alpine meadow by a cow, aggravated by the dog she was walking with. She was not properly treated, and was only operated on six months later in Vienna. She would always need a walking stick after that, making her look older than her years.

Margit continued to do what she could. She still had Finstergrün, her beautiful castle where she held receptions and welcomed guests. One such honoured visitor was the president of the CWO, Countess Carola Blome, who gave a lecture to the organisation's annual general meeting on the subject of 'Children's Welfare'. For Pentecost and the Nativity of the Blessed Virgin Mary (on 8 September), the CWO organised well-attended women's processions to the nearby villages of Mariapfarr and St Leonhard. Its grand festivities to celebrate first communions and confirmations were attended by

THE ROARING TWENTIES

bishops from Salzburg, who lent an additional lustre to such occasions. They were always welcome to stay at Finstergrün.

In 1928, when Margit was fifty-seven, Blome came to give another celebratory speech, this time on the subject of 'The education and preparation of female youth for their future careers as women, one that has been decreed by God and is yet so often neglected in our time, namely: becoming sensible, conscientious and Christian housewives and mothers.'[10] The roaring twenties seem to have bypassed Lungau, if you read this text. The Church was gaining an increasingly firm and more palpable grip on day-to-day life. Each group in society—farmers, messengers, servants, bachelors, young women—had their own separate club with its particular unique rituals. The result was a blossoming and highly ramified Catholic society life. Young girls and women received extra attention, as the future mothers of what the Church hoped would become large families: special meetings called 'exercises' were planned for their spiritual development, where they could discuss their faith with one another. The bishops sent out their own meeting guidelines to the CWO branches:

> A Catholic woman must be morally upright, and strengthened by inner religiosity; to her, Christianity cannot be merely a matter of outward trappings or habit, but rather should be a profound matter of the heart. One of the best means to achieve this is through religious reflection, opportunities for which are provided during the so-called 'retreats', and even more so during spiritual exercises.[11]

Given Margit's active, outward-looking approach to life, it is hard to imagine her having been in agreement with the above role. She doubtless found it a perfectly acceptable station in life, but one reserved for others. She was happy, however, to act as a hostess for the prelates who came to promulgate these ideas in Lungau. They long represented a seemingly innocent but deeply conservative conviction about how women should live their lives. That changed, however, when Blome's 1928 speech was followed up by a talk from CSP politican Hans Scheffel, who concluded the evening's celebrations by asking his female audience 'to support young Christian people who wish to hold their ground in red Vienna'.[12] With these words, a window to the big, wide world was thrown

115

open to the women and girls present, who only recently had walked with garlands in their hair through the undulating green hills, singing to the glory of Mary. Perhaps they had thought that all the atrocities of the Great War had become the tale of the older generation, and that peace and brotherhood once again ruled the earth in a powerful covenant guided by God Almighty. But it turned out this was an illusion. For years, unbeknownst to them, the women of Lungau had been primed as recruits for an entirely different battle: the fight against the communist peril.

There was at least one other kind of organisation that threatened the CWO's monopoly on social and civic life. This was the gymnastics association, of which there were two in the Lungau region: the German Folk and the Christian-German associations. Because the former had grown over the course of the 1920s, the latter began recruiting among schoolchildren in order to turn them into 'soldiers for Christ'. In retaliation, the German Folk Gymnastics Association organised festive activities to coincide with those of the CWO, such as children's Christmas tree–decorating parties. Such conflicts (of both a petty and more serious nature) were not uncommon in response to the growing influence of the Catholic Church over daily life, a form of resistance by a lower class that was beginning to turn away from Church and state. That same class would go on to vote in favour of national socialism, a movement that would enjoy enormous popularity in the Lungau region.

Various theories have been put forward to explain the rise of national socialism in Austria, the simplest being that Hitler grew up there. But even just looking at the developments in Lungau and the tribulations of Margit Szapáry, we can see evidence of a psychological shift, and a clash between male and female spheres of life. In Lungau, for example, it was primarily Catholic women and their organisations (such as the CWO) who enjoyed most social authority in the early years after the war, with many men—fathers—having perished or become disabled. The gymnastics associations gave young boys the opportunity to develop qualities that were regarded as masculine, such as muscular strength and speed. The figure of Samson, after all, had symbolised manly strength for centuries in

THE ROARING TWENTIES

Lungau, which had brought forth many sturdy woodsmen. (The wood from the region's trees has been an important source of income for centuries.)

The counterpart to this youth movement focused on active masculinity was the more spiritual dedication expected of women as the nurturers of future generations. The CWO excelled at developing the potential of women and girls, through its study days featuring important speakers, who were always happy to come when the invitation was sent by Countess Szapáry. Finstergrün's beautiful interior proved very useful for enticing guests, receiving company and creating a sense of community. But while the girls were praying amid the inspiring furnishings collected decades earlier from old churches and cloisters, the boys went out into the wild, pitting themselves against one another by chopping down trees or secretly shooting rabbits, foxes or deer. Their physique had already been trained during their gymnastics classes. And if they should go and enjoy a drink afterwards, then there might just 'happen' to be some cheerful men at the draughts, telling of the glorious future that awaited them all, once Austria and Germany were united under a single strong leader.[13]

When she took her head out of her many ledgers, Margit will have noticed that the world had changed. As was customary in all Germanic ledgers, hers still had the motto 'God with us' printed on the first page. More people were demanding input into urban and national governance, and a fairer distribution of power and wealth. Attached to her status as Margit was, these new ideas most likely took some getting used to. She became more introspective, made occasional notes, and cited agreement with Gandhi and his recommendation to stay mute for at least one day a week—a practice for which the high lonely mountains of Finstergrün provided ample opportunity.

Margit's daughter Jolanta, after her training in Vienna as a paediatric nurse, left for the London Nursing School to continue her studies on a Commonwealth scholarship. Attempts were made to introduce her to eligible bachelors in Vienna, which she declined. Clearly she too lacked interest in life as a good Catholic mother, and instead prepared herself for a career. Margit wrote almost daily to her 'dear *Schnuss*' in London, using the same affectionate nonsense language she had once used when writing to her own mother. Jolanta carefully stored her mother's postcards in albums. In them, Margit expresses her concern—as she always did—for the health of her loved ones. Her fear of illnesses doubtless stemmed from the many conditions that were incurable in those times before antibiotics, which claimed so many lives. The way she signed her letters, 'your old mama', was an indication of how she saw herself in this period.

* * *

For a brief time, in the early 1920s, it had seemed as though the European economy might flourish. The coincidence of a peace-loving triumvirate of three men—the English aristocrat Austen Chamberlain (half-brother of future Prime Minister Neville Chamberlain), the amiable Frenchman Aristide Briand, and the German pragmatist Gustav Stresemann—had brought stability and hopes for years of peace. In early October 1926, on board the idyllic *Orange Blossom* floating on Lago Maggiore, they cobbled together a new non-aggression agreement, the Locarno Pact, which aimed to improve relations between France and Germany. That same year, Germany even joined the League of Nations. But this stability, too, was an illusion. Major economic problems were looming in several countries, and their effects were also being felt in Lungau. In late 1925, the Ramingstein paper factory had closed its doors, leaving 170 employees out of work. Now it was their children receiving warm socks, apples and words of comfort from the ladies of the CWO.

The working classes were stirring, in Vienna especially. In 1927, a veteran member of the social-democratic paramilitary Schutzbund was shot dead with his child by members of the right-wing Heimatschutz, or 'homeland protection' movement. When the culprits were acquitted, workers burned the Palace of Justice to the ground. The police used violence to suppress the uprising, and eighty-five workers were killed. This was all before the Wall Street Crash of 1929, after which large-scale unemployment put further strain on an already-fragile democratic balance. The price of agricultural products plummeted, as did the productivity of Austrian

Fig. 1: Countess Margarethe Henckel von Donnersmarck, 1899, the year before her marriage to Sándor Szapáry. Here she is twenty-eight years old and photographed at her best, wearing the family jewels.

Figs 2–3: Margarethe's parents (above), the wealthy Hugo Henckel von Donnersmarck and Wanda Henckel von Donnersmarck-Gaschin, lived on grand estates in Upper Silesia. Count Hugo II (re)built three large palaces in the region. Brynek, today home to Poland's oldest forestry school (below), was the last to be restored. The couple only lived there for a short time, from 1904 to their deaths in 1908.

Fig. 4: Sándor Szapáry in the imperial army uniform of a Hussar commander, serving Franz Joseph I. The painting is by Sándor's wife, Margit.

Fig. 5: 'Uncle' Guido Henckel von Donnersmarck and his second wife, Katharina von Slepzow, at Neues Neudeck (the New Palace) in Tarnowskie Góry, Upper Silesia.

Fig. 6: A room at Finstergrün Castle. Watercolour by Margit Szapáry, c. 1914.

Fig. 7: Margit's identity card, c. 1910—she has become a modern woman.

Fig. 8: Margit (right) with friends, 1920s.

Fig. 9: One of Margit's interiors, Finstergrün, 1920s.

Fig. 10: Pauline Thérèse (Esther Blanche) Lachmann, known as Blanche, c. 1860. La Païva, one of the great courtesans of Paris in her day, was the beloved partner, and later wife, of Guido Henckel von Donnersmarck.

Fig. 11: This bed was one of many pieces of furniture that La Païva commissioned for the mansion Guido had built for her on the Champs-Élysées. She ended up returning the piece, but its style does match the rest of Hotel Païva's interior, which survives today.

Fig. 12: Hermann Göring, 1917, decorated with the *Pour le Mérite* he received as a war pilot. By this time, he had been coming to Lungau on holiday since childhood, staying with his godfather.

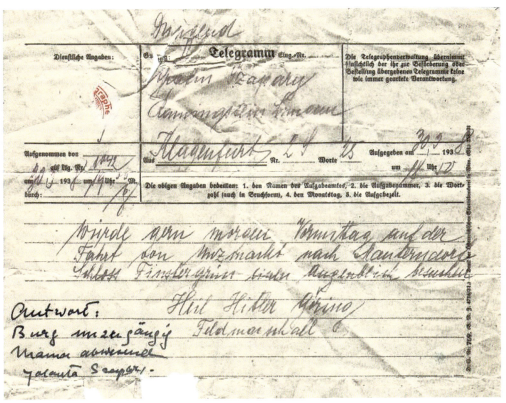

Fig. 13: Göring's telegram of 30 March 1938, announcing to Margit his imminent visit to Finstergrün, in pursuit of her furnishings. She spent the rest of the year avoiding him.

Fig. 14: The wedding of Countess Yvonne Szapáry and Prince Karl of Hesse, 18 April 1966, The Hague. This photo was taken after the ceremony, at the Szapáry family home on Van Alkemadelaan. Front row from left: Prince Philip, Duke of Edinburgh; King Constantine and Queen Anne-Marie of Greece; the bride and groom; the groom's parents, Christoph and Sophia of Hesse; and Yvonne's parents, Béla and Ursula Szapáry.

Fig. 15: After the auction of Finstergrün's contents in 1941, Margit's Gothic four-poster bed wound up at Burghausen Castle near Munich, where it is on permanent display.

THE ROARING TWENTIES

industry, dropping by 40 percent over three years.[14] The 1931 bankruptcy of one of Austria's biggest and most famous banks, the Credit-Anstalt owned by the Rothschilds, sent shockwaves through Europe, similar to those caused by the collapse of Lehmann Brothers in 2008. Margit had an account with Credit-Anstalt, and many German banks went down with it.

The more severe the crisis, the more extreme the response, and the crisis impacted Germany more deeply than Austria. Only fifteen per cent of all those unemployed in the Weimar Republic received government assistance; the other eight million lived in 'a veritable hell of meanness, oppression and disease'.[15]

On 30 January 1933, Hitler took power in Germany.

NOBLESSE OBLIGE?

Göring had a major hand in Hitler's grab for power in 1933, as has been extensively documented in various twenty-first-century studies.[1] Time and again, Göring has been uncovered as the one who made Hitler palatable to the German elite, and the nobility especially. It was Göring's efforts that granted Hitler access to the very top of society, where he found the cooperation he needed to realise his plans. Göring's efforts were at least as important as Hitler's own in rallying the German people through powerful oratory. 'Millions stand behind me' was Hitler's bluff. But the famous poster by graphic artist Heartfield places these millions in the correct proportions, focusing on the 'millions' of banknotes handed into Hitler's outstretched hand from German industrialists. Rhetorical skill and manipulation of language alone are not enough to bring about the downfall of an entire people—for that, one needs the support of big business and, at that time, the aristocracy.

Göring's early castle life at Mauterndorf and Veldenstein, coupled with his education at the Lichterfelde academy, had shaped him to favour a certain social order, with no especial provisions for equality among individuals. His marriage to Carin von Kantzow only deepened his convictions, adding an element of north-Germanic mysticism per her own leanings. With these sentiments came raging antisemitism. Such views enjoyed a positive reception among much of the German nobility, even more so when propagated by those who seemed like 'one of us'—such as the war hero Göring, husband to a countess. However, in the ten-odd years between Göring joining the party in 1922 and the Nazi takeover in 1933, that outcome was by no means a foregone conclusion.

In the summer of 1923, Hitler had heard Carin say that her new husband was prepared to die for his ideals. It would not be long before he was put to the test, during the Beer Hall Putsch—Hitler's

SECRETS OF A SUITCASE

failed coup attempt of November 1923, in Munich. Göring was shot down, and Hitler arrested and sentenced to prison.

The bizarre sequence of ensuing events is well known. Seriously wounded by a gunshot to the groin, Göring had been carried to a nearby house where the inhabitants—who were Jewish—provided first aid, buying him precious time so that he could be taken to a hospital. Carin succeeded in transporting Göring over the border to Austria, where he was operated on in Innsbruck. Because his wounds were already infected, he received two shots of morphine per day for the pain. These planted the seed of what would later turn out to be a lifelong addiction, one often cited by his biographers in connection with his later mood swings and apparently split personality.

The couple met many like-minded people in Innsbruck, who also offered financial support. Göring received so much attention, in fact, that he became a troublesome figure to the Austrians, whose Social Democrats and Christian Socialists were caught in an already-fragile equilibrium, beleaguered on both left and right by extremist factions. Göring was asked to leave, and the owner of the Tiroler Hof hotel arranged for the couple to lodge with a hotel-owner friend of his at Venice's Hotel Britannia. The Renaissance architecture and abundance of visual art in the city, combined with the pleasant climate, made Göring more of an art student than a politician at that time.

He and Carin would remain in Italy for around a year, travelling on to Florence, Siena and Rome. Their itinerary seemed rather like Göring's belated Grand Tour of the Italian art capitals; he certainly took the opportunity to expand his cultural horizons. But art was not his only priority. One of his main goals in Italy was to arrange a meeting with Mussolini, and to acquire financial support for Hitler and the Nazi Party (the NSDAP).

His plan was a complete failure. While leaving Carin with the impression that he was regularly meeting with the Duce, in reality he never made it past the doorman. Mussolini had been appointed premier of Italy in October 1922. He had the nobility and the royal family on his side, and had nothing to gain by forging ties with a group of hotheads from Munich whose leader was in prison. Despite Göring's constant stream of letters begging and pleading for an audience, Mussolini and his entourage remained unimpressed and left him hanging. It was a treatment that Göring would not soon forget.

122

NOBLESSE OBLIGE?

By that time, Göring had seen all the Titians, Tintorettos and Veroneses that Italy had to offer. Deeply humiliated, without having so much as shaken hands with Mussolini, the couple left for Sweden and waited for better times.

Back in Munich, Hitler had another agenda. He managed to leave prison within the year, but his thoughts were far from the espresso-drinking Göring on St Mark's Square, let alone with Benito Mussolini. He first needed to get his young party back on track.

In Sweden, Carin's family was shocked to see that, in the space of four years, their precious Carin's once-well-proportioned beau had morphed into a pale, sausage-like morphine addict. Carin, herself suffering from epileptic seizures and heart problems, was not faring much better. The morphine had such a hold on Göring that he was admitted on several occasions to a psychiatric hospital, where he sometimes had to be put in a straitjacket.

Göring was left in the dark as to the progress of the Nazi move-ment back in Germany, not least the impact of Hitler's book, *Mein Kampf*, written while he was in prison. But as long as Göring received no amnesty, he had no means of returning. Not until late 1927 did he manage to do so, alone. He had no employment and Carin's fortune was exhausted; they had auctioned off the contents of her home merely to make ends meet, and Hitler was unwilling to involve Göring in rebuilding the party until he had re-established a functioning network in Germany. Göring rose to the challenge: several old contacts had not forgotten him, and he succeeded in becoming a BMW sales representative. He worked day and night from his Berlin flat, with a photograph of Napoleon in front of him and a mediaeval sword behind his desk.

The ailing Carin was able to join him from Sweden, and Göring once again became an attractive figure for Hitler's organisation. While Goebbels was busy as a propagandist on the streets, Göring was engaged to canvass the villas and boardrooms, Carin at his side—he became the 'salon Nazi'.[2] Hitler placed him on the candi-date list for the Reichstag, and he was elected as a parliamentary member with a significant number of votes in 1930. Now he was assured of a regular income.

SECRETS OF A SUITCASE

Hitler knew that having Göring on hand would lend his party some style. His past as a war hero, his smooth charisma and his elegant wife were important assets, as Hitler was in desperate need of funds to keep his party afloat and achieve further electoral gains. Göring could finally demonstrate his worth, both to Hitler and for the many young sons of the nobility. These princelings often felt attracted to national socialism, but did not have the courage to join the party. They only became members once their head of house had done so, after which all members of the family would follow. Another problem was the fact that the NSDAP had always marketed itself expressly as a party for the people. Some aristocrats were even advised against joining, to avoid confrontations with the somewhat-rougher members from the party's early days, who believed that the nobility had already largely succumbed to 'Jewish influence'. To other nobles, it was suggested that the Nazis would be happy to 'help pull down the fences around their estates' for a 'scrap-metal drive', since everything was destined to become 'state-owned'.[3]

So, some sympathetic nobles decided not to become party members at all, but instead became silent backers. One of them was Guido's son, Guidotto Henckel von Donnersmarck, who ran his father's business empire in partnership with his brother Kraft. Among other positions, he was a manager of the AEG (General Electricity Company) and managed a number of Silesian businesses that ran power stations and mines. He, too, was recruited for the Nazis, during a dinner hosted by the Görings.[4] Because he was chronically ill with multiple sclerosis, from then on Guidotto and his wife, Princess Anna zu Sayn-Wittgenstein, would host the party leadership at his mansion, built by his father on the Tegernsee lake, south of Munich. This allowed him to skip party meetings while avoiding the need to defend himself against the gossip printed by Julius Streicher (publisher of *Der Stürmer*), who was wont to bring up Guidotto's 'Jewish heritage' (a reference to Guido's first wife, Blanche).[5] In the 1930s, more Nazi chiefs came to live in Tegernsee, including Himmler, and the place became something of a national-socialist resort town. There, Guidotto could casually introduce his new political friends to interested parties of the old elite.

Carin Göring, by then partially recovered, was now ready to do her part and contribute to the cocktail offensive, this time in her mod-

124

NOBLESSE OBLIGE?

est but comfortable Berlin apartment. Charming as always, Carin knew how to create a welcoming atmosphere, where both the Nazi leaders and the business and aristocratic elite gladly came to dine. Due to her fragile health, she was forced to follow the after-dinner conversation from her chaise longue. In 1931, she and her husband were even invited to visit the former kaiser for a weekend in the Dutch town of Doorn, a sign of their acceptance into the uppermost echelons of German society. Wilhelm II's second wife Hermine ('the empress' to their monarchist friends) would often leave Doorn to visit the Berlin residence of Viktoria von Dirksen, who regularly enticed top-ranking nobles to her home in Tiergarten for private discussions with Goebbels and Göring. Hermine's presence always added some lustre to the assembled company, who, after a two-hour monologue, would be eating from Hitler's palm. One attendee wrote to Guidotto: 'He did well at dinner. Went down a storm!'[6]

Such occasions were also perfect early opportunities for 'salon spies' and 'honeybees', who would become so important to the Nazi movement. One such operative was Wally von Richthofen,[7] whose husband was nephew to the Red Baron—the pilot who had inspired a young Göring. Wally organised many gatherings in her luxury villa in Potsdam. Influenced by their high spirits—and her three beautiful young daughters—guests often loosened their tongues more than they should have. It was during this time that one of Wally's daughters, Ursula, met the Dutch ambassador Godert de Vos van Steenwijk. She married him in the spring of 1933, and two years later they left for the Dutch embassy in Beijing with their newborn son, Godert Junior.[8]

'Honeybees' like Wally von Richthofen proved to be of crucial importance to the Nazis. Because they travelled a lot and had access to high society, they could gather much valuable information from the salons in London and Paris. Hitler's rising popularity among the elite was not yet universally understood, let alone appreciated. The Nazi party newsletter *Der SA-Mann* still often contained texts such as 'From blood and soil we will create a new nobility, the cream of the crop.'[9] But the cream of the old noble crop would still be a necessary ingredient to ensure total power.

The national socialists managed to give the aristocracy the impression that the heyday of the old Prussian monarchy might

125

return. The nobility had lost their position under the Weimar Republic, seen the proud 'vons' and 'zus' in their titles demoted to mere words in their surnames—in Hitler, they saw a chance to reclaim their honour. They supported him financially after the failed presidential elections of 1932, allowing him to win the parliamentary election and the Nazis to become the largest party. In January 1933, they convinced President von Hindenburg to appoint Hitler as chancellor of the Reich. Göring had worked his contacts extremely hard behind the scenes to reach this outcome, and saw in himself a veritable King Arthur, seated at the head of the Round Table. But Carin Göring, his 'Princess of the North', did not live to see it, having succumbed to her heart condition two years earlier.

She had lain in state in the family's Edelweiss chapel in Stockholm, but Göring had arrived from Germany too late to say his final farewells. During the same period, Hitler had also been emotionally distraught due to the unexpected suicide of his half-niece Geli Raubal, with whom he had had a troubling erotic relationship. She had also used Hitler's own firearm to kill herself. He had retreated to Tegernsee to recuperate, and it was for this reason that he had called Göring away from Carin's deathbed. For the rest of his life, Göring would never forgive himself. He installed a flowerbed in the form of a swastika at her grave, which would later be repeatedly destroyed. And a far more durable tribute would be built in the form of Carinhall, his country estate.

On 30 January 1933, Hitler became chancellor of Germany, and the first half of Europe's journey 'To Hell and Back' was gaining momentum.[10] It remains one of the great mysteries of history that a party led by two such unstable figures managed to rally an entire nation behind it. It says something about the breadth of support that the Nazis had attained, about the number of businesspeople and aristocrats who supported Hitler both financially and ideologically, and about the desires awoken within a people who truly wanted to believe in the violence of national socialism as the solution to all of their daily problems.

* * *

Margit Szapáry despised the events unfolding in what she still considered to be 'Prussian' Germany, and remained loyal to the

NOBLESSE OBLIGE?

Habsburgs.[11] Not only had she sent that obsequious letter of condolence on the death of Emperor Karl I to the former empress Zita and the young Crown Prince Otto, exiled in Madeira, but she also remained a devotee of the monarchy and of the social order that it represented.

The influence of the Social Democrats in Austria would increase from 1918 onwards. Although they were the largest party from 1920—in opposition, because the Christian Socialists were able to form coalition governments with smaller conservative parties—they nevertheless managed to secure a majority on Vienna's city council. In 1934, the Austrian corporatist regime (the *Ständestaat*) would be imposed; akin to the brand of fascism that took root in Italy, it was also known as Austrofascism. By that time, however, the Social Democrats had succeeded in implementing a range of social policies in Vienna. There were improvements to healthcare, better education across the population, and improvements to housing, such as the Karl-Marx-Hof built in the 1920s—which, stretching over 1,100 metres of ground, is still famous today as one of the world's longest buildings. Vienna had become 'Red Vienna'.

At the federal level, the Christian Socialists remained the dominant force in various governing coalitions. Margit, however, supported an administration based on traditional social hierarchies and classes, which would allow those 'who knew what they were doing' to govern the country using reliable Christian frameworks, preferably under a monarchy. This made her an adherent—certainly not actively, but one acting in the spirit—of what would become the Austrian corporatist state.

The notion of a corporatist state originated in Austria around 1930, in response to ten turbulent years marked by clashes between the extreme left and right and an ever-present threat of civil war. This budding movement, which would later grow into the Fatherland Front, attracted many young Christian Socialists, who joined forces in the fascism-inspired Heimwehr, or Home Guard. An initial platform in 1930 stated that they would reject the western parliamentary system. The 'socialists' were the principal ideological enemy, since they questioned Christian values—the very values that the powerful Catholic Church had worked so hard throughout the 1920s to preserve with its comprehensive network of associations.

127

SECRETS OF A SUITCASE

What is more, the socialists were often associated with the idea of a cosmopolitan, Jewish elite. While the supporters of the corporatist state united in the Fatherland Front, the national socialist movement spread like wildfire, fuelled by Hitler's success in Germany and exacerbated by the state of the economy. The conflicts became increasingly violent.

Around 1930 there were half a million unemployed in Austria—one quarter of the total labour force. And although there was some (meagre) welfare available, as there was everywhere in Europe, the eligibility criteria excluded increasing numbers from government support, including women. Social tensions rose, and with them support for the Social Democrats. The Christian Socialists were afraid of losing their slim parliamentary majority and, in 1933, Chancellor Engelbert Dollfuss used old wartime legislation from 1917 to avert a crisis: he dissolved parliament, police officers locked down the legislative buildings, and several organisations affiliated with the socialists were banned.

In February 1934, the police raided the party headquarters of the Viennese Social Democrats, triggering a brief civil war. Immediately afterwards, the SDP itself was banned, and mandatory Christian education was reinstated for all public servants. The former Social Democratic minister of education Otto Glöckl, who had removed religious education from Austrian schools, was arrested on a pretext, and would die the following year as a result of maltreatment during his detention. On 1 May 1934—a holiday of great importance to the socialists—members of the Fatherland Front celebrated their victory. The federal republic was abolished, and a Federal State of Austria declared. The new corporatist constitution was based on Pope Pius XI's 1931 encyclical, *Quadragesimo Anno*. Austria's dictatorship was Christian, authoritarian, and first and foremost anti-democratic: the government, a one-party state under the Fatherland Front, could rule by decree and, as is often the case in such situations, judicial independence was done away with.

Political opponents, whether Social Democrats or Nazis, were taken into custody; the death penalty was reinstated, and the leaders of the February rebellion were executed. The Christian Socialist Party was absorbed into the Fatherland Front. The overall aim was to reinforce a strictly Catholic state. Religious instruction was insti-

128

tuted as a prerequisite for taking final examinations; dissident teachers disappeared, and national socialist educators were banished to the most distant backwaters of the country, including Lungau. These rancorous teachers would then contribute to the rise of national socialism in such remote areas. Access to higher education was made more difficult for girls. Another goal of the corporatist state was the abolition of class warfare; labourers and businesspeople became united in cooperatives, akin to mediaeval guilds. It was disastrous for the frail Austrian economy.

Culture, too, had to submit to transformation, and aesthetic preference was given to older, more traditional styles. Modernist Bauhaus architecture, with its white walls and flat roofs—several beautiful examples of which had been built in 'Red Vienna' as social housing—were derided, with antisemitic undertones, as 'Arabian houses'. In 1934, the enthusiastic Church authorities denuded all public libraries of non-Christian books. 'Non-Christian' was given a broad interpretation, including erotic books and books by Jewish authors, such as Salten's *Bambi*. The copies were delivered to the police for destruction, and small libraries were often robbed of three quarters of their entire collection.

The role of the CWO was also destined to change. The political influence of women had grown during the First Republic, and the Viennese branch in particular opposed limits on women's influence. It claimed that 'The State' was not synonymous with 'The Men's State', and that men and women were complementary to one another. But the new leadership would have no truck with such criticism, and urged the CWO to adopt a more cooperative attitude in support of the new state structure.[12] At meetings, members were reminded of the importance of prayer for the fatherland—the idea being that, as a former territory of the Holy Roman Empire, Austria still fulfilled an important role in God's plan for salvation. The state could only do its part if every member was filled with the Catholic spirit, so that all could become apostles and influence their surroundings with Christ's word.

Though the new regime was openly based on the papal encyclical, that document merely spelled out what had already been going on for years with increasing intensity: the complete permeation of public life by the Catholic Church, as in the Lungau region. The pope was satisfied with these developments, as they would give the Austrians a means to weather the rise of Nazism, however long it might last. The predominantly Catholic Austrians saw themselves, based on their history, as the 'better Germans'. Alas, they failed to take into account the popular support for national socialism and, in an attempt to depose the government of the Fatherland Front in July 1934, the Nazis murdered Chancellor Dollfuss. He was succeeded by the young Kurt Schuschnigg, however, and the Austrofascist state continued.

In June 1937, Schuschnigg made a propaganda tour through Austria, and Lungau was on the itinerary. He was welcomed with great pomp and ceremony by the local authorities. Triumphal arches were erected in Tamsweg, schoolchildren stood along the parade route and every house was covered in decorations. The spectacle would later be described by the press as 'spontaneous demonstrations of homage by the people'. In her albums, Jolanta Szapáry carefully stored picture postcards of these tributes. Schuschnigg became an honorary citizen of eighteen Lungau municipalities, and the mistress of Finstergrün was honoured with a special role: Schuschnigg spent a night at the castle.

The chancellor's visit to Finstergrün was a highlight in the life of Margit Szapáry. She ensured that the chancellor and his entourage were treated like royalty by her staff, who had received extensive and detailed instructions. On a nearby hill, a festive effigy was made of a pair of crossed hammers (the symbol of the new state) and, at her request, her servants joined those on the streets to shout *Heil Österreich!* (Hail Austria!) and *Heil Schuschnigg!* at the top of their lungs. Although Margit gave the chancellor a royal welcome, still it had the atmosphere of a state visit from one power to another. In Finstergrün, she was the boss. And, as a member of the Habsburg aristocracy, she was—and would always remain—a monarchist.

When the CWO joined the Fatherland Front, several CWO ladies with national-socialist sympathies cancelled their memberships. With government support, another association was instituted—the Maternity Protection Organisation—and took on several duties of the CWO, such as assistance for new mothers and the provision of school meals. In 1935, Lungau received its own branch, managed by none other than the recently graduated Jolanta Szapáry. In 1936, the MPO gave every mother a Mother's Day package with groceries, a task which until then had been performed by the CWO. The corporatist state's creation of this new, almost-identical rival organisation will almost certainly have resulted in tense discussions between mother and daughter at Finstergrün. The CWO's influence on day-to-day life in Lungau was waning.

These were not joyful times for Margit, who had so hoped for a return of the monarchy in the new Austrian state. This would have allowed the exiled Prince Otto to return and restore the old ways, an eventuality for which he himself had been prepared by his mother Zita. He had studied law in Liège, Belgium, had obtained his PhD, and subscribed to pan-European ideas. He, too, saw the sense in re-establishing himself as leader of Austria, but Schuschnigg held him at bay. Otto was only permitted to enter the country for a brief visit, when his family's bank assets—frozen since the end of the First World War—were returned to him. Chancellor Schuschnigg had more pressing problems to attend to: the rise of Nazi Germany next door.

PAYING GUESTS

For Christmas 1905, back when Margit's fortune was still virtually inexhaustible, she had given her father two Ginori plates, a rare and expensive brand of eighteenth-century Italian porcelain. Her sister Sara had received a silver Secession box—evidence that Margit could also appreciate modern Viennese design—and her other sister Irmgard was gifted a Meissen porcelain vase, the pinnacle of German manufacturing. The old priest in Ramingstein was given a pair of silver sugar tongs, and the staff received a generous package of clothes. All were recorded precisely in Margit's ledgers.[1]

In 1930, by contrast, not only was the list much shorter, but the gifts were more modest. Aside from her two children, Béla (socks) and Jolanta (a hat), no other family members were included. The other lucky recipients were suppliers from Ramingstein and Margit's trusty old staff, who received bottles of wine, cigars, shoes, or a few metres of fabric from which to make clothing. The priest was not forgotten, and received a subscription to *Neues Reich*. One friend, Isabel du Cane, stands out: she was gifted a book three times the price of Jolanta's hat, which must have been a beautifully bound edition. But then, Isabel—an unmarried Englishwoman who lived with her mother and sister on a large country estate in Fittleworth, Sussex—had become an important figure in Margit's life. She had met Jolanta during the latter's studies in England, when she would travel the country to visit old castles and estates.

Isabel du Cane had become a regular guest at Finstergrün. She came from 'good stock', and had many friends and family members who also wished to stay at the castle from time to time.

Life at Finstergrün was expensive for Margit, a fact still somewhat masked by its interior. There was so much furniture that it was

133

not immediately apparent if an item disappeared—which happened occasionally, a piece or two being sold off to interested parties in Europe or the United States to supplement the household coffers. The first such sale had taken place as far back as 1922, parting with one of the most unique artworks left in the castle: the fifteenth-century altarpiece that had been central to the Maria Elend pilgrimage church in Embach. It is large, 1.8 by 1.2 metres, and richly decorated with woodcuts and paintings on a gold-coloured background. Maria holds the body of the crucified Jesus in her lap with St John and Mary Magdalene beside her; they are surrounded by various stations of the cross and depictions of the resurrection. It is not a cheerful work, and is designed to evoke a predominantly mournful sentiment. It is impressive, however, and an early work. Margit had an eye for collecting special items, as Wilczek had noted. In 1960, when it made an appearance at an auction in Vienna, the suggested price was 9.5 million Schillings (a bit less than £4 million today). The sale of this altarpiece represented a turning point for Margit. A few years later, she sold two large Persian carpets to Kunsthaus Drey in Munich; in 1931, they would make an elegant appearance in London, as part of a Persian art exhibition.[2]

Margit had been feeling the need to economise for some time.[3] It is unclear whose idea it was, but in the late 1920s the decision was made to open up Finstergrün to paying guests. It was during this period that the Salzburg Festival became a popular summer holiday destination for both domestic and international tourists, as the city hosted concerts, operas and plays throughout the month of August. The founders of the Festival, which dated back to 1920, were the theatre director Max Reinhardt, the writer Hugo von Hoffmannsthal and the composer Richard Strauss, whose aim was to bring together and present a programme of top-quality drama and music. The works of Mozart featured prominently, as he had lived and worked in Salzburg. The international interest in the festival, promoted by the arrival of mass media in the form of the radio, attracted to the region an affluent cohort of travellers who were only too willing to extend their stay.

The daily bus that ran from Salzburg to Lungau from 1921, carrying the post, improved connectivity to the north. Tourism grew, and train travel became accessible to a wider public, enticing them to spend a holiday mountaineering, or simply walking the hills and taking the clean air, in a spectacular landscape of crystal-clear mountain lakes. Austrian newspapers and journals, such as *Die Lokomotive*, were full of articles praising the pristine natural beauty of the Alps, and promoting the general notion of 'homeland beauty'.

Not everybody was warmly received, however. In the Lungau guesthouses, Jewish tourists were being refused even before the corporatist state began.[4] But this did not apply at Finstergrün: Margit used different selection criteria. She focused on the well-to-do, for whom an invigorating escape to the mountains was only appealing if spent in good company. Margit could offer her illustrious, often-international guests precisely this ambience, and in a castle that many perceived as a sort of unique and adventurous museum.

Finstergrün conjured up the kind of fantasy that had mostly only been available to previous generations through literature, in the novels of the Brontë sisters and their successors. Margit's English guests, who were often women, delighted in the castle. They were rather charmed by its candlelight, although they did find other primitive facilities—such as the poor sanitation—to be quite an inconvenience.

Margit and her daughter knew how to provide guests with a luxury welcome and, with their household staff, could offer a fine dining experience. They had built a tennis court and, according to a Lungau tourist brochure from this time, guests were able to organise their own forms of evening entertainment, such as bridge, musical soirées or costume balls. Even dancing was an option, including modern styles such as the foxtrot.[5]

Importantly, Margit also knew how to run a business and a brand. Finstergrün had become a bed-and-breakfast, but not one that was open to all. Potential guests were approached with care, and Isabel du Cane played an important part in recruiting a well-off British clientele. It seems that addresses were also acquired from the Salzburg Festival's own records, which would themselves have made use of international client lists from national music societies.

Of the recorded guests, most staying between June and September, almost all are from Britain or the United States, and their names give an impression of the sort of people the Szapárys hoped to attract. At the height of the season, eighteen of the castle's rooms

SECRETS OF A SUITCASE

were occupied. It must have been a busy time, and Jolanta, who had learned to speak good English during her years of study, played an important part as both hostess and chauffeur, going by the many thank-you cards she included in her album. The guesthouse records contain the names of many women, for whom Finstergrün must have been a reliable and trustworthy address—a must for proper ladies travelling alone, which they did increasingly in the 1930s. Long stays by a Mrs Abbott and a Miss Hemingway were noted, for example. There was also a Fräulein Krupp. It cannot have been easy for Margit to welcome a guest from a German coal-and-steel family once rivalled by the Henckel von Donnersmarcks; now her castle had been reduced to a guesthouse, while the Krupps still owned various palaces such as Blühnbach near Salzburg.

Could nobody have spared Margit this descent from mistress of the castle to bed-and-breakfast landlady? All of her siblings died during this period. Her brother Hugo III had already died in 1923, followed by both Sara and Margit's sister-in-law, Sándor's sister Ilona, in 1934; her brother Edgar would pass in 1939, and Irmgard in 1940. But Edgar, or perhaps his children, might have helped Margit out of difficulty in the 1930s—if only by selling a valuable Ginori plate from one of the display cases at Brynek, the grand Silesian palace that their father Hugo II had built and furnished at the turn of the century, when Margit was occupied with Finstergrün and the family was still flush with cash. Unfortunately for her, no such assistance was forthcoming.

Margit's son Béla also proved unable to support his mother upon his return from Canada in 1930. On the contrary, it was he who needed his mother's help with money.[6] As for more distant family, such as the Protestant Henckel von Donnersmarcks, she could expect nothing at all from them. Until 1942, her correspondence with that side of the family shows only some cards sent to Guidotto.[7] No, Margit had to tighten her own purse strings. It helped that Jolanta worked in a Vienna hospital for some time. In a few cards sent in February 1929, Margit advises her daughter not to come to Finstergrün, as she can only properly heat one room.[8]

In late 1931, Margit began advertising for winter guests openly in the Salzburg newspapers, recommending her accommodations to those who required 'nursing', for which Jolanta would have been

136

summoned back from Vienna. She was attempting to create her own version of a resort, having herself enjoyed the benefits of Abbazia long before. In summertime, she continued to target primarily British, American and select German, Hungarian or Italian guests. The advertisements stressed that Finstergrün was a 'distinguished family home' for those seeking peace and tranquillity, and highlighted the availability of an in-house apothecary and a telephone connection, allowing calls to be made 'without interruption', to put any final doubts to rest. For reservations, guests were asked to contact a 'Countess Matuschka' (not either of the Szapáry countesses), which will also have served as a barrier to any run-of-the-mill tourists. According to Margit's ledgers, guests paid a reasonable sum for a full week's room and board, around 130 Schillings (about £390 today), with surcharges for car transport, a bath, or a second egg at breakfast.

Margit had put off one of her most difficult decisions, but one that could not be delayed indefinitely: in the mid-1930s, assisted by the new Austrian corporatist state, she took out a mortgage. She also benefited from the lenient attitude towards the aristocracy shown by the board of the bank in Salzburg, which issued the loan.

This was the beginning of the end, but the writing had been on the wall for some time. The high-born had laughed, dined and danced the foxtrot on long summer evenings at Finstergrün during the early 1930s; but after the delicious trout soufflée and a few glasses of wine, they had also discussed political developments in Europe. They could keep their heads in the sand no longer. The guests all talked about it openly, in English, sitting around the open fire in the dining room, beneath those Sabbionara frescoes of mediaeval knights at the joust.

Isabel du Cane had become an annual summer guest at Finstergrün, and also travelled with Margit in the off season through southern Germany and northern Italy. This gave them both an international perspective on the political situation, which Margit shared in a letter to the editor of *The Spectator*. Her letter was published on 18 May 1934—at the start of the month, Vienna had declared the corporatist state. But that was not the subject of her submission. Margit's piece was in response to an article from two issues before, titled 'What Does Germany Mean?'. It is the only extant text in which she explicitly sets out her political views.

137

SECRETS OF A SUITCASE

Margit opens on a friendly note, saying that she has enjoyed reading *The Spectator* for some years, and wishes to make her own contribution, as she is now living in the middle of the region provoking concern for so many.[9] She wonders whether the 'English public' truly realise the threat posed by Germany, and cites the poor economic conditions that will drive Germany to war, since it has 'literally nothing else to lose'. According to Margit, England's sympathy for Austria ('for which we are deeply thankful') showed an awareness that Austria would be Germany's first victim on the path to further conquests. History was repeating itself, she warned, for Prussia had already attempted to conquer Austria once before, in 1866. Then it had been France's turn in 1870, after which the southern German lands had been 'half persuaded, half frightened' into joining the unified state. Now, sixty years later, Germany once again had its sights set on Austria, doubtless with other countries to follow, such as Czechoslovakia, the Netherlands, Denmark and Switzerland, and then France. (Not Hungary, interestingly, where her son Béla should have become a true Hungarian. Or did she still see Hungary as part of 'Austria'?)

The letter continues with a warning that Germany is 'propagating her doctrine of National Socialism' in all German-speaking regions, with the aim of triggering a rebellion that would serve as a pretext for these countries' annexation by the 'totalitarian' Nazi state. This certainly applied to Austria and, due to the country's existing national-socialist sympathies, Margit foresaw 'a Prussian government' in the near future that would take possession of all Austrian resources.

The letter shows several interesting shifts. Firstly, a distinction is drawn between 'Germany' and 'the Germans', immediately after which Germany itself is equated to an aggressive state by the name of 'Prussia'. 'Germans' are considered to be all German-speaking people, across national borders. These ethnic 'Germans' are all being intimidated by Prussia, and at risk of being subjugated. Margit contrasts an evil Germany with a good Germany, the latter of which she locates in southern and western Germany, and in Austria. It was the evil Germany (Prussia) that triggered the First World War and is now on the verge of starting a second—that is what she wishes to warn people about.

She also issues a plea in this small yet influential publication: for Britain, France and even Italy to inform Germany unambiguously

138

that any annexation of Austria would constitute a threat to stability and peace in Europe. She believes that a truce is necessary, similar to the one concluded with Poland, under which Germany would be willing to 'abstain from her Austrian ambitions' in order to prevent the 'crushing of freedom and the destruction of all we have of art and culture'. Precisely who is meant by 'we' is not clear, but likely includes at least the 'good' Germans and their Germanic culture; perhaps even Europeans at large. She concludes by saying that she is writing 'as a European who sees that the real balance of power is at stake and that the present threat to Austria is the first move towards war.' She signs off simply as Margit Szapáry, without mention of her title.

Margit was not only right in sensing the impending war and the annexation of Austria, but early too, in 1934. The rest of her arguments are open to question, however, especially in light of events at the time in Austria, where the corporatist state had only just been declared after years of violent clashes between the far left, supported by Moscow, and the far right, supported by Berlin. National socialism itself, incidentally, cannot be labelled entirely Prussian: it emerged as a political movement in Bavaria—southern Germany. Margit sidesteps this fact, and proceeds to contrast one form of nationalism, the 'good' one upheld by 'real Germans', with the 'bad' one promulgated by the aggressive 'Prussians'. She either fails to realise, or at least fails to mention, that both forms of nationalism have culminated in an authoritarian, oppressive and potentially expansivist regime.

Most importantly, her letter contains a distant echo of the old, Catholic, Silesian nobility, who had never accepted Frederick the Great's Prussian victory over the Habsburgs and Silesia. This same echo is also that of the young Margarethe Henckel von Donnersmarck, who witnessed the divide between the Hohenzollerns and the Habsburgs first-hand, within her own family, through the cool relations between the Catholic and Protestant branches. This letter to *The Spectator*, then, doesn't quite make Margit an early heroine of the resistance, which is how she came to be viewed in Lungau.[10] There is other evidence of 'social protest', like her rejection of the Nazi salute, but it's important not to exaggerate the nature of her opposition. She must have seen the national socialists primarily as barbarians who, in her eyes, had rightly been brushed aside—for now—by the declaration of the Austrofascist state.

That same corporatist state, led by the Fatherland Front, awarded Margit the Golden Medal of Honour for services to Austria in June that year, with a ceremony held in August. Her continued support for this rather problematic form of government is evident from, among other things, her enthusiastic welcome of the Fatherland Front leader, Chancellor Schuschnigg, to Finstergrün in 1936. Though she may already have considered herself a European, this act alone confirms Margit's identity as, first and foremost, a Catholic Habsburg aristocrat. Her concern for imminent war was undoubtedly sincere, and by publishing a letter under her own name in an English-language magazine, she was already doing more than many others of her class at that time. More than a few were clustering around Hitler for opportunistic reasons, or worse. On the other hand, Margit was writing for a British audience, who were not themselves entirely sure in 1934 what they should make of Hitler.

The journalist Tim Bouverie's book *Appeasing Hitler* (2019) revisits and challenges the myth that the British elite were predominantly anti-German. In the 1930s, the fear of the Russians and of Bolshevism was far greater, and many thought that Hitler might be a better option after all. There was even a 'wave of enthusiasts' who set out to experience 'Hitler's wonderland' for themselves. The Third Reich 'possessed a noxious glamour which, from its inception, attracted some of the more frivolous members of English society'.[11] Edward VIII, who became king on 20 January 1936, himself fuelled such interest, and famously believed 'that one should not meddle with domestic affairs', whether they concerned Jews or 'whatever else'.[12] He even encouraged admiration for Hitler by visiting him personally. By the time of his visit in 1937, the Nuremberg race laws denying Jews many civil rights in pursuit of a 'pure race' had been in force for two years.

Margit certainly did not belong to the group of nobles who were flirting with national-socialist ideology. Nor were her guests at Finstergrün, which is to her credit, as their (non-)allegiances must have been a known fact—otherwise, they would not have been at Finstergrün, speaking openly about their views in front of the fire while on holiday. Not even in the summer of 1934, when curiosity might have chanced them to attend a Fatherland Front rally in Tamsweg, where the Viennese 'terrorists' were denounced as public enemy number one.[13] The fact that Margit referred to herself as a 'European' in Lungau, a region drenched in Austrian and Germanic nationalism, was bold to say the least.

As sincere and alarming as the *Spectator* letter was, it suffered the fate of so many pieces: it ended up on the waste-paper pile, turned yellow, and disappeared from view. Margit had miscalculated, and there were certainly not as many British as she had hoped who thought negatively of Hitler. Her letter did not even trigger a discussion in *The Spectator*, much less a resistance movement through the organisation of a peace congress or similar. She certainly had the necessary capabilities and space at Finstergrün to host one. But perhaps, at the age of sixty-six, she no longer had the same youthful, enterprising energy she once had. She was lucky enough still to have her castle, where she could discuss matters freely with her right-minded English guests. They valued the open atmosphere, as evidenced by the memoirs of Rosemary Murray.

After the war, Murray would go on to found Murray Edwards College (then New Hall College), Cambridge, as the university's first woman to serve as college president; in 1975, she would also become Cambridge's first female vice-chancellor. In the summer of 1935, she visited Finstergrün as a fresh twenty-two-year-old chemistry graduate at the invitation of her aunt, Isabel du Cane. The young woman had a marvellous time, taking many walks through the mountains. Her diary tells of how the situation in Austria was discussed in the 'great hall' before the open fire, Dollfuss having been killed the previous summer: 'Anti-Nazi feelings ran high in Finstergrün.' She had sensed the threat of war on her journey across Western Europe: while on the train through Germany, she saw a great many uniforms, and Hitler Youth were everywhere. She was happy to disembark in the safety of London once more.[14]

The appeal of national socialism to young people must have had a particularly strong impact on Margit. In Lungau, after all, she had spent a great deal of her money and time on improving children's lives—building a school, providing them with warm clothing and food, supporting their mothers, helping to find work for their injured veteran fathers, and always on call to help solve problems. The fact that these same young people, boys especially, were now being seduced in the region and throughout Austria into following Germany's example, lured by the flags and insignias, the parades and masculine culture—and the fact that this new culture was propagated by national-socialist youth movements that had begun to supplant the old female-dominated Catholic associations—will have done nothing to ease the heart problems from which Margit already suffered.

She made one last attempt to turn the tide: a large fundraiser held at Finstergrün in 1936, to erect a statue of the late emperor Franz Joseph. The first steps for this initiative had already been taken in 1934 in the form of concerts and a lottery, to ensure sufficient funds for a worthy monument. Extensive meetings were held to determine a suitable location, the potential candidates covering fully half of Vienna. In September 1936, Margit was honoured as a distinguished benefactor, undoubtedly due to the significant financial contribution she had scraped together one month before by characteristically inventive means: on 25 August, she had organised a *Festakademie*, or a ceremonial concert. The patron of the event was Archduke Joseph Ferdinand Salvator, an old infantry general who had fought on the eastern front during the First World War and who had married into the Habsburg monarchy.

This invitation-only affair was attended by many nobles and local dignitaries, including Finstergrün's nearest neighbours: the Wilczeks of Moosham and Lilli Schandrovich, Epenstein's widow.[15] Members of the local Homeland Protection and Young Fatherland divisions were asked to provide security.[16] The honoured guests were treated to a programme of Mozart and Schubert, various opera arias and a symbolic presentation of all regions of Austria; the contributions collected were to help pay for the statue. If Margit could no longer produce the funds herself, she could at least put the castle to use as the backdrop. She garnered much recognition as a result—after the *Festakademie*, everybody who was anybody knew that Finstergrün could still be considered a bastion of monarchism, an enclave at the far reaches of Austria where a lonely countess was bravely holding the fort against the advancing hordes from the north.

PAYING GUESTS

Erecting statues was the act of a bygone era, however—one more at home in Robert Musil's great novel of the Habsburgs' decline and fall, *The Man Without Qualities*, than in Austria's interwar corporatist state. Margit's political arsenal had become rather limited.[17] (The statue was also never built.) She remained a product of her social class and conducted herself accordingly, blind to the reality that she was already living in the past. She lacked the rage, independent spirit and literary power of compatriots like the writer Joseph Roth, who continued to insist that Germany's 'freedom' was inextricably tied to its neighbours, and to European culture as a whole. From his exile in Paris, Roth—who was from a Jewish family—voiced his sorrow at the loss of what he considered to be true Germanic culture: the intellectual, cosmopolitan Austria, not the Austria of Franz Joseph and the dual monarchy. He founded the Spirit of Austria League with another Austrian Jewish writer in Paris, Alfred Polgar, and expressed his anger in fiery letters to the daily papers.

The statue fundraiser was one of the last occasions when all of Finstergrün's rooms were used in a manner befitting a castle: full of important guests, rustling gowns, civilised conversation, beautiful music and the aromas of fine dining. Those in attendance were likely aware of the poignant symbolism, and felt a definitive farewell to this grand history looming: both their own, and that of the country to which their hearts belonged.

* * *

Six months later, on 12–13 February 1938, Kurt Schuschnigg was invited to Berchtesgaden just north of Salzburg for an official retreat. At his country estate there, Adolf Hitler demanded that the chancellor agree to appoint Arthur Seyss-Inquart as Austrian minister for the interior. Schuschnigg refused. Hitler threatened not to let him leave unless he consented to the appointment, which must have sounded like a death threat, surrounded as they were by so many military units. Schuschnigg ultimately gave in to Hitler's demands, but on the return journey to Vienna was already preparing a plebiscite on the potential annexation by Germany, in the hopes of being able to turn things around. Hitler became enraged, demanding

SECRETS OF A SUITCASE

Schuschnigg's resignation and Seyss-Inquart's immediate appointment as the new chancellor. On 11 March 1938, President Wilhelm Miklas agreed.

Schuschnigg was arrested shortly thereafter, and would disappear to the Oranienburg concentration camp until the end of the Second World War. It was from there, on 12 April 1942, that he smuggled out a personal communication to Jolanta Szapáry, including a fond recollection of his welcome at Finstergrün and an enquiry after her mother's health.[18]

Under the pretext that Austria needed defending, Seyss-Inquart sent a telegram requesting German support. On 13 March, German troops entered Austria, and the annexation—the *Anschluss*—was complete. Hitler, who entered Austria via his birthplace of Braunau and his childhood city of Linz, was applauded by an ecstatic crowd at Vienna's Heldenplatz on 15th. There, from the balcony of the Hofburg, he addressed the people with the words: 'My fatherland has become part of the German Reich.' From that moment on, Austria was renamed 'Ostmark'. Roth wrote:

> A man from Braunau has Linzified Austria. (...) You can't abandon *one* country of European thought without losing the second, the third and the fourth. The joyfulness of Paris is over, ever since the Prussian boot marched into Vienna. (...) A world has been served up to Prussia (...) [and] all the witnesses of German greatness ill-treated in the concentration camp of the spirit: they have lost the last country where the great shadows of Germany could take refuge without a passport.[19]

One month earlier, Margit Szapáry had already packed her suitcases and turned her large key in the gates of Finstergrün. She avoided having to hoist the swastika flag over her castle, and spared herself the sight of all the boys, girls, men and women she knew lining the sides of the road from Ramingstein station, dressed in their Sunday dirndls and lederhosen with flags, flowers and raised right arms, welcoming the man they all saw as their saviour.[20]

But that man was not Hitler. No, it was a man they embraced as a 'son of the Lungau', the godson of Epenstein, who saw Mauterndorf Castle where he had spent so many holidays as his true birthplace. They were there to hail the Field Marshal of the Luftwaffe, the

144

PAYING GUESTS

Reich Minister for Forestry and Aviation, Master of the Hunt, Governor and Prime Minister of Prussia, and President of the Reichstag, General Hermann Wilhelm Göring.

UNWANTED GUESTS

Göring wasted no time, and requested a visit to Finstergrün by telegram that very month.[1] But Margit was not at home. She was in the Tyrol, and when it came to the field marshal, her response to the post was uncharacteristically slow. Jolanta answered in her stead, and without mincing words: 'Castle inaccessible. Mother absent', was her curt reply.

What was Göring after at Finstergrün? It can't have been a mere social visit, popping in to see an old friend and reminisce over a cup of tea. Relations between Mauterndorf and Finstergrün had never been that amiable. No, Göring had something else in mind, and was making straight for it now that he had his chance.

Göring had spent every family holiday at Mauterndorf between the ages of five and fifteen and, as we know, in adulthood he would revisit the castle whenever he needed rest or convalescence. One such occasion was his recovery from his fighter jet accident in 1916, after he had recklessly attacked the British during the First World War. During that time, Epenstein had held lavish banquets and invited neighbours to come and meet his godson, the war hero. Göring had visited again in August 1931, zooming down to Lungau for a getaway in his new luxury Mercedes convertible, a gift from Hitler to pacify him after a quarrel with Himmler. It was then that Göring had finally introduced his ailing Swedish countess, Carin, to his godfather, who was now elderly. The couple had been given another festive welcome by Epenstein and his wife Lilli, partly in acknowledgement of Göring's new position as a member of the German Reichstag. Epenstein invited all of the neighbours over for receptions and dinners.[2]

Göring's triumphal 1938 tour through Lungau came after an absence of many years. He had even missed the grand burial of Epenstein in the summer of 1934, which Margit had attended, along

147

with many other Lungau dignitaries.[3] He had met the Lady of Finstergrün several times during social events in Tamsweg and at Mauterndorf, and knew that she had furnished her castle with magnificent and valuable Gothic furniture. This suited his own taste, which he had developed via his godfather and through his marriage to Carin. He himself did not call such décor Gothic, but rather 'Germanic', in line with the jargon of the new era—but he needed it.

Carinhall, the hunting lodge he had started building after his wife's untimely death in 1934, was not the kind of home one could fill with Bauhaus products, that modernist style so reprehensible in Nazi eyes as *entartete Kunst*—'degenerate art', the label for what they considered to be a disfigurement of German culture. With this lodge, built on the 120-hectare Schorfheide nature reserve north of Berlin, Göring was creating a northern Germanic atmosphere of elevated brotherhood, a Walhalla (calling it a 'hall' was no coincidence), echoing the Nordic myth of Odin offering eternal lavish feasts to fallen warriors. For this, Göring needed more and more furniture pieces in 'Germanic' styles—such as Finstergrün had in abundance. No harm in an exploratory call on its mistress, who just happened to be in financial distress. Unfortunately for the field marshal, however, he had met with a closed door.

So, he switched targets, instead expressing his interest to Epenstein's widow, Baroness Elisabeth Epenstein Ritter von Mauternburg, better known as Lilli Schandrovich. She had become a loyal ally to Göring, had been signing off her letters with 'Heil Hitler' for some time, and regularly used Göring's name to speed up business with banks and lawyers in Lungau, sometimes referring to him as her 'brother' to exert some extra pressure. She even went to live with him for a time in Berlin, at the Reich Presidential Palace at number 30 Hermann-Göring-Strasse.[4] In August 1938, Lilli wrote to Margit saying that Göring was very interested in a Gothic four-poster bed that he had once seen at Finstergrün—might she consider selling it to him?

It was the kind of request that Margit was not in a position to refuse, as a person known for her cool feelings toward the new government in Vienna, Hitler's heavyweights. Lilli, who was on friendly terms with Margit,[5] tried to sweeten the pill. 'Oh, just go ahead and do it,' she wrote, 'you could use the money, and he won't even miss it.'[6] And so, in 1939, a magnificent piece from Finstergrün, one with great sentimental value, set off on a journey north to take its place in Hermann Göring's rapidly expanding collection of art and antiquities. But Margit still had another Gothic four-poster bed, in her own bedroom.

Knowing how beloved she was by the locals, Göring must have realised that he couldn't deal too harshly with the 'Countess of Lungau' without compromising his own esteem among the people. The farmers, however, did not qualify for such clemency, if they showed signs of anti-nationalism themselves. When one unsuspecting farm girl sent a letter to a friend criticising the new regime, and the letter 'happened' to be opened by the postman, she immediately disappeared into a jail cell.[7]

Göring generally preferred to have others do his dirty work. But the way he went about wheedling a four-poster bed out of Margit has all the hallmarks of an act of revenge, on somebody who had never accepted him or his father as equals. Demanding the bed was a symbolic act—the spoils of war. Though he paid only a small sum for it, it was a trophy, never intended for practical use. It would have been far too small for Göring anyhow—for years he had been known in some circles as 'the fat one', a man unable to hide his 308-pound frame, even in his tailor-made uniforms.

* * *

On 10 April 1938, one month after the annexation to Germany, a plebiscite was held asking the Austrians their opinion. The design of the ballot paper characterised the situation with shocking clarity. A black Gothic typeface read: 'Are you in agreement with the reunification of Austria with the German Reich that was effected on 13 March, and do you hereby vote for the list of our leader Adolf Hitler?' Below were two circles, one with the word 'Yes' above it, three times the size of the 'No' circle, which was relegated to the bottom-right corner. The name 'Adolf Hitler' was also three times the size of all other text.

Did the residents of Lungau, who had been addressed so warmly with the informal German *du* on the ballot paper, really need such convincing? Looking at the results, it would appear as though

SECRETS OF A SUITCASE

Lungau gave the final push for a landslide victory in favour of the *Anschluss*. In seventeen of its eighteen municipalities, not a single 'no' vote was cast. And of the 852 ballots submitted in Finstergrün's neighbouring villages of Ramingstein, Madling and Kendlbruck, 100 percent of voters were in agreement with 'reunification'.[8] Overall, Lungau had the highest percentage of yes-voters in all of Austria. Quite some referendum.

Margit hadn't spoiled the victory by submitting what would have been the only 'no' vote in Ramingstein. Instead she was in the Tyrol with Isabel du Cane, which also excused her from participating in the subsequent festivities, which were later described in the school newsletter as follows: 'We have become the happiest generation of the entire German people. We have all, all written our names in the book of our German history.' Nor was she subjected to the fawning welcome extended to Göring in the local press:

> Hermann Göring! To us you are not merely the Prime Minister and Field Marshall before whom the world bows in awe, admiration and envy. No, to us you are a son of the country, truly among the greatest of the land, among those whose greatness lies in the fact that they remain completely unseen to the small, the poor and the oppressed. (…) The Lungau greets you, and asks that it may call you a son. May the sense of homeland ever call you back to its remote valleys, and its pure air invigorate you time and again, that you may continue your blessed work.[9]

In the South Tyrolean town of Merano, reading the papers on the patio at Hotel Kronprinz, Margit could have studied the referendum results at her leisure; we might imagine her staring out into the valley for some time, deep in thought. When Isabel wrote to Margit announcing her own arrival at the hotel, she insisted that the countess choose a good room.[10] Margit clearly needed it. The time was long past when she had fallen for a Hungarian's charms as Margarethe Henckel von Donnersmarck amid the gentle springs of Abbazia.

When Sándor had died, leaving her with her fortune, Finstergrün and two children at her skirts, she had worked to help give ordinary folk in Lungau a better life. In 1938, many of the men and women alive there were people whose births and childhoods she had witnessed; to whom she had gifted socks, books and apples at

150

UNWANTED GUESTS

Christmas; whom she had watched rearing their own children, and keeping their lives afloat both during and after the terrible Great War. She had witnessed the misery of the Great Depression in the 1930s, caused by the Wall Street Crash. She will have understood that these people, too, wished for a better life, only they did not have the money or opportunities to realise it, as she herself had had. That was why they relied on others like her, on the social class to which she belonged, and their emperor, Franz Joseph. They had been let down. And now their despair had transformed into joy, joy at the arrival of a new leader and a new movement that promised them a bright future. They had heard Göring himself swear to build a train line to Salzburg, liberating Lungau from its isolation and improving their economic prospects. How was it possible that all of these people had allowed themselves to be taken in by such empty promises? The train line never came. To this day it has not come.

Did Margit ever experience a moment of self-criticism, and wonder whether blindly following an emperor, a pope, a bishop or a corporatist authoritarian state had left the soil all-too-fertile for such an extraordinary show of unanimity? Or did she perhaps put the referendum result down to the increased power of the media in the hands of silver-tongued demagogues, who knew how to rile up a crowd with a calculated personality cult, calls to national pride, the promise of 'putting an end to slavery' (the Treaty of Versailles) and inciting resentment of groups seen as a threat to the 'unity of the people'?

She was now sixty-eight, with walking difficulties and heart problems. A tumour had been found in her oesophagus, which limited her diet to fluids only. And her financial troubles had not left her. She wrote several letters to unburden her heart, but it is unclear whether she ever sent them.[11]

One was written to Norman Angell, the 1933 winner of the Nobel Peace Prize. In 1909 he had written a bestseller called *The Great Illusion*, in which he argued that waging war rarely brings economic benefit, and should therefore be avoided. The Englishman had become convinced that nobody could ever win a modern war, with such destructive weaponry. In the 1930s, he had been a Labour MP, and opposed the appeasement policy of the likes of Chamberlain, who, against his better judgement, continued to believe in the power of negotiation. In his *Peace with the Dictators?* (1938), Angell presents an imaginary discussion between an Italian, a German and an Englishman, elucidating their various political positions.[12] In it, he warns against the 'conditioning' of the masses through all the 'suggestive powers' of modern 'instruments', such as a 'universal press, universal radio and universal film': 'Again and again in history the demagogue has discovered that it is far easier to bamboozle than to debamboozle. (...) So the prospect that Germany will not adhere to her theory, her doctrine, her ethos, is not bright.'[13] Unlike many other Europeans, Angell had actually read *Mein Kampf*, and took Hitler's closing words seriously: 'A state which [...] devotes itself to the duty of preserving the best elements of its racial stock must one day become ruler of the Earth.'[14] Angell posited that Germany's looming territorial expansion was, contrary to Hitler's claims, utterly unnecessary to strengthen the economy, but was above all a dream with political, military and psychological motivations.

When Angell was writing the above, Margit, as a concerned resident of Lungau, wrote a letter to him, warning of a German invasion of Czechoslovakia and Hungary, both of which would involve inside assistance from German-sympathisers to avoid the appearance of an annexation like Austria's. Her letter was well-intentioned, and also accurate, but she had no notion of the forces that were guiding these events. She didn't realise that the British were aware of Hitler's plans, including Chamberlain's own cabinet. They simply weren't very concerned, since Britain 'had no interests' in Czechoslovakia, and Hungary was also quite a way from its doorstep.[15] Margit's letter was the helpless act of one who saw great danger, and knew no other way to respond than to share her concerns with those whom she assumed belonged to the same class, and would listen to sensible people like her. She seemed completely oblivious to the fact that the issue was no longer one of class, understanding or good ideas, but instead one of psychology, and the considerable interests of business magnates, including those in the German steel industry.

Margit still believed that the 'Prussian-oriented' history lessons in schools were what had chiefly primed Austria for the *Anschluss*. In her surviving notebooks, she equates Prussian people with the Hohenzollern dynasty of Frederick the Great, referring to 'Prussians/Hohenzollerns'. In her opinion, teachers should have devoted more attention to Austrian history and traditions. The irrelevance of this detail—since the foundation for events would still have been laid by the Austrofascist state and the 'official' nationalism born of the nineteenth century[16]—seemed lost on her. Margit may very well have sat in her armchair in 1934 and claimed to be a European in *The Spectator*, but that does not necessarily mean that she was one. She forgot, or was unaware, that the English also had a strong nationalist tradition. Joseph Chamberlain, politician and father to Neville and Austen (who had concluded the Locarno Pact), had written in 1895: 'I believe in this race, the greatest governing race the world has ever seen; in this Anglo-Saxon race, so proud, tenacious, self-confident and determined, this race, which neither climate nor change can degenerate, which will infallibly be the predominant force of future history and universal civilization.'[17]

There is one respect in which Margit certainly was European: she hoped that Germanic culture's contribution to the broader culture of Europe would continue to be appreciated. She now realised, belatedly, that the Christian Socialists ought to have cooperated far earlier with the Social Democrats, in order to act as a counterweight to the Nazis. It would have been possible, she wrote, since the CSP chancellor Dollfuss had been popular among broad swathes of society, far more so than the stiffer Schuschnigg, who had enjoyed such a warm reception at Finstergrün, despite her criticisms of him. But the Nazis' cowardly murder of Dollfuss in 1934 had closed off that avenue, she now realised. We can imagine Margit wrestling with her convictions here, concocting nonsensical explanations, and refusing to accept the need to abandon her beliefs. But it was all hindsight, the scribblings of one who knew the end was nigh—the end of the power dynamics in which she had grown up, of the world she had wanted to build up around Finstergrün, of her own kingdom. And of herself.

Her correspondence in these final years consisted mainly of exchanges with bishops, whose spiritual support gave her some solace. She spent precious little time at Finstergrün, spending the summer of 1938 at Haunsperg Castle in Hallein, just south of Salzburg, and at Hohenaschau Castle in Chiemgau, with Isabel.

Hermann Göring's request to visit Finstergrün in August 1938 should have set off alarm bells, and not only because of the Gothic bed he coveted. Margit had a large debt with the Salzburg State Mortgage Bank of around 60,000 Marks (around £215,000 today), and that year she started to receive requests to settle it. Göring was personally responsible for these requests, working behind the scenes to put the bank under pressure.[18] Again he set the widow Epenstein on Margit, imploring her to accept his help: he would be spending the summer at his holiday home in Obersalzberg, and could easily visit Mauterndorf to discuss the matter, Lilli suggested. But Margit was not in the neighbourhood. Indeed, her busy travels in the summer of 1938—visible in the addresses struck out and rewritten on Jolanta's collection of postcards—suggest that she was making efforts to avoid Finstergrün at all costs. But Göring had not forgotten her, despite his busy schedule in Berlin.

After the annexation of Austria, the next item on Hitler's agenda was the invasion of Czechoslovakia. Neville Henderson, the new English ambassador to the Third Reich and a passionate hunter, often visited Göring at Carinhall as part of Chamberlain's appeasement policy, which essentially boiled down to prolonging discussions in order to avoid war. But in Göring's map room, he happened to notice that the borders between Germany, Austria and Czechoslovakia had mysteriously disappeared. When asked about it, Göring's response was: 'A good hunter knows no bounds.'

'Peace for our time' was Chamberlain's triumphant verdict after signing the Munich Agreement on 30 September. But he was mistaken. Hitler did not want peace at all. Only Göring had misgivings about war, as he was afraid to lose all the wealth he had amassed over the years. But, just at this moment, when his connection with Hitler—the most important relationship in his life—had waned somewhat, Göring was forced to take a step back. In early 1939 he started yet another treatment programme in an attempt to keep his morphine addiction under control, and also to lose some weight. With his second wife Emmy Sonnemann and their newborn daughter Edda, he travelled to Tripoli via Naples, to combine business—strengthening ties with Libya—and pleasure. He had hoped to continue on to Franco's Spain, but was called back in early March 1939. Hitler wished to expedite the full occupation of Czechoslovakia, and wanted Göring's talents as a pitbull during the final 'negotiations'. On 15 March, this second annexation became a reality. Göring was sent to Rome, to at least keep Mussolini friendly. Early in the summer he again fell ill, and recovered in San Remo.

This brief summary of events between late 1938 and mid-1939 suggests that Göring might have had more important matters to attend to than the badgering of a widowed Lungau countess in financial difficulty. And yet that is what he did. His grudge must have been sizeable indeed. During these few months, Göring increased the pressure from his offices. His secretary wrote to the bank in Salzburg, saying that the Szapáry matter required 'resolution', on the unjustified pretext that, under the corporatist state, she had obtained the loan via her personal bank contacts without providing adequate collateral.[19] An old, draughty castle would never have counted. Margit had a representative negotiate a solution with the bank on her behalf, but not quickly enough for Göring, who demanded an immediate resolution in October 1939. Exactly why is unclear, since a part of Margit's inheritance amounting to approximately 32,000 Marks (more than £120,000 in today's money) was located in Polish Silesia, which had been under German occupation for a month by that time. The funds were used to service some of the debt. But Göring continued to push via the bank for the modest remainder to be paid off.[20]

Frequent correspondence continued into late 1941 between Margit and Gisela Limberger, Göring's personal assistant for art-related matters.[21] Between 1940 and 1942, several letters were also exchanged with a certain 'Riegele' in Berlin; this must have been Göring's sister Olga Riegele, who managed some of his affairs. Alas, only the entries in Margit's correspondence records have survived.[22] The topic of the letters with Gisela Limberger will have been 'art', however, for that was her only remit, and she always signed off her letters as 'Librarian'.[23]

Limberger was extraordinarily busy during the early years of the Dutch and French occupations, which began in the spring of 1940. Göring made short work of all the major arthouses in Amsterdam and Paris, sending Berlinwards a veritable tsunami of works that were either purchased—often for a pittance—or stolen outright from Jewish estates. Between November 1940 and November 1942, Göring visited Paris no fewer than twelve times to view expropriated and stolen art at the Jeu de Paume, where the pieces were selected for him in advance. Art acquisition held increasing importance in the field marshal's life at the time.[24] All of the pieces were either given a home at Carinhall, or put into storage for a future museum—the pretext under which Göring had brought to Carinhall 4,249 artworks that would be registered after the war, including many Bruegels, Cranachs, Rembrandts and Tintorettos. Margit knew nothing of all this; she was concerned only with the correspondence addressed to her, which was pressing enough. She was conscious of what had happened to her brother Edgar's family in Silesia.

Edgar, who had died in 1939, left Brynek Palace to his son Karl. Immediately after the German invasion of Poland in that year, Karl was conscripted into the army, where he would die in 1940. His wife and three daughters were chased out of Brynek's main building, forced to leave behind all of their personal possessions. The pride and joy of Margit and Edgar's grandfather, Hugo II, was then converted into the Adolf Hitler School for the Hitler Youth, and a Hitler Library was established in the chapel. A large proportion of the Upper Silesian mining and steel industry, in which the family still held some assets, was also appropriated by the Germans after the invasion of Poland. The enterprise was renamed *Bergwerksverwaltung Oberschlesien G.m.b.H. der Reichswerke Hermann Göring* ('Upper Silesia Mining LLC, Hermann Göring Reich Works'). With a stroke of the pen, much of Hugo I's life's work to build his family fortune disappeared anonymously into Göring's ledgers, devoured by the great glutton of Carinhall.

Margit was completely on her own—yet another reason to avoid a visit from her former summer neighbour. She must have suspected what fate might await Finstergrün in the near future. Her debt to the bank in Salzburg, which had already shrunk significantly, can't have been the only reason why she invited Karl Garzarolli-Thurnlackh, an art historian and museum curator from Graz, to view her collection and provide an estimate of the total worth. If she hadn't known already, his visit will have made clear that, by selling just a few pieces, she could have repaid her debt and lived modestly from the remainder. She would not have been able to afford staff, but even if she had, where was she supposed to find any reliable personnel, now that virtually the entire region had become national socialist?

156

UNWANTED GUESTS

Weighing all of these considerations, Margit decided to pack up the entire contents of her home and send them off for auction, right down to the last candlestick and pewter plate. It was partly a response to Göring's threats, an attempt to spare Finstergrün from meeting the same fate as Brynek. Besides, the interior furnishings were not part of the family's estate, and so contained no heirlooms cherished through the centuries. She had assembled them all herself, and was at liberty to dispense with them as she pleased.

Still, the decision remains a curious one, coming from a woman of a social class that placed such importance on castles, estates and material inheritance. Perhaps she did it for her two children, for whom she likely still had motherly concerns, despite the fact that they were now both adults. Béla Szapáry, who was nearly 40, lived in Budapest and was still unmarried. His inability to help his mother at this crucial time was an indication that he himself had no access to sufficient financial means. And Jolanta, likewise unmarried, was working as a poorly paid paediatric nurse.

GOING ONCE, GOING TWICE

In November 1941, Margit began preparing to sell off her valuable interior furnishings, via Munich's Adolf Weinmüller auction house. Its reputation was already controversial by this time, as the contents of many Jewish estates went under the hammer at Weinmüller's; but it was also a specialist for interior and art collections, the closest one to Finstergrün.

Weinmüller was proud of this auction. He had been a Munich art dealer for years, and had benefited from the 'aryanisation' of the Jewish auction houses, a process set in motion by the 1934 Nuremberg race laws, which aimed to siphon off all Jewish property into the hands of the Nazis. As minister of economics and leader of the four-year-plan, Göring bore final responsibility for these confiscations, which (per Evans) would ultimately constitute the greatest act of theft in history—not only of art and antiques, but of virtually all businesses that could be labelled 'Jewish'. Weinmüller was a relatively small figure within this overarching policy, though he certainly profited from it. He had become an early member of the NSDAP in 1931, and after Hitler's ascent to power in 1933, he had been tasked with bringing the Trade Association of German Art and Antiques into line with Nazi policies and ideologies—a process known as *Gleichschaltung*, a euphemism for 'Nazification'. He had become national president of the association, and in 1934 had collaborated on a law governing the auction system.

When a large, Jewish-owned auction house had run into difficulties in 1936, Weinmüller had taken over the enterprise. With this move, he had become so powerful that he could compete with the other 'Aryan' auction houses, ultimately holding a monopoly in Munich. He had reopened the business, formerly the Kunsthandlung Hugo Helbing, as the Adolf Weinmüller Munich Art Auction House, based in the imposing Leuchtenberg Palace. After the

Anschluss in 1938, he had opened a second auction room in Vienna, acquiring the aryanised enterprise of the Jewish Kende family. By the time Margit came to him in 1941, he was on a committee that went to inspect stolen Jewish cultural heritage at the Gestapo headquarters in Prague, a minor portion of which would be auctioned off at Weinmüller's. Among others, his clients included Martin Bormann and Maria Almas-Dietrich, who purchased artwork directly for Adolf Hitler.

When the auction house was bombed in May 1943, Weinmüller was forced to split up his collection for storage. Immediately after the war, he went into hiding at his home in Tegernsee. He avoided prison by being deemed an accomplice rather than a major perpetrator, which ultimately saw most of his property restored to him. He reopened his auction house in 1949, and would continue to run auctions until his death in 1958. The Weinmüller name would remain associated with the business for another twenty years thereafter, until 1978. But the records from the war years—a subject of much interest among all organisations involved in restitution of former Jewish property—were nowhere to be found. Weinmüller had always maintained that the papers had been lost. That was still the story in 2013, when a number of boxes were discovered in the cellar beside the house's boilers, which until then had been overlooked. They contained the Weinmüller auction catalogues from 1936–45, including the documentation listing all of the vendors, buyers and prices.

It was a major find; the files were immediately safeguarded and later indexed by Meike Hopp. The catalogues and their accompanying documentation were then digitised in 2014, and made public in 2015 via www.lostart.de, a website which already offered information on German and international auction houses that had dealt in artwork stolen by the Nazis. This site, which anyone can consult, is the fruit of hard work by all those who continue to search tirelessly for the belongings of their robbed, deported and murdered families, over seventy years after the war. On my first visit to the website, I held my breath, thought of this history with admiration for the descendants' tenacity and determination, then gingerly searched the names 'Weinmüller', 'Szapáry' and 'Finstergrün'. The auction results for the entire contents of Finstergrün appeared on my computer screen.

160

GOING ONCE, GOING TWICE

I zoomed in on photographs of Margit's candlesticks, crucifixes, pewter plates, blanket chests, chairs, tables, and her remaining four-poster bed, 410 pieces in total, each with its own lot number, all of which had once stood in Finstergrün. Though black-and-white, the catalogue looks richly illustrated. My thoughts were with Margit, who had collected all of these pieces in remembrance of her husband, to serve as the décor for her solitary life after he died so young. These were not furnishings intended to impress visitors, for Finstergrün rarely hosted receptions. No, it was a private home, albeit a very large one, and only began to see guests in large numbers out of financial necessity at the last. And after that, when Margit sensed that it was truly over, she had once again meticulously catalogued the entire contents herself, giving every item a reserve and estimated price, then packing and loading everything up to be sold off in Munich.

Margit Szapáry was not a victim of the Nazis, like so many Jewish families. Until the very end, she was free to travel and do as she wished, and even to auction off her property when she thought the time was right. She did not have to watch in horror, after an unexpected knock at the door, as the Gestapo cleared out her home within the space of a few days. She too had been forced to part with her belongings, however, her livelihood threatened by the warnings and reminders from the bank—prompted by Göring, and forwarded to her by Jolanta via registered post.

Finstergrün symbolised the marriage between Margarethe Henckel von Donnersmarck and Sándor Szapáry. The castle was an integral part of Lungau, a region that disappeared for Margit around 1940, when the ideals of the people who lived there were no longer her own. She was unsure of what to do with her convictions: she was trapped in a museum for a home, a queen without a people. In such a situation, Finstergrün could no longer serve as a symbol of her independence, not even if Béla and Jolanta decided to live there after her death. Whatever the case, her children would still have a castle, with some land and a few farms to fall back on. Her wish was to keep it until her dying breath, for to her, it was land—hers and theirs. This was a sentiment she shared with all major landowners of her

SECRETS OF A SUITCASE

class and generation. She had no idea how the war would unfold, she was seriously ill, and so she committed to one final act. That act required strength, which she thankfully still possessed: she had decided to make herself, and the contents of her home, disappear.

And so Finstergrün's furnishings were sent to Weinmüller's Leuchtenberg Palace, where they were sold off over the course of two glum days in November. Although Margit's collection was the highlight of the auction, consisting of 410 items, Weinmüller auctioned other artworks during the same two-day period. They came from Prague and also numbered just over 400, but nearly all were paintings.

The catalogue text for Margit's possessions was quite bombastic: 'With this collection from Finstergrün Castle, the Adolf Weinmüller Auction House offers a series of late-Gothic furniture items and other valuables, in such a volume and quality as is seldom seen at auction.'[1] The introduction explains that the collection was assembled by 'Count Sándor Szapáry and his wife', aided by Count Wilczek, 'whose own art collection at Kreuzenstein Castle is renowned far and wide'. Evidently, Wilczek's name was still synonymous with quality. Margit herself is not named at any point, let alone by her maiden name of Henckel von Donnersmarck. Perhaps it would have done harm to the sale price if it had been revealed that the owner was a woman. The omission may also have spared the national-socialist branch of the family at nearby Tegernsee— Guidotto and his princess in particular—a few awkward inquiries.

The art historian employed at Weinmüller's, the Nazi Eberhard von Cranach-Sichart, took great pains to describe each item, with a clarity and precision usually reserved for museum collections, adding to the almost solemn tone of the catalogue. It is astounding that Margit had managed to amass such a collection within forty short years. It wasn't only the antique Gothic furniture and its intricate woodcarvings that made the auction so special. There were also several ornamental pieces that lent elegance to the collection, in counterpoint to the stark wooden furniture. A small, fourteenth-century northern German oil lamp, in the shape of a fantastical elephant approximately one foot tall; some florid cast-iron Italian gates from the fifteenth century, lacking in religious symbolism, but representing a wonder of design from such an early period. The

162

saints' statues were exceptional, as they had been selected based on the human emotions present in their facial expressions, rather than their pious demeanour. The catalogue said that they were from 'Ostmark', Austria's new name under the *Anschluss*, thus robbing them of their Central European, in some cases Austrian, origins. In a foreword, art historian Hubert Wilm mentions the collection's qualities as more reflective of the present period: 'Herein lies the secret as to why all pieces of old German craftsmanship, wherever they may stand, spread an atmosphere of bourgeois comfort and refined taste even today.'[2]

'Wherever they may stand'—no longer at Finstergrün, for which no reason was given. This text was an invitation to the *nouveau riche*, wherever their money may have come from, who could gift themselves tasteful surroundings by bidding on such pieces. Wilm's assessment of the second large lot, the artworks from Prague, was noticeably less verbose, likely because there was no private vendor to wax lyrical about. These pieces had come from the German government, and more specifically the Prague division of the Gestapo, which had looted artworks from Jewish citizens upon the annexation of Czechoslovakia. After the Nazi leaders had taken the prize pieces for themselves, Weinmüller had been invited to Prague to see if there was anything he liked. The leftovers proved none-too-shabby: mostly Dutch paintings by artists such as Judith Leyster, Cornelis de Heem and Jacob Jordaens—and a Bruegel.

The sale of the Finstergrün collection was a success for Margit, yielding over 200,000 RM—a little less than £700,000 in today's money. Under normal circumstances, the sum would have been far greater. The pieces that fetched the most, well exceeding the estimated price, were the lamp in the shape of an elephant (6,500 RM), a large lectern (9,000 RM), a carved cabinet (8,000 RM), a finely crafted clothing chest (15,000 RM), and the four-poster bed (5000 RM), all from Central Europe and dating back to the fourteenth and fifteenth centuries. Margit now had enough to pay off the mortgage, and since almost everything of value had been sold, she would also have some money to leave to her children.

Who bought Finstergrün's greatest pieces? For privacy reasons, that information is not available online. But in response to my requests, I received from the researchers at Maagdenburg's German Lost Art Foundation a copy of the pages showing several winning bids; and the Central Institute for Art History, the organisation that manages the original Weinmüller catalogues, sent a document listing the buyers of every single lot. The names are a large assembly of international collectors, merchants and museum curators, who had registered for the auction. The collector Prince Friedrich Leopold of Prussia (1895–1959) was in the room, acquiring two chairs for his imperial collection at Gut Imlau in Werfen. The Munich-based collector and beer-brewer Mr Grandauer was present, as was Baron Erwein von Aretin—a powerful monarchist who had opposed Nazi collaboration among the nobility of Bavaria in the 1930s.[3] The German Gothic-furniture merchant Julius Böhler, who worked for Hitler, bought a single item, as did the German traders Zinckgraf and Roselius, and the Dutch trader Hermsen. The elephant lamp went to 'Metz'—a clear reference to the still-extant Musées de Metz au Musée de la Cour d'Or, where a mediaeval exhibition is on permanent display in the renovated Metz granaries. Most of the pieces, however, including the fifteenth-century canopy bed, lot number 354, were purchased by a Mr Kreisel.

Kreisel bought no fewer than eleven prize pieces from the furniture collection. According to another auctiongoer,[4] he had been forced into a bidding war with a representative of Göring—most likely Böhler, who had worked for the field marshal as well as the Führer. Göring was evidently in the market for yet another four-poster bed; one was no longer enough for him. Nevertheless, it was Kreisel who won the bid, also taking Margit's other, larger items of Gothic furniture. Göring had undoubtedly admired these pieces in the past, so the fact that his dealer let them slip away is a sign that he had adapted his tastes to suit the new climate. Besides, Göring must hardly have known where to put all of his looted art. On 5 November 1941, two weeks before the Weinmüller auction, twenty-three crates of paintings and other artworks had been delivered to Göring at Carinhall, including an eighteenth-century French secretaire and four commodes, all from the Rothschild collection in Paris.[5] Perhaps, in the wake of these prizes, Margit's collection no longer held such great appeal for Göring.

Mr Kreisel must have been pleased with his purchases. He was not just anybody—at the time of the auction, Kreisel was curator

164

GOING ONCE, GOING TWICE

for the Bavarian Administration of State-owned Palaces, Gardens and Lakes, or the Bavarian Palace Administration for short. One property under this administration was Neuschwanstein Castle, another fairytale palace from the nineteenth century that was built by King Ludwig II of Bavaria, and which served as the storehouse for many of Hitler and Göring's artworks during the Second World War. Between 1939 and 1941, Kreisel fought as an officer in France, Poland and Russia, but afterwards went back to looking after his Bavarian palaces. As soon as the war was over, he would be dismissed and forced into retirement by the Americans due to his membership of the Nazi Party, his Wehrmacht record, and his involvement in the acquisition and storage of stolen art.[6] His memoirs, largely a recollection of his experiences on the eastern front, would become a best-seller. He was permitted to return as early as 1948, however, and in 1968 he would publish a ten-centimetre-thick, three-volume history of the art of German furniture, which is still in use as a standard reference work today.[7]

Among the nearly 700 museum-worthy masterpieces included in the book, all mediaeval or early Renaissance, were Margit's canopy bed and one of her woodcut clothes trunks. The photos are dutifully labelled 'from the Finstergrün collection',[8] and are accompanied by explanatory notes as to why he found the pieces so special. The ornate oak trunk, which was probably made as a lady's bridal chest, combines German and early-Renaissance Italian motifs, a rarity for the time.[9] The bed, however, is the *pièce de résistance*: it is South Tyrolean, and similarly Italian-influenced. It may not be as elaborately decorated as the chest, or even seem particularly well made by twenty-first-century standards, but there is one standout element: it has a slanted rooftop, instead of the usual four pillars supporting a baldachin. This suggests that it once stood in a poorer household, whose roof was not entirely water-proof, as was the case in many mediaeval homes. A slanted surface atop the bed offered additional protection during inclement weather—a roof within a roof.[10]

The Bavarian Palace Administration was in charge of thirty-two estates, one of which must have had a fitting spot for the pride of Margit's collection. Whatever the case, the old lady will have been pleased with the bed's final resting place, as painful as the auction

165

had been: from that moment on, nobody else would ever sleep in her bed, since it had been purchased by a museum.

After the auction, Margit herself never returned to Finstergrün. There was nothing left for her there. Winter was coming, and the home she knew and loved was no more.

In July 1942, it became clear that Margit was not fully free of Göring's clutches after all. He had plans to use Finstergrün as an educational institution for NSDAP teachers. Without her signature, a lease agreement was reached with a Silesian party member who claimed authority to act on her behalf as manager of the Henckel von Donnersmarck family's assets. From then on, Margit was unable even to enter her own castle.

Then, Margit had a stroke. She clearly had not much longer to live, and in April 1943 she expressed a wish to return to Ramingstein. There, in the Premhaus farm building where she had lived during the First World War, she died on 17 May, at the age of seventy-two. The entire population of the Lungau region turned out for her funeral. She would have been pleased to know that they had not forgotten her, despite the altered circumstances.[11]

Two days later, swastika flags could be seen flying from the towers of Finstergrün—the future Nazi Party instructresses had arrived. They complained about the cold, and the castle's mediaeval facilities.

THE COLLECTOR

Moosham, Finstergrün and Mauterndorf were all full of fourteenth-, fifteenth- and sixteenth-century furniture that their owners had painstakingly collected from across Central Europe and put on display. Not for nothing were the castles referred to as the 'museums of the Lungau'. In the Middle Ages, a dowry chest—an intricate piece of wooden furniture, sometimes topped with expensive porcelain vases—was simply more important than a painted artwork, even in the Netherlands, where the art of painting had flourished so grandly.[1] Paintings that hung in sixteenth-century houses were either religious scenes, portraits of the prosperous inhabitants, or neat compositions of flowers prone to wilting, or of fruit that must eventually decay—a common theme symbolising life's short and fragile nature. Furniture items were counted among the most valuable contents of a home. These included beds, which—far more than in later centuries—were a major focal point of any interior. This was where heirs were conceived and born, ensuring the continuation of the dynasty; where people received their last rites, and passed away in dignity. The art of furniture-making was one in which Central Europeans excelled, with woodcuts and inlaid panels of the various woods abundant in their forests. The religious interiors of churches, monasteries and abbeys, with their sacristy stalls and lecterns, were translated to secular spaces as chests, cupboards and writing desks.

It was with such pieces, therefore, that Göring had begun his collection in 1933, when his appointment as prime minister of Prussia granted him access to a generous budget for the construction and furnishing of Carinhall. The first time he had beheld such an interior was at his godfather's castle; Epenstein himself had got the idea from Wilczek. Like Sándor and Margit, they had followed the nineteenth-century trend of renovating mediaeval castles and mov-

167

ing in to 'live like a king'. Epenstein had left his own mark by including rooms full of souvenirs from his time in Africa. But he had carefully noted what his illustrious neighbour had done before him. Wilczek had originally helped Epenstein to create an even-more-authentic 'reconstruction' of Mauterndorf: at an art dealership in Graz, he had discovered floral bedroom-wall panels that came from Mauterndorf, and had had them brought back.[2] Wilczek had gladly shared his knowledge with all, helping both Epenstein and Margit with the 'Gothic' decoration of their castles.

That the style might also have been called 'Germanic', or simply 'German', did not even occur to him at that time. He was a cosmopolitan and curious *homo universalis*—an art connoisseur and adventurer. He was somebody. Wilczek was not interested in playing a part—he had no need of one. Epenstein, however, did. Despite his social successes as a doctor and businessman, he was a poser, an attitude that Göring also adopted. This 'legacy' from his godfather had shaped the impressionable young Göring into the man he would later become—a process marked significantly by the mediaeval castles he had come to know in Lungau, including Finstergrün.

There is a curious novel about Göring's life titled *The Knight, Death and the Devil*, by American author Ella Leffland (1990). For years she conducted research and spoke to many people, including close family members and staff who had worked with Göring personally. Unfortunately, instead of writing it as non-fiction, Leffland took her fine research and turned it into a novel, immediately raising doubts as to the authenticity of her claims. Some descriptions, however, do give an impression of the way Göring must have looked up to his godfather. One example is Leffland's narration of a family dinner at Mauterndorf, while the Görings were holidaying with Epenstein in 1904: 'Each day dinner was announced by the blast of a hunting horn [...] Pate [Godfather] ate a great deal of the food. He finished every course and at the same time he gave all his views on politics and history and also managed to keep the footmen on their toes by barking at them. [...] After dinner Pate leaned back in his polished throne of a chair and continued his speeches.'[3]

Epenstein created the kind of ambience at Mauterndorf that gave the master of the house a sense of the almighty, an ambition that went far beyond decorating the house according to his aesthetic preferences. Within Epenstein's walls, and later Göring's, all others were reduced to walk-on parts, including close friends and family. They had to play along with a game that was created for them, in front of the scenery provided.

Göring built Carinhall as a series of stages on which he was to play the lead role, not as a comfortable home to live in. It was not only a hunting lodge, but also an indoor amusement park, with model train sets and rooms for model aeroplanes, a cinema, a swimming pool and a gymnasium. In the garden was a miniature Trianon (modelled after Marie Antoinette's pleasure pavilion at Versailles), built for Göring's daughter Edda. He also bred his own 'Germanic' game animals, and introduced them to the surrounding forests.[4]

Carinhall became the official residence for Nazi receptions, as Hitler preferred to remain unencumbered by such distractions. Göring assumed the role of host, which immediately presented the attractive prospect of paying all of Carinhall's expenses from the government budget. He welcomed government leaders, diplomats and businesspeople, entertaining them with a hunt or in his many gaming rooms, then giving them a guided tour before holding the meetings and serving dinner. Later descriptions by his guests indicate that he did so using the kind of theatrics he had witnessed at Mauterndorf when younger, including costumes for himself and his servants. After 1940, he would also show guests his rapidly growing collection of valuable paintings, for which a long gallery had been specially built.

The way Göring went about obtaining Margit's four-poster bed in 1938 seems like an early, perhaps even his very first, attempt at a general approach that he would later implement on a far greater scale. Looking at the lengths he went to, to wrestle the bed from Margit and then to appropriate her castle amid all his other commitments, it's clear how important it must have been for him to bring the Countess of Lungau to her knees. As we know, she eventually sent him the bed in 1939, and would never receive payment for it. Göring rarely kept his grandiose promises.

The bed settled a score that went all the way back to Göring's youth. Although he had grown up in stately homes, still he was reliant on the good graces of his mother's lover Epenstein, himself only tolerated in higher circles because of his wealth. Margarethe Szapáry-Henckel von Donnersmarck, with her rigid traditional elitism and her noble heritage dating to the 1400s, had no doubt made this very clear to Epenstein and his makeshift family. Her aversion, of course, was repaid tenfold, for the canopy bed was not the end of the story. But Margit at least seemed to have beaten Göring to the punch in late 1941, auctioning off her possessions before having to give him anything else. Anyway, by that time, Göring had bigger fish to fry.

The paintings, furniture, tapestries, carpets, dinner sets and other trinkets that the field marshal began transporting from Vienna in 1938, and in increasing quantities from Amsterdam and Paris after 1940, were no more 'Germanic' than the many jewellery items he commissioned using gemstones purchased in Amsterdam, Antwerp and Paris. If Carinhall itself could still be called 'Germanic' at all, it was in its location and design, and the many animal species in the forests of the surrounding private nature reserve, Schorfheide, which Göring had gathered and protected for his organised hunting parties: bison (including European bison), wild bears, wild geese and elk. With these hunts, he laid claim to an ancient privilege of the nobility—and anyone who could brandish a hunting rifle, and drive powerful, dangerous creatures like stags into a corner to be shot down, might easily nurture an elevated opinion of themselves.

Göring had shot his first buck in Lungau when he was thirteen, guided by his godfather Epenstein. This episode is described vividly in Leffland's novel. The historian Fabrice d'Almeida, in *High Society and the Third Reich*, paints an even clearer picture: 'In contact with wild animals and the earth, the Aryan ideologists saw a validation of their prejudices. [...] This belief was so widespread in German society that, in visual representations, the image of a hunter was soon conflated with that of Nazi soldiers.'[5]

The portrayal of Göring as the sovereign exercising his hunting rights was a common thread that pervaded the building and the grounds at Carinhall. A photo book from 1999, now in its eighth edition, is judiciously titled *Göring's Reich: Self-Portrayals at Carinhall*.[6] What the field marshal did between 1933 and 1940 was to give

170

THE COLLECTOR

shape to his ideas of nationalism and Germanic culture. He had a sentimental notion of German history and the German character, a 'superficial belief in a Germany that was predestined, through a historical process, to become the standard-bearer of a superior culture.'[7] This was a view that he had developed even before the First World War, through his contact with Epenstein and his castles. He later supplemented the nationalism with a virulent antisemitism, and a disdain for international Marxism, while simultaneously working to shut reality out of his personal living environment.[8] From 1940 onward, Göring lost all control amid the opportunities he suddenly saw to multiply his possessions, in the regions newly occupied by Germany.

His collection began to resemble an illustrated encyclopaedia of the greatest names from Western art history—not because he appreciated them, but because they were among the most priceless artworks in the world. He padded out his gallery with more modern pieces, such as works by Cézanne, Courbet, Monet and Sisley. Although considered 'degenerate' by Nazi standards, they were still useful as bargaining chips; besides, his second wife Emmy liked them. Their presence in his collection demonstrates that, from now on, Göring was concerned only with amassing property, for which his appetite was seemingly insatiable. The works he had shipped to Germany—including, oddly enough for a Nazi, much early Christian art, such as Madonnas and statues of Christ—were stripped of their own, distinctive meaning. Their unique portrayals of the human condition, and the reflections they inspire on the highs and lows of existence, were rendered impotent by their display at Göring's Walhalla as the spoils of war. The artworks had become commodities, packaged up like herring and shipped to Berlin in overstuffed trains to serve as wallpaper. Göring was only interested in their value as showpieces, their ability to impress, and their investment value. The walls of Carinhall were thus adorned with Reichsmarks, in their millions.

* * *

Amassing European art's greatest hits since the fourteenth century under one roof is only worthwhile with an audience, people to view

SECRETS OF A SUITCASE

the artworks and appreciate their value. International diplomats from nearby Berlin made excellent fodder in this regard. Göring regularly invited them to Carinhall, making them complicit in the crimes that allowed his collection to be assembled.

Most of the diplomats were amused and shrugged their shoulders at Göring's obvious staging, although they will have appreciated the art nonetheless. Some, however, perceived the dangerous aspects of Göring's playground early on. In 1934, for example, after his first hunt at Carinhall, the British Ambassador Eric Phipps wrote an official communiqué to his government that became known as the 'bison dispatch', which concluded as follows:

> The whole proceedings were so strange as at times to convey a feeling of unreality; but they opened, as it were, a window on the Nazi mentality, and as such were not, perhaps, quite useless. The chief impression was that of the almost pathetic naivety of General Goering who showed us his toys like a big, fat, spoilt child: his primeval woods, his bison and birds, his shooting-box and lake and bathing beach, his blonde 'private secretary', his wife's mausoleum and swans and sarsen stones, all mere toys to satisfy his varying moods, and all, or so nearly all, as he was careful to explain, Germanic. And then I remembered there were other toys, less innocent, though winged, and these might some day be launched on their murderous mission in the same childlike spirit with the same childlike glee.[9]

Although the message was encrypted, it was intercepted and deciphered almost immediately by Göring's own secret service at the Luftwaffe, the Forschungsamt (known in English as the Research Bureau). Phipps was not invited to Carinhall again. Later, in the spring of 1937, and much to Göring's delight, he was replaced by Neville Henderson, who found hunting with Göring much more enjoyable than his predecessor.

Carinhall represents Göring's attempt to compensate for an upbringing in which he always lived on the threshold of the big, wide world, without ever being wealthy or possessing a noble title himself.[10] He was convinced of his entitlement to prosperity, as restitu-

172

THE COLLECTOR

tion for the 'humiliations' he believed he had suffered in his youth. The injured vanity of a narcissist never heals. Acquiring valuable artworks as cheaply as possible was the ingenious mechanism he developed for stroking his ego.[11]

He started in Vienna, where he initiated the 'transfer' of Jewish-owned property on 26 April 1938. Under the Nuremberg race laws, anybody who could be considered 'Jewish' and who owned more than 5,000 RM was required to surrender their possessions to Germany. For days thereafter, the Gestapo ransacked the homes of the major Viennese Jewish families and confiscated all of their other possessions, from paintings to dresses. The most beautiful items disappeared into the personal collections of Hitler and Göring, while the rest were auctioned off at ridiculously low prices to Austrian supporters of the *Anschluss*, who flaunted their new acquisitions. The Rothschilds' belongings were purloined on the pretext that the bankruptcy of the family bank, the Credit-Anstalt, had supposedly been responsible for the economic crisis in Germany and Austria. The palace of another banker, Ephrussi, was cleared out on the basis that he was a suspected Schuschnigg supporter. The lack of protest meant that anybody with any wealth—unless they harboured overt national-socialist sympathies—could become the target of a raid. The harassment of Margit, who had offered Schuschnigg such a grand welcome at Finstergrün, fits this model.

In 1939, once war had broken out after the invasion of Poland, Göring had a free rein with his collecting habit, and was happy to travel for it. First he would 'pop in' on an art dealer or individual as though by chance, take a good look around, and note the items he wanted. On a follow-up visit, the alarmed proprietor or resident would have to hide their most valuable pieces. Göring would ask where the items were and, in the absence of a satisfactory answer, would send someone along to complete the purchase for him, at far below asking price, of course. Occasionally he would propose a trade for a less-valuable artwork from his collection. If that did not work, the vendor would receive open threats, including the suggestion that his wife, children or Jewish friends might meet with some unpleasantness.[12]

It was in this manner, in the Netherlands and Paris especially, that Göring appropriated a great number of paintings, including the entire collection of the Dutch Jewish art dealer Jacques Goudstikker, which was internationally renowned and included many Old Masters. Göring quickly switched to deploying intermediaries, such as the formerly Hague-based Berlin art dealer Walter Andreas Hofer and, in Amsterdam itself, the banker Alois Miedl. In Paris, he even had an entire bureau at his disposal, the Reichsleiter Rosenberg Taskforce, whose art hunters, such as Kurt von Behr and Bruno Lohse, were not averse to deploying criminals like the Bony-Laffont gang to track down hidden Jewish art. In Berlin, Hofer was given an office and an impressive title: Director of the Reich Marshall's Art Collections. Hofer's wife Berta aided him by restoring the paintings, so they both earned a little extra from the enterprise.[13]

By adorning his homes with artworks, Göring hoped to imbue himself with a kind of 'eternal life', just as his beloved knights lived on through the legends that survived them. In this respect—and including in this book, alas—he still gets to this day what he so craved during his lifetime: attention.

* * *

Before bidding farewell to our dangerous, fantasist murderer-thief, and returning to the fate of Finstergrün, its mistress, her possessions and her family, it's worth looking at the way Göring thanked the widow Epenstein for all that her deceased husband, his godfather, had meant to him. This was a special parting gift, and one that I happened to stumble across during my search for information on Mauterndorf.

February 2019. It was cold, and the wind pierced through my jacket as I stepped out of the S-Bahn at Berlin-Köpenick, a part of town rarely visited by tourists, and which formerly lay in East Berlin. It's impossible to escape history in this city: many of the streets still contain uneven and poorly aligned cobblestones, bricks, tracks and sections of asphalt in places where East and West Germany were reunited after 1989. The past is often still visible through the plasterwork used to cover up the bullethole-ridden walls. And the road from the S-Bahn to Friedrichshagenerstrasse was no exception on that chilly winter's day.

THE COLLECTOR

The area first appeared to be a Biedermeier town, made up of nineteenth-century bourgeois homes painted in hues of blue, yellow and pink, and festooned with kitsch embellishments. But that changed as soon as I crossed the river beside the Spree, entering a dilapidated industrial park that was mostly abandoned. The unused smokestacks of the half-collapsed redbrick buildings still reached up into the sky, as they had done for decades. Graffiti on the walls and the makeshift road signs were an indication of the many squatters in the neighbourhood. But some work had already been done on the other side of the street, which featured a large shopping complex of the type common to outer suburbs, the convenient car park making it easy to unload a full cart of goods.

I made my way towards a DIY store. As various men of nondescript age hurried past me in grey-green fleece pullovers, on their quest for discounted cordless drills, my gaze was fixed on the ground. It took some time for me to find it, but suddenly there it was: a *Stolperstein*. Literally a 'stumbling stone', these brass-coloured street stones are ominous markers that can easily trip one up in many European cities. Each displays the name of a Jewish man or woman who never returned from the Nazi extermination camps, placed at the site of the victim's last known address. They are also emblematic of Western civilisation restored, once the barbarism had ended. This particular stone is an exception, however, as it is dedicated to a man who did manage to escape, although he had to leave behind everything he owned. The stone reads: 'Here worked Julius Fromm. Factory aryanised 21–7–1938.' This was where Fromm's factory had stood until 1945, when it was destroyed by the Russians. He had been forced to sell in 1938 due to his Jewish heritage.

Fromm's factory was not just any factory. The goods he produced had been known for years throughout Germany as 'Fromms' (or 'Frommser' in Berlin dialect). He was the country's most prolific condom manufacturer, so much so that his name had become synonymous with the product itself. He had worked hard to get where he was, having grown up impoverished in the area around Berlin-Alexanderplatz, a slum full of prostitution and crime at the turn of the century. He had educated himself, taking chemistry classes in the evenings after his shifts in a cigar factory, and had founded a small workshop in 1912 where he started producing rub-

175

ber goods, mainly condoms. At that time, condoms were only sold under the counter at hairdressers and pharmacies, and the quality was poor. Only the rich could afford the high-quality rubber versions that actually prevented sexually transmitted infections and unwanted offspring. These were first produced in the early twentieth century thanks to Charles Goodyear's work on the vulcanisation of rubber. Fromm's factory met a great need, especially during the difficult interwar period, when the Church's prohibition on contraceptives was ignored, and women who had long suffered near-continual pregnancy became aware of an alternative—provided their husbands were willing to cooperate.

By 1920, Fromm was already producing 100,000 condoms per day, and he had factories in Breslau, Cologne and Hannover. Five years later, he had three international locations. Fromm had become a rich man, and a respected figure in Berlin. He witnessed the rise of Hitler with astonishment, and could not understand why Jewish people were being labelled the greatest threat to humanity. But when the Nazis came to power in 1933, Fromm sent his three sons abroad as a precaution. After the ban on contraceptive advertising in 1934, he produced advertisements for 'Fromm's rubber sponges' and once again sold his wares via hairdressers and pharmacies, relying on his widespread name recognition. The ruse worked for a time. But the Nazis wanted to turn women back into birthing machines, and so contraceptives were banned outright, as is often the case under reactionary regimes. On 21 July 1938, Fromm found himself before a civil notary, finalising the forced sale of the business he had worked so hard to build, with its 800 employees. Only then did he learn the identity of the lucky new owner: a noblewoman from Mauterndorf, Austria.

Hermann Göring must have selected his gift with care, as there were thousands of other confiscated Jewish businesses for him to choose from. Of all of the assets at his disposal, it was the successful Fromm's Act Rubber Works that became the property of Lilli Epenstein Ritter von Mauternburg, widow of his mother's lover, and mistress of Mauterndorf Castle in Lungau.

Fromm received 300,000 RM for his business. He still had to pay the 'departure tax' charged to all Jews wishing to leave the country. Fromm and his wife escaped Germany flat broke, but with their

THE COLLECTOR

lives. They went to live with their son in London. There, as Fromm opened the curtains on the morning of 15 August 1945, he suffered a heart attack upon hearing on the radio that the Second World War was over. His sons eventually continued the family business—but only after having suffered another expropriation, by the Russians.[14]

DISPLACED PERSONS

'Hunger' is written in large letters in the household ledger of Jolanta Szapáry, who inherited her mother's exactitude. She was cold in the harsh winter of 1944–5, as the war was nearing its end. Since 1943, the Lungau population had seen regular B-17 and B-24 US bombers flying over their plateau, en route from Italy to Bavaria. They had sought refuge as bombs fell on their sparsely populated region, leftovers loosed by the Americans dropping weight on the return flight. In 1944, many locals still took some pleasure in the aerial battles between the Americans and 'their' Hermann's Luftwaffe, and still chose to side—against their better judgement—with the Nazis, whom they had all embraced in 1938. But some did secretly take in injured American pilots who had been shot down.[1]

Jolanta lived in the Premhaus farm building, having continued work as a paediatric nurse for several years with her own surgery in nearby Tamsweg.[2] We can safely assume that she was quite busy with the local mothers, many of whom had broods so large as to qualify for the national-socialist Mother's Cross award.[3] For the remainder of the war, Finstergrün was barely used by the Nazi Party's teacher training, due to the complaints about inadequate facilities. It was clear that Göring's appropriation of the castle had been primarily an attack on Margit, launched via his favourite warmongering tactic: bureaucracy. In late 1944, a Hitler Youth motorcycle unit was accommodated in the castle. They, too, saw how the American bombers engaged in combat with Göring's Luftwaffe above Lungau. Down on the ground, the boys made their own contribution to the war effort by imprisoning the grounded US pilot John McGill at Finstergrün and subjecting him to serious abuse.[4]

Jolanta's brother Béla was living in Budapest. Hungary was still under German occupation in early 1944, with dire consequences for the Jewish community, who had thought themselves safe there during the early years of the war, but were persecuted from that time on. They were forced to live in ghettos, and became the victims of arbitrary massacres committed by both Germans and their abettors, the Hungarian Arrow Cross Party, a paramilitary group acting as a terrorist unit.[5] The Nazi regime had forced the Hungarian nobility to withdraw to their country residences. When the Soviets arrived, the nobles were chased off their land and stigmatised.[6] By then, some 565,000 Hungarian Jews had been murdered.

Béla had barely seen Finstergrün since the age of six.[7] During his time as a gentleman farmer in the vast fields of Canada, he and his friend Pallavicini had grown wheat and corn—with varying degrees of success—using new agricultural machinery that was partly manufactured in Hungary. In 1930 they had returned to Budapest, where Pallavicini's mother believed it was high time for her son to marry. Béla, who had no family fortune, earned his living as an insurance agent. He did have social capital, however, and the business thrived thanks to his extensive network of Hungarian aristocratic families wishing to insure their buildings, harvests and factories. He lived a pleasant life as a bachelor, supported by his many friends and the more affluent branches of the extended Szapáry family. His mother's address book lists him at 'Nemzeti Casino', one of Budapest's most prestigious gentlemen's clubs. It was comfortably furnished, offered accommodation for extended stays, and boasted a famous library; many names of the grand Hungarian nobility were on the members' list. In one of the few photos of Béla from that time, we see him well-dressed and smiling happily, sitting on a garden bench with two of his cousins, shaded by the trees. He seems not to have become the fervent nationalist his father had had in mind on his deathbed in 1904, when he asked his wife to send their son away for a Hungarian upbringing.

During the 1920s and '30s, under the leadership of Miklós Horthy, an authoritarian corporatist state emerged in Hungary comparable to the Austrian regime before the *Anschluss*, or that of Spain under Primo de Rivera. Jews were oppressed and forced to assimilate into Hungarian culture—whatever that meant, given the multitude of nationalities in Hungarian society. The wealthier among the Jewish population fled to Western European countries. But because Béla's insurance business meant that he associated primarily with major Catholic landowners, he was barely confronted with this reality.

DISPLACED PERSONS

He did not marry until 1942, at roughly the same age as his father. His bride was the widow of the Dutch ambassador in Budapest, Godert de Vos van Steenwijk. Margit's health and the political situation prohibited her from attending the wedding, and she died the following year, too late to witness the birth of her first grandchild, Yvonne, on 4 April 1944.

Baroness Ursula de Vos van Steenwijk, née von Richthofen, had a history of her own. She was the second of three daughters born to the Nazi 'honeybee' Wally von Richthofen. Before the war, Wally's villa, which served as a meeting place for Berlin's diplomats, had been bugged by the Gestapo.[8] Her daughter Ursula had married Baron Godert de Vos van Steenwijk there in 1933. Godert and Ursula had had two children when the ambassador, serving in Budapest from 1940, died suddenly of acute appendicitis. Ursula kept her husband's heritage alive for her children, giving them a 'proper Dutch' upbringing: they were tutored at home by a Dutch governess, and when they were allowed outside, their mother made them wear pins on their coats displaying the Dutch flag.[9] After two years of widowhood, she married Béla.

When the Russians were nearing Budapest in late 1944, Béla and his new family fled to Austria. And where better to seek refuge than in the castle his father had bought forty-five years earlier to give his branch of the Szapárys a fresh start? Finstergrün, however, turned out still to be under Nazi occupation, and uninhabitable besides. Dishevelled, tired and confused, Béla and his family gathered with Jolanta and several other relatives and friends in the Premhaus building, where their mother had always spent the winter. Everybody in the area was hungry, and many did not know the whereabouts of their loved ones.

The number of war refugees, or displaced persons, was enormous. The policy was to allow everybody to return to their place of birth; but in families with so many different birthplaces—like the Szapárys—that was easier said than done.

The chaos reached its apex when the Americans advanced into Austria. Nobody knew who could be trusted and, as in all war zones, everything in Lungau was a shambles. Scores were settled, great and petty, and things got even more complicated when Göring himself suddenly turned up at Mauterndorf, on the run, like an animal seeking cover back in the burrow where it came from. He was under the misapprehension that he might still become the successor to Adolf Hitler, and conduct peace negotiations with the Americans.

He did enjoy a brief moment as Sir Hermann of Mauterndorf, when some returning German soldiers recognised him from the road and asked him to pose with them for photographs. But that was that, and shortly afterward he was arrested by the Americans. His wife Emmy and daughter Edda, whom he had left behind in a hotel in Innsbruck, were also approached by the Americans—to recover the last paintings the Görings had tried to take with them. They included a fake Vermeer. Emmy, too, was arrested.

* * *

When the war ended, Jolanta was immediately put to work as a translator for the occupying Americans. She also gave lectures in Salzburg on the subject of 'Women in Social Work',[10] and returned to her profession as a paediatric nurse, making research trips to England and the United States. Scotland was also once again on her itinerary, after a decades-long hiatus, where she visited several of Finstergrün's former paying guests, with whom she had kept in touch all those years. In 1953, she took early retirement for health reasons, and that is when she began creating her albums.

The photographs were small, blurry and often damaged. Later on, she would add descriptions in large blue, green and red lettering and, where possible, outline her mother's most notable activities. Together with the 'Szapáry papers' in the Salzburg archives— Margit's drawings, ledgers and carefully preserved renovation records—these albums conjure up a distant memory of the fairytale castle of Finstergrün as it was for several decades, proof of a woman's ability to single-handedly forge a new world for herself. Jolanta would continue to live in Ramingstein until her death in 1987.

Béla—who also spoke good English, thanks to his years in Canada—became a translator for the Americans in Lungau, too. They

DISPLACED PERSONS

assigned him an additional role as estate manager of Mauterndorf. The castle suited him, and he allowed his stepson, Godert de Vos van Steenwijk Junior, to spend a night in 'Göring's bed'. Even at eleven, the boy knew full well who that was. The Szapárys witnessed the American confiscation of Mauterndorf's contents as 'enemy property'; the collection was transported to Munich, where the Americans had set up an organisation called the Central Collecting Point.[11] This was where all of the Nazis' stolen art was catalogued and, where possible, immediately returned to original owners who could prove that it had been either stolen outright or obtained by unfair means.

Several clergymen from Salzburg wrote that Göring had taken possession of Mauterndorf illegally, appropriating five valuable antique chasubles in the process. In fact, Göring had simply inherited the castle from Lilli Epenstein, who had died unexpectedly in late 1939 shortly after being gifted Fromm's condom factory. The Americans believed the clergymen, and even returned the chasubles.[12] It had been some time since churchmen had enjoyed a sense of superiority in Lungau, and their assessment of good and evil was accepted without question.

In the autumn of 2019, in the Dutch province of Drenthe, I paid a visit to Baron Godert de Vos van Steenwijk and his wife Clara (née van Pallandt). Today Béla's stepson manages part of Margit's personal archives. Godert followed in his father's footsteps with a diplomatic career, but since his retirement from his final posting as ambassador to Moscow, the couple have bred special Russian horses on their family estate. They were surprised to hear about the Gucci suitcase and the boxes that had come into my possession at the Sotheby's auction, and asked me whether I knew how they had made their way to Amsterdam. Clara suggested that perhaps Yvonne Szapáry, Godert's half-sister, might have some information.

Otherwise, we discussed the history of Central Europe and the situation in the Balkans. As a former ambassador to both Russia and Hungary, Godert was only too familiar with the situation there, and still wrote a column on the subject for several provincial papers. As for his opinion of Margit Szapáry: 'Oh, power women are nothing new. History has seen so many of them. My own mother was also a power woman.'

* * *

In the immediate postwar period, Austria found itself caught in a tug-of-war between east and west. A demarcation zone ran right through the centre of Vienna, which itself became the subject of Carol Reed's beautiful film *The Third Man*, starring Orson Welles. The Austrians had lost everything; not only their grand empire, but now also their honour. They would later attempt to rewrite history by repeatedly suggesting that Austria, too, had been a victim of unwanted occupation, and had suffered under the Nazi regime. It's true that there had been wholesale robbery of all people in occupied Europe who were not Nazi Party members or sympathisers.[13] Many nobles had lost their property: the once-prosperous Schwarzenberg family—who had owned so much land in the Habsburg era and who had commissioned the train line connecting Ramingstein to Vienna—had lost everything, and would have to wait until the 1980s for compensation. But Austria's small group of royalist, Catholic aristocrats had generally remained safe within their palace walls. The country's real 'suffering' seems to have been 'limited' to Jews, socialists and all the others who were dispossessed, imprisoned and/or sent to concentration camps.

Austria would struggle with poverty and hunger for many years, prompting an interesting exchange between the restored republic and the Netherlands immediately after the war. The Dutch were lacking the construction materials necessary to rebuild their bombarded cities, not least housing for the postwar baby boom. Austria, on the other hand, was in dire need of food, but had plenty of building materials due to its extensive forests. Trains began shuttling between the two countries: dried vegetables, preserved fish and seeds were loaded on at one end, while at the other, construction materials for entire homes were strapped onto freight carriages, two being required for each flat-packed house. In total, 800 Thermohaus construction kits were shipped to the Netherlands, 100 of which were assembled in the new town of Emmeloord. Concrete foundations made the homes quick to assemble, and provided space for all of those starting a new life. And because nothing is more permanent than a temporary home, they remain standing to this day. They are even lovingly cared for, and have been celebrated for their energy efficiency.

There was little left for Béla, Ursula and their three children in Austria. Their plan was to leave for the Netherlands, where Ursula's former in-laws lived. Little Godert was to attend a good Dutch school, and Béla needed a way to earn a living. But he was kept out of the country for several years, as he had become a naturalised Austrian in 1945 and was thus deemed a former enemy. At the time, Austria was severely reproached for the 1938 annexation: it was impacted by Western sanctions and a lack of foreign currency, and would be occupied by the four Allied powers until 1955. Not even Ursula escaped the stigma, her marriage putting her Dutch finances at risk of appropriation as 'enemy capital'.[14] Thankfully, with assistance from her Dutch family and the Pels Rijcken law firm, she was able to prove that she was, and had remained, Dutch through her first marriage, and had a Dutch diplomatic passport. She moved to The Hague, close to her son, who was living with his legal guardian and attending school in Drenthe. But she also often visited Austria, where she had left behind Béla and her younger children, Marieliese (the ambassador's daughter, born in Beijing) and Yvonne (born to Béla and Ursula in Budapest, but naturalised as Austrian with her father in 1945).

Béla tried to make the best of things. In 1949, as owners of the castle, he and Jolanta gave consent for a monument to the fallen 'heroes of the last war' to be built at the foot of Finstergrün's hill—honouring the 100 or so soldiers from Tamsweg who had gone to fight for Hitler. Jolanta had already made some land available for the Wehrmacht's use in late 1943.[15]

In 1950, Béla and Jolanta were finally granted entry to the Netherlands, where they moved into a simple apartment in The Hague. The family would still holiday regularly in Lungau but, as a father, Béla never talked about his past. He established several businesses in The Hague, including a timber merchant that traded with Austria and proved lucrative in the early postwar years. That would change once Norway recovered from occupation, as Norwegian wood was much cheaper. In the late 1950s, however, he received sizeable compensation for the Henckel von Donnersmarcks' Silesian assets that had been confiscated by the Germans.[16] The old homeland of Hugo I thus came fleetingly back into Béla's life, easing his troubles somewhat, as it had done for his parents before him. Otherwise, he divulged nothing about his family history, concentrating on his new Dutch life and his beautiful young daughter Yvonne, referred to affectionately in the family as Pinky. He gave her a good upbringing. And when she was twenty, she introduced her parents to a special boyfriend of hers.

A ROYAL WEDDING

In the spring of 1966, the 'Stan Huygens Report'—the society and gossip column of the largest newspaper in the Netherlands, *De Telegraaf*—made the front page: a local girl from The Hague was to wed a German prince. This event would give the city the 'royal wedding' it had missed out on when the future queen Crown Princess Beatrix had decided to marry Claus von Amsberg in Amsterdam on 10 March that year. The headlines read: 'Hitched—The Hague Way', 'Wedding and Birthday Coincide', 'Princely Wedding in The Hague', 'A Glorious, Endless Day', and 'Little Miss Pinky and Her Prince'.

Stan Huygens had already introduced his readers to 'Miss Pinky' once before, playfully referring to her by her old teenage nickname as though she were a character from *The Baby-Sitters Club*. Two years earlier, in 1964, he had reported her attendance at a 'fairytale ball with our Princesses Beatrix and Margriet' at Denmark's Fredensborg Castle, for the Danish Crown Princess Margrethe's twenty-fourth birthday. She had found it quite exhausting, Pinky told the journalist, and for that reason would be leaving immediately with her parents to visit her 'father's estate' near Salzburg. She had also met somebody at the ball with whom she would make a more intimate acquaintance over the ensuing years during their 'winter holidays'. This was the man she would marry on 18 April 1966, at the age of twenty-two.

On a dreary Monday, before representatives from half of Europe's royal houses, Countess Yvonne Margit Valéria Szapáry de Muraszombath, Széchysziget et Szapar was wed to Prince Karl Adolf Andreas von Hessen-Kassel. The wedding, held at The Hague's Great Church (also known as St James's), was not only covered by *De Telegraaf*, but inspired fifty-three articles in other Dutch newspapers, and even one in Curaçao. Most of the press talked about the future princess herself, who, after a year of finishing school in

SECRETS OF A SUITCASE

Lausanne, had been working since the age of eighteen as a designer at the renowned jewellery house Schaap. Huygens characterised her as 'an athletic girl, who has barely spared a thought for the fact that she will soon be a princess'. The reports covered her time at boarding school in Britain and her year in Lausanne, where she had met and befriended the Danish Princess Benedikte. They also mentioned her mother Ursula, widow of the former Dutch ambassador Godert de Vos van Steenwijk—making the half-German, half–Austro-Hungarian Yvonne something of a Dutch princess herself.

As for the father of the bride, the papers described Béla as a 'retired businessman'. The family was living in a sizeable villa on the corner of Van Alkemadelaan and Waalsdorperweg. For the wedding, Béla had a couple of large marquees put up in the garden, so that there could be food and dancing in the evening. The garage beside the house, which provided garden access, served as the 'entrance hall'. A candle-lined red carpet led guests in from the footpath, adding some ambiance. The police were occupied with security for the house for weeks.

And so Yvonne Szapáry, like Princess Beatrix the previous month, married her German prince. But Yvonne's had a far more impressive pedigree than Claus von Amsberg. Karl Adolf Andreas von Hessen-Kassel came from the royal house of Hesse, who for centuries had ruled over an important part of Germany including cities like Frankfurt, Wiesbaden and Kassel. His grandfather had been Kaiser Friedrich III, and he himself was the eldest son of Prince Christopher of Hesse and Princess Sophia of Greece and Denmark. Sophia, the daughter of Princess Alice, was sister to the United Kingdom's Prince Philip. In other words, 'Pinky's Prince' was nephew to the Duke of Edinburgh, husband of Queen Elizabeth II.[1]

Much of Europe's past was assembled in the Great Church that day, people whose personal histories had been deeply scarred by the two world wars. A large proportion of the wedding guests had witnessed the loss of their estates and power; for some, their noble name was all they had left. But on 18 April 1966, it was time to celebrate and look to the future, as Yvonne and Karl got married. The weekend prior to the ceremony, the guests had already gathered for a lavish reception at Friedrichshof Castle in Kronberg, near Frankfurt, where part of the Hesse family had been living since the

188

A ROYAL WEDDING

end of the nineteenth century. Friedrichshof had become a hotel, and Prince Karl was set to join its management. But not yet. First, he had a two-day wedding reception to get through, on 16 and 17 April. King Constantine of Greece was there with his wife, Princess Anne-Marie of Denmark, as well as his sister Sophia and her husband, Prince Juan Carlos of Spain. Of course, as a close friend of the bride, Princess Benedikte of Denmark was also in attendance.

Afterwards, the entire Hesse family and all of the guests flew together on one plane to Amsterdam, for the church wedding in The Hague the next day. With so many high-profile guests, that Sunday must have been a unique day at Schiphol airport, the more so because no special protocols had been put in place. King Constantine took charge upon landing, deciding who would travel in which car. Prince Philip, uncle to the groom and the most distinguished guest, was scheduled to arrive later at Ypenburg by private plane, with his mother Princess Alice. To explain the vast array of dignitaries present, the *Volkskrant* newspaper proudly reported that the groom was 'related to the royal houses of England and Greece'.

The next day, all of The Hague turned out for this momentous occasion. There was an enormous crowd at the church, cheering the honoured guests and especially the petite, graceful bride, who wore a dress that 'showcased refinement down to the finest detail', in the words of *De Leidse Courant*. The happy couple exchanged their vows in a church adorned with flowers, accompanied by three choirs. The service—held in German—was led by the Reverend Grabowski, an old Hesse family friend. One of Yvonne's witnesses was the then-prominent right-wing politician Harm van Riel, another 'friend of the family' who had known the de Vos van Steenwijks since his childhood in Drenthe. In the 1960s, he was almost a neighbour of the Száparys on Van Alkemadelaan. The *Leidse Courant* pointed out that the service was 'almost identical to the marriage service of Princess Beatrix and Prince Claus'. The only downside was that it finished fifteen minutes early, necessitating a mad search for the cars that had been parked elsewhere to take the wedding party on to the reception at the Haagsche Club—a crisis resolved in a typically informal Dutch fashion.

A buffet followed that evening in the Szapárys' decorated garden, where the company posed happily for a photograph in the marquee

SECRETS OF A SUITCASE

erected in front of the living room. One can just discern the festive lanterns in the press images. The happy couple's parents stood proudly near their children, though they did make room for King Constantine and his wife, who had the bride on one side and Prince Philip on the other. They were the guests of honour, after all, in a group where each distinguished guest was keenly aware of everyone else's heritage and status.

It was 'a glorious, endless day' for the bride, as Pinky later told Stan Huygens from *De Telegraaf*. There was just a single fly in the ointment, one that both of the major papers had called attention to: where was the Dutch royal family? Not a single royal representative was to be found on the extensive guest list, to which *De Telegraaf* had been given exclusive access. Huygens theorised that it came down to envy: Prince Philip hadn't attended Beatrix's wedding the month before, yet had seen fit to fly in for his cousin's marriage to this young Hungarian countess. Everybody seemed to understand, and none of the journalists pressed the matter. Why would the local royalty have come to the wedding of a couple completely unknown in the Netherlands?

The Second World War archives might easily explain why the Dutch royals were content to stay away that day, miles from the nuptials—particularly after Princess Beatrix's wedding in March, when the anarchistic protest group Provo had launched a smoke bomb into the ceremony, as a clear signal that not everyone in the Netherlands approved the match. Claus von Amsberg had been a member of the Hitler Youth, and had served in the German Wehrmacht for some time. He had been assigned to a tank division in Italy at the end of the war, where he claimed 'not to have fired a single shot'. A segment of the Dutch population responded rather crudely to this information with 'Raus, Claus!' Although the matter would ultimately be resolved, once Claus managed to endear himself to the wider public, that was certainly not the case in 1966.

* * *

It has been nearly sixty years since these marriages took place. Today, especially in view of the research conducted by Stephan Malinowski, Fabrice d'Almeida, Jonathan Petropoulos and Karina

190

A ROYAL WEDDING

Urbach, it is far clearer than it was in the postwar period how the German nobility was used, knowingly allowed itself to be used, or even actively participated, in Nazi practices during the Hitler era. The Hesse princes were in the latter category, having joined the NSDAP early on and become officers in the Wehrmacht. Yvonne's late father-in-law, Prince Christoph von Hessen-Kassel, who had died in 1943, was, along with his brother Philipp, among the highest-ranking Nazi aristocrats. He had worked for Göring's Luftwaffe, and been involved in the preparations for the bombing of Rotterdam. He died after an aircraft accident in northern Italy, under circumstances that were never fully explained. He was survived by his young wife Sophia, who had married him at age sixteen, and their five children (Sophia was pregnant with the youngest at the time of the crash). Shortly after the war, Sophia had celebrated her second marriage, to Georg, Prince of Hanover, grandson of the last German Kaiser, Wilhelm II. For a long time, Sophia and Georg's children knew nothing of what had transpired within their family. When they found out, they felt ashamed and struggled to come to terms with it.[2]

Yvonne is supposed to have described her new family as 'a big, friendly bunch'. If those were truly her words, then it was a rather carefree summation of the family's chequered history. On the other hand, who among the German nobility of the 1950s and '60s didn't have a chequered family history? There were plenty of fathers, uncles and cousins who had perished at the whims of Hitler and his Nazis, and those who had survived needed constantly to justify their former support for the Third Reich. Half of the aristocracy had joined the Nazi Party.[3]

Their children were, of course, blameless—the choice had not been theirs to make, and it was mainly their parents who had a fraught past to contend with. After the war, these families picked up where they had left off, many having lost much of their property either due to their own war activities, or at the hands of the liberating Russian and American forces. Some wrote their memoirs, cherished their family history and resorted to ancient noble traditions and rituals, or occasionally newly invented ones, seeking to salvage something of their lost status and convert it into cultural capital—a cachet of the new, symbolic kind, for which there proved to be rising demand in an increasingly individualistic Europe.[4] Others from the old families preferred a quiet life.

The nobles adapted to their new circumstances. If their castles were still standing, they converted them and ran them as hotels. A disproportionate number were given jobs at banks or large companies, where their names and international backgrounds lent prestige to the business. They placed their hope in their children, who might, with a good education and the right match, restore some of their former glory. Occasions such as Karl and Yvonne's wedding were a rare opportunity to once again be *entre nous*, even if it meant turning up to a wedding reception that, by their standards—and possibly our own, in the age of slick media saturation—was a bit of a shambles, winding up in a circus tent on somebody's back lawn in The Hague. For the Dutch royal family, it would have been one hornet's nest too many, after the smoke bomb in Amsterdam.

Karl von Hessen-Kassel (whose middle name was 'Adolf') was among those who preferred to let his family's history lie undisturbed. The British press had already looked into him as their own Prince Philip's 'Nazi nephew', even though Karl had been a toddler when his father died. He avoided the media, preferring not to air the family's past in public. At the time of their wedding, Yvonne too preferred to speak of the future—the splendid future that awaited them at Friedrichshof Castle, where Karl was to become a manager.

What she neglected to mention was the exciting history of Friedrichshof itself, which would come in useful for the hotel's marketing: the place owed its fame principally to the great jewel theft that took place there just after the war had ended, when it was serving as the headquarters and officers' mess for the US army. One night in 1946, after being tipped off by some local workers, several of the top officers went down to the basement in search of the Hesse family jewels rumoured to have been hidden there, bricked up into the walls. They found them, proceeding to remove the diamonds and other gemstones from their eighteenth-century settings—quite brusquely, according the later evaluations—and then sold them for millions. What the Russians called 'looting' was known as 'collecting souvenirs' among the Americans; perhaps an excessive level of souvenir collection, given that 252 treasures were taken as spoils of war, some of which were considered to be among the German Crown Jewels.[5] Only some of the precious gems were restored to the von Hessen-Kassels, the rest being sold to anonymous buyers. In 2009, a (rather bad) Belgian film called *The Hessen Conspiracy* was made about this colourful episode in Friedrichshof's history, dominated by a love story between two of the American officers.

Juicy stories do help to lure visitors to castles such as these. But none of these details appeared in the newspaper articles from the 1960s on Karl's marriage—only the sentiment that a beautiful future awaited Yvonne Szapáry as 'Princess of Hessen'. She was described using the simple yet evocative language increasingly common in the postwar popular press, which allowed readers to share in the joy of those whose lives were, in reality, quite far removed from their own. The cult of celebrity was in full bloom, and sought its objects of adoration in broader and broader circles. Film stars, pop stars and media stars were revered with almost as much devotion as the 'true' nobility.[6] But, of course, if a genuinely blue-blooded person presented themselves, then they would still automatically get top billing in these postwar years. And so Countess Yvonne Szapáry briefly rose to stardom in the early 1960s, becoming the untouchable fairytale princess who had gone off to live in a castle.

Thankfully, the media reassured readers, she was also an ordinary person, one who needed to learn to cook for her future husband, as she told *De Telegraaf*—a skill that she had obviously not learned in Lausanne. Her 'new furniture' also had to be put in storage in Munich, as there were some problems with the move to Friedrichshof. Such articles always made effective use of the everyday juxtaposed with the sublime, allowing the readership to identify even more closely with their idols.

In reality, though, the great and good were only becoming even more inaccessible. Any mundane, intimate information would always be followed by details of precisely the kind of lifestyle the general reading public was not destined for. The reporting on 'Princess Pinky' had referred to the area south of Salzburg—where Yvonne had spent her holiday before getting married, and where she had become better acquainted with her future husband while hunting—as her 'father's estate'. At the mention of this phrase, audiences who had grown up in the 1950s with movies about Empress Sisi of Austria could let their imaginations run wild, as the press carefully noted.

Yvonne and Karl belonged to a new generation of aristocrats, who would adopt a different approach to the management of their estates, to the use of their names and titles, and to what it meant to lead a good life. At least, that is, until half a century later, when I unexpectedly stumbled across a history of the far more complicated lives lived by princes and princesses, counts and countesses—especially those in central Europe in the early twentieth century. On realizing this, the fantasy world of the modern nobility disappears as if by magic, replaced by stories that are not limited to the Second World War, but have deep roots extending back into the nineteenth century. Under the pressure of the more practical and occasionally barbaric interests of Central Europe, *noblesse oblige*—that ancient duty of the aristocracy to improve their own lives and those of others—had proved to be mere driftwood swirling in the maelstrom of history, and a cover that could be used to desperately save one's own skin.

Keeping up appearances after the Second World War became more of a burden than a privilege, as we can see in the youth of Yvonne Szapáry. The estate where she had so enjoyed holidaying was no palace for the likes of Sisi. In the early postwar years when Yvonne partly grew up at Finstergrün, it served as a military field hospital. Later it became a hostel for boy and girl scouts and for Christian youth, who used the former 'great hall' and the surrounding rooms as a kind of dormitory during their summer camps.[7] The antiquated wood furnaces meant that it was far too cold to spend even a single night there in wintertime. The castle was therefore closed for that part of the year, and the Szapárys spent their postwar holidays in a nearby hunting lodge. One still on their land, at least.

Before her wedding in 1966, Yvonne had taken Karl to Finstergrün for that centuries-old royal pastime, the hunt. *De Telegraaf* described the trip as follows: 'One hobby shared by the bride and bridegroom is a love of hunting. Prince Karl has spent much time hunting in Scotland, and Miss Pinky has cultivated a competent shooter's hand during many hunting parties on her father's estate, where deer and chamois frolic in the wild.' If they could have read these reports, the hearts of all Lungauers, and those of Ramingstein in particular, would have nearly burst with pride, though they would of course have been fully aware that Yvonne's holiday home was not exactly an ancestral estate. Nor was it even her 'father's estate', but rather her grandmother's. Finstergrün was always Margit's creation.

By contrast, Friedrichshof Castle, where Karl of Hesse had grown up, and where he and Yvonne threw a party on the eve of their marriage, was far more impressive, and had already served as the décor for a charming wedding in 1930. Then, too, a special photograph was taken. It shows Karl's father and mother, Prince Christoph and Princess Sophia, with the bridal party. The nine-year-old Philip of Greece and Denmark, later Duke of Edinburgh, sits at the feet of his sister Sophia like a page boy. Their mother Princess Alice sits beside her daughter, at a time in her life when she still wore beautiful gowns. Not until after the war would Alice permanently don the habit as a Greek Orthodox nun, shunning the gruesome world around her.

Behind them is Christoph's brother Philipp of Hesse, who had then only just joined the Nazi Party. Carin Göring herself had encouraged him during the intimate dinners of the German aristocracy in her Berlin apartment ('Wouldn't you also like to be a part of this grand movement?').[8] A year after Christoph's marriage to Sophia, he would also join the party, and in 1935 even became head of Hermann Göring's Research Bureau. Göring and the Hesse brothers already knew one another from Lichterfelde, the military academy in Berlin. Christoph's appointment to such an esteemed position is unsurprising, given Göring's penchant for surrounding himself with old friends of high birth. At his wedding to Emmy Sonnemann, for example, Christoph and Sophia were seated at the bridal table, opposite Hitler. They were often spotted in Göring's box at the Berlin opera, and the family were regular guests at Carinhall, where the children were allowed to play with Göring's pet lion cubs.

These warm relations came to an end in 1940, when Hitler ordered in the *Prinzenerlass* decree that members of the noble elite that had governed Germany until 1918 were no longer to be trusted on the front lines. In 1943, the increasingly paranoid Hitler forbade German princes from serving in the Wehrmacht at all, blaming the rising casualties in Russia partly on the international contacts of the extensive royal families—the Führer titled his edict the 'Decree of the Führer on the Exclusion of Internationally Affiliated Men from State, Party, and Armed Forces'. Christoph, who was already critical of the senseless loss of life and resources on the North African front, had only a brief window to express his displeasure, before his aeroplane disappeared above the Appenines in 1943, his body never to be found.

His brother Philipp fared little better: he was arrested in 1943. His wife Mafalda, Princess of Savoy, was sent to Buchenwald when her father, Italy's King Victor Emmanuel III, had fallen from Mussolini's good graces. Mafalda died in Buchenwald in 1944, during an Allied bombardment. As a former Nazi, after the war Philipp was tried and sentenced to prison, primarily for having looked the other way when Jews in Hesse—and the large Jewish community in Frankfurt especially—were persecuted and sent to concentration camps.

After his release, Philipp was reportedly a broken and bitter man,[9] who dedicated himself to the restoration of the family's estates. He would divest himself of several properties in order to retain the most important. Interior design had been his greatest passion even before the war, and Fasanerie Castle became his masterpiece, though he also turned Friedrichshof into something special. While most of the castle was still occupied by the Americans, he retreated to one of the towers. After a bombardment that destroyed the castle's chapel, which contained a family tomb to which he would bring Mafalda's body from Buchenwald for reburial, he decided to dedicate it as a monument to loss. He deliberately left the roof unrepaired and allowed ivy to cover the ruin, so that the chapel ultimately resembled a painting by Caspar David Friedrich.

By the 1960s, of course, Karl von Hessen-Kassel was to manage Friedrichshof as a hotel, with Yvonne set to play hostess to new affluent guests, just as her grandmother had done at Finstergrün when funds had run dry. Friedrichshof, by contrast, was ten times

A ROYAL WEDDING

the size, and boasted a history as the residence of an empress. A golf course had even been built, at the behest of the American general and future president Dwight Eisenhower, while he had his headquarters there. 'Pinky' had taken a big step into the world, and her parents had reason to be happy. But what would her grandmother Margit have thought? Yvonne had married into a house that had given generous support to the regime that destroyed her life at Finstergrün. Karl was the son of one of Göring's closest men. While Margit might have realised that children cannot be held responsible for the sins of their parents, she would surely have had reservations about her granddaughter marrying a Prussian, and a Lutheran besides, for whom Yvonne had converted.

Their daughter having concluded a fruitful marriage, Béla and Ursula left the Netherlands, settling in the region his own father Sándor had chosen for his descendants. They moved into Göriach, the lodge in the hunting region chosen by his father in the Göriachtal valley, a few kilometres from Tamsweg. Living at Finstergrün was still too problematic, especially in winter, and the castle would have been costly to maintain as a residence. After its early postwar years as a home to boy scouts in the summer, from 1949 it was leased to the youth division of the Evangelical Church, as a venue for children's activities. Jolanta continued to receive guests for a time in the castle's private quarters. Yvonne's half-brother, Godert de Vos van Steenwijk, would even live there for a while with his wife and four small children after returning from India in 1964, where he had worked as a Dutch foreign correspondent. 'It was an interesting experience,' Godert's wife Clara told me when I visited. 'It was freezing cold. And a twenty-metre walk to an old kitchen to warm up a bottle of milk.'[10]

In 1972, Jolanta and Béla decided to sell Finstergrün to the Christian youth division, which took some effort, as castle upkeep would be expensive for such an impoverished organisation. Fifty years later, after some major renovations, it has been transformed into an attractive holiday destination for children, a youth hostel, and a budget bed-and-breakfast where families can stay in special family rooms. It has also been made available for hire as an event space, though there was little demand. Lungau is still a very out-of-the-way place.

Béla and Jolanta still had one final task: honouring their mother's memory and the fate that befell her. Where was the four-poster bed that Göring had swindled out of her and never paid for? It had been valued at 3,000 RM, which was quite a meagre sum compared to the 5,000 RM fetched by the second bed at auction in 1941. But Margit's children were unaware of these sums, which only came to light when Weinmüller's records were discovered in 2017.

Like so many others, whose losses were often far greater than theirs, the Szapáry siblings submitted an application for compensation or restitution.[11] It was rejected, on the grounds that they could not adequately demonstrate that the bed had belonged to them, and that it had been forcibly taken from Margit. They were also not really 'war victims' per se, compared to the multitudes who had lost their families in concentration camps. The most valuable items sold off in 1941 only appear in a few small photographs carefully preserved by Jolanta, and these would certainly not qualify for restitution, as Margit had sent them to auction of her own volition, even if the tenacious Göring had left her little choice.

Jolanta died, unmarried and childless, in 1987; Béla in 1993; and his widow Ursula in 2002. All three are buried beneath the family tombstone in Ramingstein with Finstergrün towering above; most space on the stone is taken up by Ursula's many names—Szapáry née von Richthofen, the widow de Vos van Steenwijk. Margit, whose name is at the top, would seem to have drawn the short straw in that regard.

The Premhaus farm building was cleared out. The family found boxes of old lace kept in used containers from a Dresden salon, and a few albums full of picture postcards of mediaeval castles in France and England. Junk. They were stuffed into moving boxes, along with an old 1960s Gucci suitcase, some riding jackets, whips, fur collars and cocktail dresses fitting a slender woman, and sent to Sotheby's in Munich in 2004.

At that time, Sotheby's happened to be preparing a 'German Noble Sale' in Amsterdam. When the auction came around, I happened to be sitting in the hall, took an eye to the Gucci suitcase, and won the bidding. A few cardboard boxes were included with the lot. Back at home I noticed a small, half-torn label on the handle of the suitcase. The only legible words were 'The Prince' in English and 'Castle' in German, '*Schloss*'.

During my visit to the Lungau region, I was told that Princess Yvonne of Hesse was living in Munich, working as an interior design consultant. I found a business named 'Hessen Interior' based in Munich, and while on a work trip to the city in 2015, I decided to drop by, assuming that it was a business address. I called the number I'd found and, to my surprise, Yvonne herself answered the phone. I asked whether I might come by for a visit, mentioning that I had found some old postcards and photographs in a cardboard box from an auction in Amsterdam, and that I was curious as to how they had ended up in the Netherlands. At the time, I was still travelling around, trying to decide whether I might write about the life of Margit Szapáry, and I had only scant knowledge of the family's post-war life in the Netherlands. If only I'd thought to search 'Szapáry' on the *Delpher* online newspaper archive, I would have been better prepared for my visit.

I was cordially received by a slender woman who looked a young seventy, on the ground floor of a modest '50s low-rise block, in Munich's Schwabing district. The space teemed with rolls of fabric, but she made some room for me on the sofa. I showed her a few photos and postcards from the boxes that I had thrown into my luggage—because 'you just never knew'—and told her how they had come into my possession. We spoke German and English, since I still knew nothing of her Dutch background, and she said nothing to enlighten me. 'How did these albums end up in the Netherlands?' I asked. 'That must have been my sister-in-law's doing', Princess Yvonne replied firmly, referring to Clara de Vos van Steenwijk. And yes, she said, Finstergrün had belonged to her grandmother, who was once very well known in the Lungau region.

She told me that I should seek out a young academic from Graz, a Mr Blinzer, who had written his doctoral thesis on Margarethe and had once curated an exhibition about her in Tamsweg. I made the suggestion that it might be worthwhile writing a biography about her. The princess took another sip of tea, stared out into the distance for a moment, and said: 'Oh, so much has already been written about my grandmother.' I thanked her for her time, apologised once again for the visit at short notice, and was back outside within half an hour. On the doorstep, I noticed that three of the four letterboxes were labelled 'Hessen'. Princess Yvonne and her family had clearly not remained at Friedrichshof. The cocktail dresses must have looked beautiful on her.

On my way back to the Netherlands, the day after my visit to the Hessen Interior showroom, I opened up an abandoned copy of *Bild Zeitung* magazine on the train. It contained an article about a garden party that had been held the day before, in honour of Queen Elizabeth II and Prince Philip's state visit to Germany. There was a photograph of Philip greeting a woman, the caption identifying her as his niece, Countess Irina von Schönburg-Glauchau, a Hesse princess by birth. It was Yvonne's daughter, the great-granddaughter of Margit Szapáry, reconnecting with a distant relative. She had married Alexander von Schönburg, a *Bild* journalist who had incorporated the trials and tribulations of his own 500-year-old aristocratic family into a bestseller titled *The Art of Stylish Impoverishment*.[12]

Back at home, while Googling 'Hesse' and 'Lungau', I came across yet another enterprise that would have generated some income for the 'impoverished' royal house, and one that—like interior design—shared a history with Finstergrün. It was a holiday home, called Premgut Hessen Royal Rental. The online gallery showed one room with a salon table boasting a signed photograph of King Charles III, then Prince of Wales, and Queen Camilla, then Duchess of Cornwall. On closer inspection of the house and its surroundings, it seemed to be the Premhaus farmstead, where Margit always spent the harsh winters. It was also where she had wished to return at the end of her life, and where she ultimately died of her heart condition. The name change to 'Hessen' had severed any last ties with Lungau's anti-Nazi countess.

I filled in the contact form asking for more information, such as the nightly rate, but received no reply; only a notification that one first had to obtain access to the 'member zone'. The website disappeared not long afterwards when the property was sold, and it now belongs to a German family. But one can still hire the *Premhütte*: a small, sparsely furnished hunting cabin located higher up the mountain, which was used by Sándor during his hunting days. The owner recommends the cabin for its the surrounding calm and tranquillity, and the opportunity to 'unplug' from the twenty-first century. There is no phone reception.

AFTERWORD

Margarethe Szapáry made deliberate choices that shaped her life. She used her wealth independently for a purpose that was rare among women of means in the early twentieth century: to improve the circumstances of those around her. She chased after no grand, long-term ideals, but instead did what she believed needed to be done, right in her own backyard. She did what George Steiner believed is virtually the only thing one can do, in an examined life: be there for others.[1] She experienced setbacks, as everybody does. She became the victim of envy, a devastating and often underestimated emotion. She made mistakes and errors of judgement, and her family background did nothing to protect her against it all. She was a living example of Robert Musil's summation in *The Man without Qualities*: 'Aside from the extremely fortunate and very unlucky, all people lead equally poor lives, though they do take place at different levels.'[2]

Margit's problem was that she could not disassociate from the community she considered herself a part of, the Habsburg empire's high nobility, and frequently had to challenge her own worldview. She remained a Catholic, monarchist, Habsburgian aristocrat, aware of her dependence on a structure in which—to paraphrase Montesquieu—a king is nothing without the nobility, and the nobility cannot survive without a king. But from the moment she began living independently in her castle, as a widow, she did start pushing the limits of her role. She was the architect of her life from then on, and ultimately left the stage with a grand gesture: bidding farewell to the home she had created for herself, which had fit her like a glove.

Margit's life story is about the loss of money and power, and the transformation of Europe amid the constantly shifting borders of the twentieth century. What was once Central Europe became either

SECRETS OF A SUITCASE

East or West. And while concepts such as 'nationality' became fluid on the one hand, on the other they served as a final lifeline for those who'd lost everything else from which they drew their identity.

The palatial homes that the Middle European nobility had built and furnished with unlimited means in the nineteenth century reflected a dream held by many in society: a place of one's own, where one can reign supreme. But then the fortunes extracted from Silesia's mines that had financed such lavish estates went up in smoke. During and immediately after the Second World War, most of the Silesian properties were looted, set alight or left to nature's devices for decades thereafter. It was from the wreckage of these estates, and the lives once lived there, that a new Europe arose— one with a fairer distribution of wealth, and where more people could shape their homes as they wished, though often on a much smaller scale. 'My house is my castle' appeared frequently on door plaques, as a kind of protective talisman. Not insignificantly, the motto often appeared in English, the language of the soldiers who were seen as the liberators of the Second World War.

* * *

What happened to all the castles, palaces and other stately homes described in this book, the residences that played—and sometimes still play—such an important part in the lives of the noble families I encountered during my travels through Central Europe?

The children who came to Finstergrün for scout camps or Christian camps would not have had much at home in Austria's poor postwar years. For almost seventy years now, such children have enjoyed carefree holidays in Margit's castle, but they have also received some valuable life lessons along the way. When it came time for the Church organisation to describe its activities in the catalogue for the 2007 Margit Szapáry exhibition, Reverend Manfred Perko wrote that the team was inspired by the biblical mandate to 'beat swords into ploughshares'. Perhaps he was referring to the mediaeval knights whose swords and cuirasses were once on display in the castle's great hall. But it's in the context of Austria's and Finstergrün's twentieth-century history, and the country's struggles with a conservative past—not least Lungauers' widespread admira-

204

AFTERWORD

tion for the Nazi regime—that makes young people's use of the castle especially interesting. The opportunity for these children to 'contribute to building God's kingdom' has a flipside, though, requiring some critical reflection up there on the mountain: in German, God's kingdom is also a 'Reich'.

Still, it is difficult to argue with the famous saying by Martin Buber, the Austrian Jewish philosopher who inspired all the youth activities: 'An "I" can only take shape in the presence of a "Thou".' Finstergrün still provides opportunities for solidarity, surrounded by the majesty of nature, to all who are willing to set their defences aside for a moment and extend a brotherly hand. It is, after all, a place that flourished through the ordinary love between two human beings, and where hunting—the thing that had originally piqued Sándor's interest in this spot, before he met Margit—ultimately faded into the background. Hunting animals for sport is also regarded as a less civilised pastime now, for nobility and for everyone else. In the castle's brochure, from 2016, the emphasis lies more on the seven Christian, chivalrous virtues taught to the children at Finstergrün: temperance, courage, wisdom, justice, faith, hope and love. All fine principles for leading a good life. Margit would have agreed wholeheartedly.

Provided that buildings have good capacity, high ceilings and spacious rooms, they can serve different purposes over time, as Finstergrün's story shows. Their unique stately staircases, ornamental doors, windows and wall or ceiling decorations can move with the times, for new generations with new purposes and new ideals. In this sense, many modern, more purely functional buildings, including twentieth-century homes, have far less to offer. They are also usually demolished far sooner than their centuries-old counterparts, which—provided they have been well-maintained—are always ready for a new life, and can inspire an interest in history among younger generations.

The children of Ramingstein who now attend the castle-like community school that Margit built for them in 1912 benefit from its history. In the late 1990s, it became one of Austria's first IT specialist schools. Today's digital curriculum, occasionally customised for individual students, fits perfectly into this 'castle of learning'; its niches and challenging outdoor areas are easy to retreat to with an iPad or a cellphone.

SECRETS OF A SUITCASE

And what of the other buildings that feature in this story? Margit's birthplace, Siemianowicz, has had a turbulent history. Although she received a splendid photobook of it when she married Sándor, her family had essentially already abandoned it by that time. Her father, Hugo II, sold it off when he needed funds for his grander palace, Brynek. It remained a luxury country estate until a rather sinister fate befell it during the Second World War. The railway lines laid into remote Silesia half a century earlier by magnates like Hugo and Guido, for transporting their zinc and iron products, were used by the Nazis to perpetrate their crimes against humanity: the extermination camps for European Jews, Roma, homosexuals, the mentally ill and all others whom they regarded as inferior beings. Even today, the name Auschwitz—located not far from Siemianowicz—still says all that needs to be said.

Although the death camp was built in the city itself, there were many auxiliary sites that belonged to the complex, which together formed a coordinated whole. These included various kinds of work camps, where the vast range of 'enemies of the Reich' were exploited as free labour by the industrialists who profited from Hitler's regime—ThyssenKrupp, IG-Farben, BMW, Miele, Siemens, Volkswagen, and others. In addition to serving as barracks, existing buildings were also used as private residences or dormitories for soldiers and officers. With the surrounding region designated the location for Auschwitz's labour camps, Siemianowicz itself was earmarked as a home for the Wehrmacht. After the war, it fell into severe disrepair under the communist regime, and classic Eastern Bloc prefab apartments were built beside it. But after Poland joined the EU in 2004, funds were released to aid the restructuring of neglected regions, and Siemianowicz was rescued just in time. In 2018, a brand-new brewery opened in the first of the palace's restored spaces, part of an ambitious, far larger plan to convert it into a conference centre.[3]

Villa Rosalia in Abbazia, where Margit and Sándor first met, was renovated and reopened sixty years later as a luxury casino, designed to attract high-rollers as a means of boosting tourism to Croatia. It may have been destructively capitalistic, but it also brought a welcome injection of foreign funds, of which the Yugoslavians behind the Iron Curtain were in dire need. In the

AFTERWORD

twenty-first century, 'Casino Rosalia' has been integrated into a modern hotel, putting its splendour within reach of mere mortals. These include many former inhabitants of the USSR, who were able to travel freely after 1989.

Krowiarki, where Margit and Sándor were married and where Jolanta and Béla were born, did not fare so well. Two world wars, Stalinist socialism and lack of occupancy during the twentieth century have all taken their toll. Edgar, Margit's older brother, took ownership after their father's death in 1908, and moved between Krowiarki and Brynek until his own death in 1939, at which point his son Karl inherited Brynek. Krowiarki passed to the descendants of Margit's uncles, Lazarus and Artur (brothers of Hugo II). Johan Henckel von Donnersmarck, Karl's brother, was the last of the family to live there—until March 1945, when he fled by bicycle to the train station as the Soviet troops approached, narrowly making the last train to Czechoslovakia, the best escape route. One's life could not be guaranteed in any other direction, as many eyewitness accounts had warned. Johan left everything behind, and would emigrate to Brazil with his wife not long afterward.

After the war, Krowiarki, now in Russian-occupied Poland and plundered of its contents, became an educational institution for (communist) political activism, and a children's home in 1947. In 1963, it was transformed into a rehabilitation centre, but when more efficient accommodations were built for the centre in 1970, it was abandoned and fell into disrepair. In 2009, it was put up for sale by a Polish real-estate agent for the bargain price of one million Euros. Since then, it has been undergoing renovations, but with many setbacks. The dilapidated palace now serves principally as a backdrop for romantic wedding photography. Krowiarki is also deserving of a hefty European subsidy, to restore it to its former glory.

As for Finstergrün's neighbours, Moosham—where Sándor and Margit lodged during the construction of their own home—is still the private property of the Wilczek family. Part of it is a public museum space, where daily tours are held. Mauterndorf is now a tourist attraction for families wishing to experience a day in the life of the Middle Ages. The museum offers no account of the castle's twentieth-century history, and Göring's name is nowhere to be found—thus preventing the place from becoming a Mecca for neo-Nazis.

SECRETS OF A SUITCASE

Of all the Silesian properties owned by the Henckel von Donnersmarcks, Brynek is the one to which fate has been kindest. Margit's nephew Karl only briefly enjoyed his inheritance, however, as he died early in the war, in January 1940. He passed ownership to his wife and three daughters, but they had already been ousted from the castle in 1939, as soon as Poland was invaded by the German Wehrmacht, due to their lack of national-socialist sympathies. They moved into the groundskeeper's hut, and the palace itself was converted into the Adolf Hitler School for the Hitler Youth. The chapel became a Nazi library.

One of the daughters, Karolina, married a German major in 1944, Count Clemens von Kageneck. He was a richly decorated Nazi war hero, son of a general and a nephew to Franz von Papen, last chancellor of the Weimar Republic, who had famously persuaded President von Hindenburg to replace him with Hitler. Von Kageneck served as commander of a tank division deployed in Russia, and was known to carry out secret missions as an intelligence officer. Little imagination is required to surmise what kinds of missions these were: the Nazis were responsible for countless massacres in Ukraine and other locations in the USSR. After suffering multiple serious injuries at the Battle of Belgorod, von Kageneck arrived at Brynek, supposedly while retreating with the Wehrmacht. And it was there that he entered into an improbably beautiful marriage at the end of the war.

Averting one's gaze from von Kageneck's uniform, and the prominent black cross on his neck, he and Karolina Henckel von Donnersmarck made a most handsome couple. Karolina does not seem to have been forced into the marriage, though appearances can be deceiving. Perhaps she thought they were a good match, of which there were few to be had in Silesia—let us hope she did not know too much about his activities in Ukraine. Only a few months later, however, von Kageneck was called away to the artillery and tank-crew training institute at Bergen-Belsen, where he was captured after the capitulation in 1945. Like so many others, he came away relatively unscathed, and was offered a position as a banker in the 1950s that he held until the 1970s. He died in 2005, having survived by a long shot his unfortunate brothers (including a Luftwaffe pilot, Erbo). But their story must be told elsewhere.

208

AFTERWORD

Karolina's marriage meant that the castle was not returned to the family. As the Russians approached Brynek in 1944, the Henckel von Donnersmarcks fled all the way across Germany to Westphalia, leaving behind the fruits of their forefathers' money, care and dedication and the labours of the industrial workers who had toiled in their mines and factories. Although the palace was looted by the Red Army, the building itself and its fixed furnishings survived intact. It became a secondary school, and then—appropriately—a vocational college for forestry and ecology, the oldest forestry school in Poland. Nowadays it is a public monument, and its unique collection of stuffed mammals, birds and insects and its herbaria make it worth a visit. The palace building itself is currently set up as a dormitory for the forestry students, who attend classes in an uninspiring structure next door. They use the lush ambience primarily for wild post-exam parties, as can be seen in various YouTube videos. In 1994, the entire Catholic branch of the Henckel von Donnersmarcks gathered at Brynek one last time, to celebrate Karolina and von Kageneck's fiftieth wedding anniversary.

Uncle Guido's Silesian inheritance met with a worse fate. At the end of the war, both the Old and the New Palace at Neudeck were burned to the ground by the Soviets, including all valuables that had not already been plundered. The grounds, landscaped in the English style, are now a large public park. The remains of ponds, lanes and a few sculptures have sparked the imaginations of many Polish visitors to produce digital reconstructions of what was once their 'little Versailles'.

Guido's Palais Blücher apartment on Pariser Platz, not far from the Brandenburg Gate, was hit during the Battle of Berlin. It then ended up in the postwar Russian zone, and remained a ruin for years, until the Berlin Wall was built and it was razed to the ground. The new American embassy has since been built in its place.

Hotel Païva in Paris, on the other hand, is still standing, having miraculously survived two world wars and escaped subsequent dilapidation. Sadly, the unique furniture items commissioned by La Païva have now been scattered across the globe by numerous estate sales and auctions—but the locations of most pieces are still known. Although the grandeur of the façade has been diminished somewhat by the presence of the cocktail bar now located on the ground floor, the house behind it was recently restored. It has remained in perfect condition since 1904, when it became home to the Parisian branch of the Travellers Club, where affluent (male) tourists can hide away from the City of Lights. It is open to the public several times a year, though bookings are required months in advance. In fact, Hotel Païva may recently have been visited by a young Earl of Derby—if so, he would have seen the ultimate culmination of La Païva's imposition on his great-uncle in London. The Tories have closer connections to the continent than they would care to know.

Friedrichshof Castle suffered a major fire in 1967, was restored and is now a five-star hotel. It was renamed Schlosshotel Kronberg, after the nearby city. In March 2019 it was absorbed into the over-arching Prinz von Hessen brand, an umbrella group for other activities run by the Hessian House Foundation, including estate open days and a cultural foundation. The other successful hotel run by the foundation is the Grand Hotel Hessischer Hof in Frankfurt. Their website says, ever so modestly: 'The Prinz von Hessen brand transcends generations, making a lasting cultural and economic impact both in Hesse and beyond. Our brand is defined by extraordinary products, strong name recognition, and values that help shape identities', in the words of Prince Donatus, the president of the Hessian House Foundation, who is also the head of the House of Hesse. In 2019, the then-president of the European Central Bank, Christine Lagarde, held her first meeting with all of her colleagues at Schloss Kronberg.

The Tegernsee villa near Munich is also still standing. But Uncle Guido's most democratic contribution to urban design is Berlin's planned quarter of Frohnau, designed after the English garden cities of the early twentieth century in a 700-hectare area that was formerly part of the Stolpe estate and hunting grounds. Shortly before his death in 1916, Guido built a 300-bed centre here for the first injured soldiers returning from the First World War, for which he renovated a station building. He also founded a research institute, with a starting capital of four million Marks, to investigate the effects of chemical weapons. Guido was no supporter of the war provocateurs surrounding Wilhelm II, having already spent the end of his life regretting his involvement in the Franco-Prussian conflict of the 1870s, after he realised that this had foreshadowed the First World War.

AFTERWORD

Today, the House of Donnersmarck Foundation is a sizeable rehabilitation institute for the disabled. It has 600 employees across multiple locations in Berlin and beyond, including a hotel for people with disabilities. In 2016, the foundation celebrated its centenary, commemorated with the publication of a thoroughly researched history of the organisation. The Nazi years were not overlooked, a period that the institute miraculously survived, thanks in part to the friendship between Guidotto Henckel von Donnersmarck and Hermann Göring. Because Göring had used part of the foundation's land to build a field hospital for the Luftwaffe, no further claim on it could be made by the local authorities, thus securing the income for the foundation.[4] Representatives from the Henckel von Donnersmarck family still sit on the executive board today.

The S1 (Oranienburg) light-rail connection makes Frohnau—like all products of the garden city movement—easily accessible by public transport. The station's tower is a living reminder of Guido's activities in the area. The fact that it all still stands is a final testament to his business acumen, and his forethought for the future development of his land: were there perhaps a few doctors who wanted to build a villa closer to their place of work? The result has made Frohnau a pleasant place to live to this day.

The Szapáry villa in The Hague where Yvonne and Karl's wedding was so joyfully celebrated in 1966 was the property of the Kenyan embassy for many years. The International Criminal Court sits diagonally opposite.

* * *

And what of the four-poster bed that Göring coerced out of Margit? In German, the word for 'canopy bed'—*Himmelbett*, literally 'sky bed' or 'heavenly bed'—took on dramatic meaning during the Second World War, when Göring was in charge of the Luftwaffe. *Görings Himmelbett* was the name given to the string of radar-linked searchlights that ran from Denmark to France's North Sea coast— their purpose was to detect British bombers at night so that they could be brought down. Many such crews fell victim to Göring's 'bed of lights'.

As for the real bed, alas, it was never found. It did not feature in the inventories of Carinhall, which mostly contained paintings, nor

SECRETS OF A SUITCASE

did it appear on the cargo lists of the nearly 5,000 artworks and artefacts of Göring's collection that were prepared for transport to Berchtesgaden in February 1945, so that they could be hidden away in Neuschwanstein Castle and in the old salt mines around Salzburg.[5] The collection was loaded onto two trains and three 'auto carriers', but delays meant that the trains were shunted into the depot at Berchtesgaden, where they were partly looted by locals, who made off with Göring's expensive whiskeys and shredded Aubusson tapestries. Most likely the bed disappeared or was lost when Göring abandoned Carinhall in 1945, fleeing from the advancing Russian army. He had the complex destroyed. The Luftwaffe levelled Carinhall completely, so that nobody else could ever live there.

Thankfully, at least one important piece of furniture from Finstergrün has been properly preserved. When I wrote to the manager of the Bavarian Palace Administration, asking whether any of the items auctioned by Weinmüller were still in their collection, I received an immediate reply from both her and a pleasantly surprised curator. For years, Margit's second canopy bed has been part of the permanent exhibition at Burghausen Castle, east of Munich. The castle is listed in the *Guinness Book of Records* as the longest in Europe, exceeding one kilometre with six courtyards and numerous gardens. These were once used to grow vegetables, enabling the household to survive prolonged enemy sieges. It is no fairytale castle: since the thirteenth century, it has belonged to House Wittelsbach, which produced many Bavarian dukes and duchesses, princes and princesses, kings and queens—from the Habsburg Empress Sisi to the eccentric Ludwig II of Bavaria, the mastermind behind Neuschwanstein Castle.

In any event, Burghausen has plenty of space for grand furniture. In the permanent exhibition, Margit's bed has a room of its own. A chest table stands beside it, topped with a jug and a candelabra that also once belonged to her. A Gobelins tapestry hangs on the wall, portraying a landscaped garden with peacocks. It lends an Orientalist ambience, and is not from Finstergrün's collection. The bed is covered with a sky-blue sheet. There is no reference to Margit Szapáry anywhere, and nobody has ever asked where the bed came from.

212

AFTERWORD

ACKNOWLEDGEMENTS

In writing the tale of Finstergrün, my research was greatly facilitated by the foundations laid by Lungau's own Christian Blinzer, who has also ensured the preservation of many materials in the Salzburg Provincial Archive. During his time as a history teacher at Vienna's Sacré Coeur Institute—once attended by Jolanta Szapáry—he raised his pupils' awareness of Austrian history, starting with a project investigating the terrible history of their own school: a place where the mentally ill were committed and murdered by the Nazis during the Second World War. He is now the director of Hak, the business school (*Bundeshandelsakademie*) in Tamsweg. I am extremely grateful for his generous assistance.

Christian's old teacher, Dr Klaus Heitzmann, now headmaster of Tamsweg's grammar school, must have been a major source of inspiration for him. His hefty chronicle of the town, written while he was director of its museum, is frequently cited in this book.

I am also much obliged to all of the Wikipedians who selflessly populate thousands of entries per day with their knowledge. In the time since my impulse buy at Sotheby's in 2004, a wealth of new information has been added illuminating the history told in this book, from all corners of the world.

My search would have been equally fruitless without the help of all the private businesspeople who run online bookstores, doubtless for little or no profit, giving them flowery names to cover up the fact that their sales are all processed at kitchen tables. These individuals make it possible to obtain within a few days second-hand books that have already vanished from libraries; as such, they too are acting as custodians of European civilisation. Although one can never rely blindly on these often-incomplete and occasionally contradictory accounts, collectively they do paint a picture that allowed Finstergrün and its illustrious mistress to take shape in my work.

ACKNOWLEDGEMENTS

My continued thanks go, first and foremost, to Mai Spijkers, managing director of Prometheus Books in Amsterdam, for his immediate enthusiasm when I spoke to him of my book-to-be. I am grateful to my helpful and accurate editor at Hurst Publishers in London, Lara Weisweiller-Wu, for her invaluable critiques, and to my friends (and guinea pigs) Sabine Horsting, Françoise Kappé and Thea Summerfield for their wise remarks.

There are also a large number of friendly people who were so kind as to open their archives for me, or send me all kinds of information on request. First on this list is Dr Gerda Dohle from the Salzburg Provincial Archives. I would also like to thank Baron Godert de Vos van Steenwijk Junior, for agreeing to an interview with him and his wife, and for his letter afterwards, which clarified many details. Furthermore, I thank Dr Manfred Rasch, Guido Henckel von Donnersmarck's biographer; Dr Alison Wilson at Cambridge, biographer of Rosemary Murray; Dr Sebastian Weinert, the archivist of the Fürst-Donnersmarck Foundation in Berlin and author of the chronicle published to mark its centenary; Lisbeth Bednar-Brandt, the current custodian of Finstergrün; Dr Andrea Baresel-Brandt from the German Lost Art Foundation; Dr Christian Fuhrmeister, director of Munich's Zentralinstitut für Kunstgeschichte (Central Institute for Art History); Dr Gudrun Szczepanek, director of the Bavarian Palace Administration, and Dr Matthias Memmel, curator of the palaces' furniture collections; and Dr Sebastian Karnatz, manager of Burghausen Castle, who was prompt in sending me several photographs of Margit's four-poster bed on display, just before the closure of his museum due to COVID-19.

Lastly, I wish to thank Princess Yvonne von Hessen-Szapáry and her family for sending the Gucci suitcase to Sotheby's, so that it could come into my possession. Margit and Jolanta's belongings are a daily reminder to me that the here and now is only ever a moment in world history.

But, above all, this book could not have been written without the care and attention of the love of my life, Gerard de Vries.

pp. [8–15]

NOTES

THE SEPTEMBER AUCTION

1. Christian Blinzer (ed.), *Unentwegt, bewegt. Margit Gräfin Szapáry (1871–1943)*. Tamsweg (W. Pfeifenberg) 2008, 2nd edition. Exhibition catalogue (2007); Christian Blinzer, *Unermüdlich tätig zum Wohle der Anderen. Sozialfürsorgliches und politisches Handeln von Margit Gräfin Szapáry (1871–1943)*. PhD thesis (unpublished), Charles Francis University Graz, 2009.
2. The Weinmüller auction house.
3. Monique de Saint Martin in: Yme Kuiper, Nikolaj Bijleveld, Jaap Dronkers (eds), *Nobilities in Europe in the Twentieth Century: Reconversion Strategies, Memory Culture and Elite Formation*. Leuven (Peeters) 2015, pp. 307–11.
4. Peter Sloterdijk, *You Must Change Your Life: On Anthropotechnics*. London (Polity) 2014, ch. 3.

PALATIAL HOMES

1. Usually abbreviated in German as *k.u.k.*: imperial and royal.
2. Richard Barkeley, *The Road to Mayerling: Life and Death of Crown Prince Rudolph of Austria*. London (Macmillan) 1958, ch. 12; Judith Listowel, *A Habsburg Tragedy: Crown Prince Rudolf*. London (Ascent Books) 1978, pp. 83, 84.
3. M. Czaja, *Der industrielle Aufstieg der Beuthen-Siemianowitzer und Tarnowitz-Neudecker Linie der Henckel von Donnersmarck bis zum Weltkrieg*. Doctoral thesis, LMU Munich, 1936, p. 14 ff.
4. Rudolf II is best known for the alchemy experiments he carried out in the Habsburg palace in Prague, where he curated an impressive 'chamber of wonders' (*Wunderkammer*): Martyn Rady, *The Habsburgs, The Rise and Fall of a World Power*. London (Penguin/Allen Lane) 2020, pp. 107–15.
5. M. Rasch, *Der Unternehmer Guido Henckel von Donnersmarck. Eine Skizze*. Essen (Klartext) 2016, p. 16.
6. Rasch, p. 20.
7. The following passage is largely based on Rasch; on P. Rother, *Chronik der Stadt Konigshütte Oberschlesien*. Munich (Laumann) 1994; and on Czaja.

217

pp. [15–22]   NOTES

8. Here and throughout the book, the values of the German Mark, Thaler and Reichsmark (RM) are based on the historical purchasing-power data calculated by the Federal Bank of Germany for the period between 1810 and 2019: 'Purchasing Power equivalents of historical amounts in German currencies', available at www.bundesbank.de—this takes the price of a kilogram of potatoes as its basic unit of measure. What these purchasing-power overviews fail to consider, and which they themselves acknowledge as a problem, is the cost of labour. Over the centuries, labour has become considerably more expensive, making the relative value of currency, then and now, difficult to calculate. In any event, even though these are only estimates (on the conservative side), they give an impression of equivalent wealth and worth. Another approach is to compare the richest individuals from the respective periods. With 250 million RM, Guido Henckel von Donnersmarck was the richest person in Prussia in 1910, and the third-richest man in Germany in 1914 (with an additional annual income of over 13 million RM in the intervening years—see Rasch, p. 9). His entire fortune would be worth around £4.3 billion today. He would still need tens of billions more to compete with today's German top ten, however.
9. Rother, p. 46 et seq.
10. She is known primarily for comments about bloodlines.
11. William D. Godsey, *Aristocratic Redoubt: The Austro-Hungarian Office on the Eve of the First World War*. West Lafayette, IN (Purdue University Press) 1999.
12. Salzburg Provincial Archive (Salzburger Landesarchiv, hereafter SLA), Szapáry papers, Box B.
13. Arnout Weeda, *Het mysterie van Wenen*. Amsterdam (Bezige Bij) 2011, p. 15.

FINSTERGRÜN

1. Anja Thaller, 'Burg Finstergrün', in: Blinzer, 2007, p. 59 et seq.
2. Godsey, p. 4.
3. Elisabeth Kinsky-Wilczek, *Hans Wilczek erzählt seinen Enkeln Erinnerungen aus seinem Leben*. Graz (Leykam) 1933, p. 63. Wilczek was also the first to suggest to banker Nathaniel Rothschild that they address each other informally, using the more familiar German *du* instead of the formal *Sie*. Wilczek even gave Rothschild a pet name, Nattie, which was a common practice among many noble family members, helping to distinguish between the many individuals with similar names. There were other such exceptional cases at the Viennese court, such as the influential Princess Pauline Metternich, a good friend of Wilczek, who facilitated Rothschild's

NOTES pp. [23–28]

entry into the Viennese elite by inviting him to dinners and parties at her residence. Martina Winkelhofer, *Das Leben adeliger Frauen. Alltag in der k.u.k. Monarchie*. Vienna (Haymon) 2016 (2011), pp. 108, 145 et seq.

4. Edmund de Waal, *The Hare with the Amber Eyes*. London (Vintage) 2010, p. 162.

5. The terms 'early Renaissance', 'South Tirolean' and 'Gothic' were used rather interchangeably by Wilczek and his fellow castle lords, and their usage is reflected here. What they designate is the stylistic period between the Roman Empire and the Renaissance. The use of the word 'Gothic' to describe the interiors of Moosham and Finstergrün seems to be a reference to Central European styles from the fifteenth and six-teenth centuries. Later on, Göring & co. would further pare down this term to 'Germanic' or 'Teutonic', appending a nationalistic connota-tion to the style that it certainly did not originally possess.

6. Conversion of the old Austrian currencies was facilitated by the Historic Currency Calculator (*Historischer Währungsrechner*) of the Austrian National Bank: www.eurologisch.at.

7. Kinsky-Wilczek, p. 258 et seq.

8. Josef Steiner-Wischenbart, 'Finstergrün' in: *Österreichische Illustrierte Zeitung*, 2–6–1912, p. 11.

9. This was the pseudonym of Siegmund Salzmann, who co-authored the pornographic novel *Josefine Mutzenbacher* with Schnitzler, among other works.

10. Felix Salten (trans. Whittaker Chambers), *Bambi, a Life in the Woods*. New York (Simon & Schuster) 1928.

11. Winkelhofer, p. 66.

12. Godsey, p. 24 et seq.

13. Richard J. Evans, *The Pursuit of Power: Europe 1815–1914*. London (Allen Lane) 2016, p. 289.

14. Funded by the Schwarzenberg family, among others.

15. Kinsky-Wilczek, p. 383: see use of '*wir*' (we) with regard to the pur-chase of Finstergrün.

16. SLA, Szapáry family archive, Box A.

17. SLA, Szapáry papers, Box 1, book 1. Letter dd. 28–7–1900.

18. It would become the property of the Krupp family after the First World War. The castle can be seen in a documentary about the final Krupp res-ident available on YouTube: *Herr von Bohlen Privat*, filmed by André Schäfer (Germany, 2015). Much later, Blühnbach was owned by the American art lover and philanthropist Frederick Koch, until his death in 2020. He was the estranged brother of the Koch oil family, well known as Trump financers. All of this gives an impression of the scope and grandeur of the estate.

219

pp. [28–42]   NOTES

19. Evans, p. 363.
20. Salten, p. 12.
21. SLA, Szapáry papers, Box 1, household ledger 1901 et seq.
22. Kinsky-Wilczek, p. 383.
23. Wilhelm Deuer, 'Der Umbau von Schloss Wolfsberg in Kärntner Lavanttal durch einen Schlesischen Magnaten als Zeittypische Aufgabe des romantischen Historismus', in: Claudia Fräss-Ehrfeld, *Kärnten und Böhmen, Mähren, Schlesien*. Klagenfurt (Geschichtsverein Landesmuseum Kärnten) 2004, pp. 151–61.

A GOOD GIRL

1. SLA, Szápary papers, Box 1.
2. On the role of resort towns and 'the management of pain', see: Evans, p. 418.
3. Monika Kubrova, 'Vom guten Leben. Adelige Frauen im 19. Jahrhundert' in: Heinz Reif (ed.), *Elitenwandel in der Moderne*, vol. 12. Berlin (Akademie) 2011; Winkelhofer.
4. Isabel Hull, *The Entourage of Kaiser Wilhelm II, 1888–1918*. Cambridge (Cambridge University Press) 1982, p. 109.
5. We can deduce this from the handwriting, which is almost identical to that on the postcards. The descriptions themselves also offer clues. Her husband's expenses are listed under 'Sándor', for example, a familiar form of address that a subordinate would never have employed. Her own expenses, on the other hand, are reported neutrally, such as 'Abbazia trip'. Finally, there are no indications that the Szapárys ever employed a bookkeeper.
6. Kubrova, p. 115; and Marion Kaplan, *The Marriage Bargain: Women and Dowries in European History*. New York (Haworth Press) 1985.
7. Winkelhofer, p. 37.

A GOOD NAME

1. SLA, Szapáry papers, Box 1, book 1.
2. Rasch, p. 130.
3. Rasch, p. 43.
4. These writings were most prevalent in reports from Paris under the pseudonyms of 'Marquise de Fontenoy', appearing in *The Chicago Daily Tribune*, and 'Heloise Countess d'Alemcourt' in *The San Fransico Chronicle* and elsewhere, in the first few years of the twentieth century (source: Fold 3/Newspapers.com).
5. Virginia Rounding, *Grandes Horizontales: The Lives and Legends of Marie*

220

NOTES   pp. [42–52]

Duplessis, Cora Pearl, La Païva and La Présidente. London (Bloomsbury) 2003, p. 281.

6. Email to the author from M. Rasch, August 2019.
7. Evans, p. 318.
8. Dolores Augustine, *Patricians and Parvenus: Wealth and High Society in Wilhelmine Germany*. Oxford (Berg Publishers) 1994.
9. Evans, p. 291.
10. Hull, pp. 39, 64.
11. This industrial boom in Silesia and other regions saw inordinate dividends of 10–20 percent. See also: Rasch.
12. Bozena Lebzuch, 'The role and the meaning of a colour in creating parks and palaces of the Henckel von Donnersmarck family', in: Maria Godyn (ed.), *Colour, Culture, Science*. Krakow (Jan Matejko Academy of Fine Arts) 2018, pp. 239–47.
13. In Central Europe, at least, onion domes were indicative of Catholic buildings, which undoubtedly played a role here, too.
14. The same happened to filmmaker Florian Henckel von Donnersmarck upon the release of his film *Never Look Away*, about the artist Gerhard Richter and his father-in-law, a former Nazi gynaecologist. Henckel von Donnersmarck was berated for not having incorporated his own family history into the story, with journalists presupposing that his relatives 'also included prominent Nazi figures'. He had to explain to them that he belonged to the Protestant, Beuthen branch of the family. The press remained skeptical.
15. Winkelhofer, p. 71.

WHERE IT WAS

1. Hans Dieter Rutsch, *Das Preussische Arkadien*. Hamburg (Rowohlt) 2014.
2. Evans, p. 283.
3. After the Second World War, quite a number of displaced Silesians researched and documented the history of the region and their birthplaces. One such figure was the Silesian former tax inspector Paul Rother, who produced an extremely detailed account of the rise of the mining industry in his *Chronik der Stadt Königshütte Oberschlesien* ('History of the City of Königshütte, Oberschlesien'), his hometown. For more information, see Rother.
4. Rother, p. 16.
5. Rother, p. 19.
6. Rother, p. 27.
7. Tatjana Tönsmeyer & Lubos Velek (eds), 'Adel und Politik in der Habsburgermonarchie und den Nachbarländern zwischen Absolutismus

pp. [52–59] NOTES

und Demokratie' in: *Studien zum Mitteleuropäischen Adel*, *Vol. 3. Adel und Politik*. Munich (Meidenbauer) 2011, p. 79.

8. Calamine is an ore that combines with copper to produce brass. The resulting alloy is more durable than copper and easier to polish to a sheen, and so was often used in altarpieces, chandeliers and household items, as well as clocks, firearms and cannons. In Silesia, production was in the hands of Georg Giesche for two centuries, and the name Giesche became synonymous with brass. Rasch, pp. 22–9.

9. Ibid., p. 55.

10. Ibid., pp. 239–41.

11. This is according to Czaja, a researcher who conducted this study in 1936, and who was likely not entirely free from the national-socialist sentiment that Silesia should return to German rule, for which she provides several exaggerated arguments.

12. For information on the origin of the term 'crime against humanity', see: Philippe Sands, *East West Street*. London (Orion/Weidenfeld & Nicolson) 2017.

WILL AND FATE

1. Alfred Döblin, *Reise in Polen*, Olten (Walter) 1968 [Fischer 1926], p. 235. This book is available in English as Alfred Döblin (trans. Joachim Neugroschel), *Journey to Poland*. London (I.B. Tauris) 1991.

2. For information on the dangers of childbirth faced by women even in the highest social circles, see Winkelhofer, pp. 197–201. Vivid descriptions are also provided in Julian Barnes's *The Man in the Red Coat*, a book on the nineteenth-century Parisian gynaecologist Dr Pozzi. London (Jonathan Cape) 2019.

3. SPA, Szapáry Family Archive, Box A, postal card dated 15–4–1903.

4. 'He had quit smoking by switching to chocolate, and when he was away hunting in Hungary, in his letters he would ask for bars of chocolate again and again, which my mother would send to him', from *Lebenserinnerungen Jolánta Szapáry, Erinnerungen der Tante Jolinka, aufgezeichnet für Christoph und Irina*, p. 1 front. Cited in: Blinzer, 2009, p. 28.

5. Ibid.: 'He was under constant treatment for his heart, but the real cause was self-induced poisoning, due to excess eating (his colossal appetite earned him the nickname The Tiger)[,] eating too quickly, and too little exercise, after having given up riding a[nd] sitting a[nd] drawing all the time.'

6. SPA, Szapáry Family Archive, Box A.

7. Author interview with Godert de Vos van Steenwijk, 13 November 2019.

8. Noble widows around 1900 were expected to observe 'deep mourning'

222

NOTES pp. [59–70]

for at least three months, receiving no guests and undertaking no travel. Those who disregarded this convention were subject to strong public criticism. Winkelhofer, p. 217.

9. Kaplan, 1985; Horst Bienek, *Birken und Hochöfen. Eine Kindheit in Oberschlesien*. Berlin (Corso bei Siedler) 1990, p. 44.
10. Winkelhofer, p. 213–18.
11. Evans, p. 297.
12. György Dalos, *Ungarn in der Nussschale. Ein Jahrtausend und zwanzig Jahre*. Munich (Beck) 2004, p. 71.
13. Rasch, p. 42; Rother, pp. 15–16, 76–7.
14. Winkelhofer, pp. 117, 190.
15. E.J. Hobsbawm, *The Age of Capital, 1848–1875*. New York (Scribner) 1975, p. 279.
16. Hobsbawm, p. 281.
17. Hull, pp. 14, 70.
18. In the nineteenth century, the Neo-Gothic style emerged after Neo-Classicism. In Britain, the style was introduced by Augustus Pugin. He originally designed opera houses, but worked under his master Sir Charles Barry on the Palace of Westminster, rebuilt in Gothic Revival style after the fire of 1834. The Houses of Parliament were then superseded in grandeur by Budapest's parliament building, again Neo-Gothic, and built in 1895–1904 by Hungarian architect Imre Steindl. The Neo-Gothic trend also led to the heritage-preservation movement. Evans, p. 453.
19. Early film footage of the anniversary celebrations shows just how popular these ceremonies were. Thomas Ballhausen, *Krieg der Bilder. Filmdokumente zur Habsburger Monarchie im Ersten Weltkrieg*. Incl. Hannes Leidinger, 'Jubel und Elend. Illustrationen zum Zeitgeschehen', DVD 2. Vienna (Austrian Film Archive) 2004.
20. SPA, Szapáry Family Archive, Box A.

MODERN WOMEN

1. The following is based largely on Odile Nouvel-Kammerer (ed.), *L'Extraordinaire Hôtel Païva*, Paris (Les Arts décoratifs) 2015; and on Rounding.
2. Orlando Figes, *The Europeans: Three Lives and the Making of a Cosmopolitan Culture*. London (Allen Lane/Penguin) 2019, pp. 95, 98, 298.
3. Nouvel-Kammerer, p. 25.
4. Another great admirer of Baudry was the Parisian *netsuke* collector Charles Ephrussi, the subject of Edmund de Waal's *The Hare with Amber Eyes*. Ephrussi wrote Baudry's biography. De Waal, p. 86.

223

pp. [71–88]   NOTES

5. Rounding, p. 262.
6. Ibid., p. 271.
7. Rasch, p. 100.
8. Adolf Loos, 'Ornament und Verbrechen'. Lecture series 1908–1913, Vienna, published in: Adolf Loos, *Sämtliche Schriften*, vol. I. Vienna (Glück) 1962, pp. 276–88.
9. One Housing Arlington, 'Arlington's history', https://arlington.org.uk/arlington-homeless-accommodation/arlingtons-history (accessed 8 April 2024).
10. Josef Steiner, 'Finstergrün' in: *Österreichische Illustrierte Zeitung*, 2–6–1912, p. 11.
11. Heinrich Kreisel, *Die Kunst des deutschen Möbels. Von den Anfängen bis zum Hochbarock*, vol. I. München (C.H. Beck) 1968, p. 45 et seq.
12. Nora Watteck, 'Gräfin Margit Szapáry. Ein Lebensbild' in: *Mitteilungen der Gesellschaft für Salzburger Landeskunde* vol. 119 (1979), pp. 261–79.
13. SPA, Szapáry papers, Box 3, letters dated 18–2–1913; 3–2–1914.
14. Winkelhofer, p. 118.
15. SPA, Szapáry Family Archive, Box A; Josef Steiner-Wischenbart, *Burg Finstergrün in der Lungau*. Graz (Paul Cieslar) 1911.
16. Beatriz Colomina, *Privacy and Publicity: Modern Architecture and Mass Media*. London/Cambridge, MA (MIT Press) 1996, p. 283 et seq.
17. Rasch, p. 126.
18. SPA, Szapáry papers, Box 1.
19. Cited in Evans, p. 310.

A CRUMBLING EMPIRE

1. The Katholische Frauenorganisation (KFO).
2. SPA, Szapáry papers, 'Erinnerungen', vol. 4.
3. Author interview with Godert de Vos van Steenwijk, 13 November 2019.
4. Ibid.
5. Kubrowa, p. 97 et seq.
6. Dalos, p. 71.
7. Eva Philippoff (ed.), *Die Doppelmonarchie Österreich-Ungarn. Ein politisches Lesebuch (1867–1918)/L'Autriche-Hongrie. Politique et culture à travers les textes (1867–1918)*. Dual language text, Villeneuve d'Ascq (Presses universitaires du Septentrion) 2002, p. 24.
8. Evans, p. 329.
9. Evans, p. 306.
10. Cited in Blinzer, 2008, p. 16.
11. Kinsky-Wilczek, p. 163.

NOTES pp. [91–103]

DOUBLE-ENTRY BOOKKEEPING

1. Watteck, p. 261.
2. Robert Musil, *Der Mann ohne Eigenschaften*. Hamburg (Rowohlt) 1970 [1930–52], p. 175.
3. Ian Kershaw, *To Hell and Back: Europe 1914–1949*. Houten (Spectrum) 2015 [London Penguin], ch. 2.
4. Lenzbauer private collection, *So sollen wir leben in der Kriegszeit. Gräfin Margarethe Szapáry-Henckel von Donnersmarck auf Burg Finstergrün im Lungau*. Cited in Blinzer, 2009, p. 60.
5. Rasch, p. 133; SPA, Szapáry Family Archive, Box 7.
6. SPA, Szapáry Family Archive, Box 7.
7. Kershaw, ch. 2. Martyn Rady writes that, by the end of the war in 1918, of the original eight million Habsburg recruits (from a total population of nearly thirty million), one million had died, two million had been mutilated, four million had been admitted to a hospital or another institution, and 1.5 million taken as prisoners of war. Rady, p. 320.
8. Blinzer, 2009, p. 54.
9. Blinzer, 2009, p. 55.
10. Czaya, p. 98.
11. Philippoff, p. 158.
12. This was the first place in Austria where ordinary women could be trained as nurses (from 1880), and was also the first private hospital in Austria, besides the older institutions run by religious orders.
13. National Archive, The Hague, Dutch Management Institute, access no. 2.09.1613, file no. 164516.
14. Ibid.
15. Since nearly all of the hunting grounds in Lungau had been let to the major landowners, when times were hard the poorer populace had little choice but to hunt illegally. Poaching was subject to severe penalties: in 1936 and 1937, for instance, poachers were treated as thieves, and were sentenced to two months' harsh imprisonment for shooting a deer in Margit's hunting grounds (*Salzburger Volksblatt*, 31–7–1936 and 27–2–1937). Their line of defence, that they would rather hunt than beg, fell on deaf ears.

THE ROARING TWENTIES

1. The account in this chapter is based closely on the version of events given in the following Göring biographies: François Kersaudy, *Hermann Göring. Le deuxième homme du IIIe Reich*. Paris (Perrin) 2013 [2009]; Roger Manvell & Heinrich Fraenkel, *Goering*. London (Greenhill) 2005 [1962]; Richard Overy, *Goering*. London (Phoenix Press) 2000 [1984].

225

pp. [104–125]   NOTES

2. Manvell & Fraenkel, p. 136.
3. After the death of her sister, Countess Fanny von Wilamowitz-Möllendorf became an important 'honeybee' for Göring and Hitler. See Karina Urbach, *Go-Betweens for Hitler*. Oxford (Oxford University Press) 2015, p. 170.
4. Salzburg Provincial Archive and Laurin Luchner, *Schlösser in Osterreich. Zweiter Band*. Munich (Oscar Beck) 1983, p. 282.
5. See the 1911 publication on Finstergrün by Josef Steiner; and Weinmüller's foreword to the 1941 auction catalogue, among others.
6. Blinzer, 2009, p. 122.
7. Ibid., p. 124 et seq.
8. Ibid., p. 110.
9. *Salzburger Wacht*, 9–10–1924.
10. Blinzer, 2009, p. 131.
11. Ibid., p. 134.
12. Ibid., p. 131.
13. In 2019, Dr Klaus Heitzmann discovered that an underground Nazi organisation had existed in Lungau since 1930, which used planned tactics to spread Nazi ideology in the region, creating a bridgehead for the NSDAP, and later for the *Anschluss*. The technique capitalised on Hermann Göring's popularity, who was increasingly revered in this part of Austria as 'our Hermann', a reference to his regular stays at Mauterndorf. *Salzburger Nachrichten*, 6–10–2019.
14. Kershaw, pp. 237–9.
15. Ibid., p. 241.

NOBLESSE OBLIGE?

1. See, for example, Stephan Malinowski, *Vom König zum Führer*. Frankfurt (Fischer) 2004 [2003]; Fabrice d'Almeida, *La vie mondaine sous le nazisme*. Paris (Perrin) 2006; Jonathan Petropoulos, *Royals and the Reich*. Oxford (OUP) 2006; and Karina Urbach, *Go-Betweens for Hitler*. Oxford (OUP) 2015).
2. Manvell & Fraenkel, p. 68.
3. Stephan Malinowski, *Vom König zum Führer*. Frankfurt (Fischer) 2004 [2003], p. 548.
4. Manvell & Fraenkel, p. 69.
5. Rasch, p. 12.
6. Malinowski, p. 556.
7. Fabrice d'Almeida, *High Society in the Third Reich*. London (Polity) 2008 [Paris (Perrin) 2006], p. 192.
8. His birth was even reported in the society column of the *Wiener Salonblatt*

NOTES pp. [125–139]

on 15–7–1934, stating that his grandmother Wally had 'a delightful abode' in Potsdam.

9. Malinowski, p. 544.
10. Kershaw.
11. Margit deployed her daughter Jolanta to attend a 'secret' meeting on 11 October 1933 in Budapest with the former empress Zita and other members of the Habsburg high nobility. Zita was on her way to Italy, where she planned to propose to the royal house of Savoy a marriage between her son Otto and one of the Italian king's daughters. *Süddeutsches Tagblatt/Grazer Tagblatt* 12–10–1933, p. 1.
12. Blinzer, 2009, p. 151.

PAYING GUESTS

1. SPA, Szapáry Family Archive, Box 1B.
2. The Kunsthaus A.S. Drey collection was confiscated in 1938 as a result of the Nuremberg race laws, and the tapestries ordered to be auctioned in Berlin. The (Jewish) Drey family fled to England and the US. After the war, the Drey collection fell largely into the hands of Dr Gau, who donated his art collection to Unicef. After recovering pieces following the state restitution of stolen art, the Drey family gifted a further part of the collection. Deutsches Zentrum Kulturgutverluste, 'Lost Art-Datenbank', https://www.lostart.de/de/start (accessed 9 May 2024).
3. Here, the term 'economise' is used relatively. Throughout the 1930s, Margit continued to travel, and to lodge in the most expensive hotels and resorts in Vienna, Klagenfurt, Salzburg and the Tyrol, as recorded both in the society column of the *Neues Wiener Journal*, and by the addresses on the postcards Jolanta sent her, among other sources (author's collection).
4. K., A. and J. Heitzmann (eds), *Tamsweg. Die Geschichte eines Marktes und seiner Landgemeinden*. Tamsweg (Pfeifenberg) 2008, p. 398.
5. Cited in Blinzer, 2009, p. 34.
6. Author interview with Godert de Vos van Steenwijk, 13 November 2019.
7. In a later card sent to Jolanta, dated 17–12–1942, one year after the furniture auction, someone who signed only their initials noted that they had visited Guidotto at Tegernsee. (Author's collection.)
8. Author's collection, 15–2–1929.
9. *The Spectator*, 18–5–1934, available at https://archive.spectator.co.uk/article/18th-may-1934/17/letters-to-the-editor (accessed 9 May 2024).
10. Blinzer, 2009, p. 208.

pp. [140–147]   NOTES

11. Tim Bouverie, *Appeasement: Chamberlain, Hitler, Churchill and the Road to War*, London (Penguin Random House) 2019, ch. 7.

12. Ibid.

13. The *Salzburger Chronik für Stadt und Land* (3–7–1934) reported on a number of large-scale propaganda meetings run by the Fatherland Front in Lungau, stating that the 'English summer guests from Finstergrün' also took part.

14. Alison Wilson, *Changing Women's Lives: A Biography of Dame Rosemary Murray*. London (Unicorn) 2014, pp. 65–6.

15. *Neues Wiener Journal*, 13–9–1936, p. 20.

16. *Salzburger Chronik für Stadt und Land*, 28–8–1936.

17. Consider Hull's remarks on the excessive quantity of imperial monuments erected during the nineteenth and early twentieth centuries: 'The monarchy attempted to do with ceremony what it should have done with politics, namely, integrate large sections of the population comfortably into a stable but changing order. … [It] substitute[d] poorly for genuine political solutions'. Hull, p. 44

18. Facsimile reproduced in Blinzer, 2009, p. 276.

19. Joseph Roth, 'Requiem Mass', *Das neue Tage-Buch*, Paris 19–3–1938. Cited in: Joseph Roth, *On the End of the World*. London (Pushkin Press) 2019, p. 35.

20. This festive parade was documented in an amateur colour film from 1938, which can be viewed on the website of the United States Holocaust Museum at: USHMM, 'Goering visits small towns in Austria', https://collections.ushmm.org/search/catalog/irn555346#rights-restrictions (accessed 9 May 2024). There is a surprising amount of security on the roadside, which prompts Manvell & Fraenkel to suggest that this warm welcome was perhaps not as spontaneous as it appeared: 'Goering enjoyed receiving admiration and applause in the places where he had once been undistinguished, and to make sure that the village was crowded and gave him a fine welcome he brought with him a large number of soldiers.' Manvell & Fraenkel, p. 186.

UNWANTED GUESTS

1. 'Urgent: Countess Szapáry Ramingstein Lungau, Klagenfurt […] 30–3–[193]8 […], 6:50 pm. Tomorrow late morning, on the way from Unzmarkt to Mauterndorf, I would like to visit Schloss Finstergrün for a moment. *Heil Hitler*, Göring, Field Marshall [handwriting unknown]'. De Vos van Steenwijk private archive, dated 30–3–1938. Reproduced in: Blinzer, 2009, p. 276.

228

NOTES pp. [147–164]

2. François Kersaudy, *Hermann Göring. Le deuxième homme du IIIᵉ Reich*. Paris (Perrin) 2013 (2009), p. 140.
3. *Salzburger Volksblatt*, 15–6–1934.
4. SPA, Epenstein Papers, correspondence.
5. Postcard from 31–12–1933 (author's collection).
6. Blinzer, 2009, p. 84.
7. Heitzmann, p. 392.
8. Ibid.
9. *Tauern Post*, 30–3–1938.
10. Author's collection.
11. Blinzer, 2009, p. 167.
12. Norman Angell, *Peace with the Dictators? A Symposium and Some Conclusions*. London (Hamish Hamilton) 1938, p. 15.
13. Ibid., p. 55.
14. Adolf Hitler (trans. James Murphy), *Mein Kampf*. London (Hurst & Blackett) 1939, available via Project Gutenberg of Australia at https://gutenberg.net.au/ebooks02/0200601.txt (accessed 8 April 2024).
15. Manvell & Fraenkel, p. 196.
16. Benedict Anderson, *Verbeelde gemeenschappen/Imagined Communities*. Amsterdam (Jan Mets) 1995 [New York (Ithaca) 1983/1991], p. 82.
17. Cited in Evans, p. 684.
18. Blinzer 2009, p. 189 et seq.
19. Blinzer 2009, p. 192.
20. Margit sought representation in the matter from an anti-Nazi lawyer, Ludwig Kastl of Munich, with whom she corresponded very frequently in 1940 and 1941, until the auctioning of her furniture. See ibid., pp. 190–1.
21. Ibid., p. 183.
22. SPA, Szapáry Family Archive, Box 1B.
23. Fold 3, Ardelia Hall Collection, *Correspondence Göring* 1940–1943.
24. Les Archives diplomatiques & Jean-Marc Dreyfus, *Le catalogue Goering*. Paris (Flammarion) 2015, p. 75 et seq.

GOING ONCE, GOING TWICE

1. *Möbel, Plastik, Kunstgewerbe (Burg Finstergrün). Gemälde alter Meister. Farbstiche. Teppiche. Auktion xxv*. Weinmüller Catalogue 28, 13/14 November 1941. Munich, 1941.
2. Ibid., p. iv.
3. Didier Lancien & Monique de Saint Martin (eds), *Anciennes et nouvelles aristocrates. De 1880 à nos jours*. Paris (Éditions de la Maison des sciences de l'homme) 2007, p. 95.
4. Watteck, p. 272.

229

pp. [163–171]   NOTES

5. Fold3 archive, Ardelia Hall Collection: Correspondence Göring 1940–1943.
6. Fold3 archive, Ardelia Hall Collection, Bureau München 1946.
7. Its authority is evidenced by the large number of references to Kreisel's opus in the Amsterdam Rijksmusem's *Aspects of the Collection* series: Reinier Baarsen, *Duitse meubelen. German furniture.* Amsterdam/ Zwolle (Rijksmuseum/Waanders) 1998.
8. Kreisel, vol. I, pp. 50, 60, and image 132. Here, the canopy bed is attributed—erroneously—to the collection of the Austrian Miller zu Aichholz family (who, incidentally, had never lived at Finstergrün).
9. Ibid., p. 60.
10. Ibid., pp. 17, 57.
11. In June of that year, an 'In Memoriam' piece appeared in the *Neues Wiener Tagblatt* (4–6–1943, p. 3), adapted to the new political climate. Margit Szapáry was honoured primarily for her assistance to the farming community. Her maiden name, Henckel von Donnersmarck, was not mentioned, unlike the 'authentic' mediaeval architecture of Finstergrün, which was praised as a counterpoint to the 'imitation Windsor-Gothic' style that had supposedly swamped Europe. The *Salzburger Zeitung* (22–5–1943) merely printed an entry in the obituaries section. The national-socialist *Ramingsteiner Heimatbrief* (20–5–1943, p. 2) reported her death in the 'Premvilla' after 'a long period of absence', and that the countess had 'always worked to do good and offer a helping hand'. A notification that her body would be transported to Hungary, for burial beside her prematurely deceased husband Sándor, was struck out.

THE COLLECTOR

1. Interview between Reinier Baarsen and Pauline Terreehorst (included CD), in: W. Fock, *De verzamelingen van het Centraal Museum Utrecht. Part 8, Furniture to 1900.* Utrecht (Centraal Museum) 2005.
2. Luchner, p. 282.
3. Ella Leffland, *The Knight, Death and the Devil.* New York (William Morrow) 1990, p. 41 et seq.
4. The dramatised documentary about Hermann Göring's brother Albert, *Der gute Göring* (Kai Christiansen, ARD/Arte, Germany, 2016) provides a detailed reconstruction of these environments.
5. D'Almeida, p. 171.
6. Volker Knopf & Stefan Martens, *Görings Reich. Selbstinszenierungen in Carinhall.* Berlin (Ch. Links) 2019 [1999].
7. Merlijn Schooneboom, *Een kleine geschiedenis van de grootste Duitse worsteling.* Amsterdam (Querido) 2019.
8. Overy, pp. 13–15.

230

NOTES pp. [172–184]

9. Bouverie, p. 174.
10. Manvell & Fraenkel, p. 114.
11. Dreyfus, pp. 31, 43.
12. Ibid., p. 43 et seq.
13. Fold3 archive, Ardelia Hall Collection, Correspondence Göring 1940–1943.
14. Götz Aly & Michael Sontheimer, *How Julius Fromm's Condom Empire Fell to the Nazis*. New York (Other Press) 2009.

DISPLACED PERSONS

1. Heitzmann, p. 404.
2. *Wochenblatt der Bauernschaft für Salzburg*, 10–8–1940, p. 16.
3. Women were awarded the cross for having four (bronze), six (silver) or eight (gold) children. In Tamsweg, a total of over 200 women qualified for the decoration.
4. Heitzmann, p. 397.
5. Among many others, see: János Köbányal, *Agnes Heller. Het levensverhaal van de Hongaars-Joodse filosofe*. Amsterdam (Boom) 2002 [Budapest 1998], p. 30 et seq.; Sándor Márai. *Journal. Les années hongroises 1943–1948 / A teljes Napló, 1943–1948*. Paris (Albin Michel) 2019/[Budapest (Helikon Kiadó) 2006–2008]; Arno Geiger, *Unter den Drachenwand*. Munich (Carl Hanser) 2018, ch. 'Goodbye to Vienna'.
6. Victor Karady in: Kuiper et al., p. 34.
7. Before WWII, the travels of the aristocracy (for touring holidays, resort stays, etc.) were documented fairly meticulously in local and national newspapers. Yet there is only one mention of Béla to be found in the Austrian papers, noting his attendance at a New Year's Eve celebration in 1937, organised by the British socialite Lady Doverdale in Kitzbühel in honour of King Leopold of Belgium (*Salzburger Volksblatt* 4–1–1938). These types of reports were probably less common for personal visits. Another article concerns his hunting rifle, which was stolen from Finstergrün during his time in Canada (*Salzburger Wacht* 13–11–1926).
8. Urbach, p. 167 et seq.; Petropoulos, p. 123; d'Almeida, pp. 190–2.
9. Author interview with Godert de Vos van Steenwijk, 13 November 2019.
10. *Salzburger Volkszeitung*, 6–9–1946, p. 5.
11. The start of this process is portrayed—and highly romanticised—in George Clooney's movie *The Monuments Men* (2014).
12. Fold3 archive, 'Ardelia Hall Collection, *Correspondence Göring 1940–1943*'.
13. Dreyfus, p. 24.

pp. [185–200]   NOTES

14. National Archives, The Hague, Dutch Management Institute, access no. 2.09.1613, file no. 164516.
15. *Ramingsteiner Heimatbrief*, 26–11–1943, p. 1; *Salzburger Volkszeitung*, 22–11–1949, p. 4.
16. Ute Palmetshofer & Monika Eichinger, 'Provenienzforschung an der Universitätsbibliothek Salzburg—Ein Werkstattbericht', in: *Mitteilungen der VÖB* vol. 65.1 (2012), pp. 22–38.

A ROYAL WEDDING

1. Karl von Hessen was not unknown in the Netherlands. In 1961, for example, he had attended a garden party at Soestdijk Palace for Prince Bernhard's fiftieth birthday. He also attended several royal parties in Greece and Denmark during that period, and had been romantically associated with both the Dutch Princess Irene and Princess Irene of Greece. *De Volkskrant*, 30–6–1961; *Trouw*, 14–12–1961.
2. Katrin Rössler, 'Interview Rainer Prinz von Hessen' in: *Frankfurter Allgemeine Zeitung*, 14–4–2008, pp. 48–9.
3. Jonathan Petropoulos, *Royals and the Reich: The Princes von Hessen in Nazi Germany*. Oxford (Oxford University Press) 2006, p. 5.
4. Kuiper et al., p. 25.
5. The culprits were Colonel Jack Durant and Captain Kathleen Nash. Durant received the most severe punishment, and was sentenced to fifteen years' hard labour in 1947. The fascinating reports of the investigations highlight the Americans' skepticism regarding the rightful property of the house of Hesse—especially the interviews with Princess Sophia (Karl von Hessen's mother), who had to prove that her family owned the jewels.
6. Richard Dyer, *Stars*. London (British Film Institute) 1979.
7. The *Niederösterreichischer Grenzbote* (12–10–1947, p. 1) offers an enthusiastic report of the impression left by Finstergrün on the young girl scouts.
8. Petropoulos, p. 3.
9. Rössler, 2008.
10. Author conversation with Baroness Clara de Vos van Steenwijk, 13 November 2019.
11. Palmetshofer & Eichinger, pp. 32–3.
12. Alexander von Schönburg, *Die Kunst des stilvollen Verarmens*. Hamburg (Rowohlt) 2006.

NOTES

pp. [203–212]

AFTERWORD

1. Wim Kayzer, *Nauwgezet en wanhopig* [Meticulous and Desperate]. *VPRO televisievertelling in 4 delen. 1989 (2 April, 9 April, 16 April, 23 April).* Transcription of interviews, Part 4, p. 14.
2. Musil, p. 427.
3. It would seem that the Polish have recently rediscovered Silesia's ruined palaces as a part of their cultural heritage. A large number of recent videos have been circulating on YouTube in recent years, made by passionate amateurs and semi-professionals using drone footage to create nostalgic, occasionally magnificent 3D reconstructions of the palaces built by the Henckel von Donnersmarcks, such as Siemianowicz, Krowiarki, Brynek, Neudeck and Neues Neudeck. These videos also show that family members are welcomed as royalty whenever they visit for events on their former estates.
4. Sebastian Wienert, *100 Jahre Fürst Donnersmarck-stiftung 1916–2016.* Berlin (FDST) 2016, p. 45.
5. Fold3 archive, Ardelia Hall Collection, Correspondence Göring.

SOURCES AND FURTHER READING

Archive

Dutch National Archives, The Hague
Fürst-Donnersmarck Foundation, Berlin
National Library of Austria, Vienna
Salzburg Provincial Archives, Salzburg

Online archive

Austrian National Library, ANNO Historische Zeitungen und Zeitschriften (Austrian Newspaper Online: Historical Newspapers & Magazines): www.anno.onb.ac.at
Fold3 international database of military records, Ardelia Hall Collection: www.Fold3.com
German Centre for Losses of Cultural Property (Deutches Zentrum Kulturgutverluste), Lost Art-Datenbank: www.lostart.de
Royal Library of the Netherlands (Koninklijke Bibliotheek), *Delpher* database of media publications: www.delpher.nl

Documentary and dramatic film

Anonymous, *Goering visits small towns in Austria 1938*. Archive, United States Holocaust Memorial Museum.
Thomas Ballhausen, *Krieg der Bilder. Filmdokumente zur Habsburger Monarchie im Ersten Weltkrieg*. DVD 2. Film Archive Austria (2004).
Paul Breuls, *The Hessen Conspiracy*. Corsan (2009).
Marie-Pierre Camus & Gérard Puechmorel, *Durch Mord zur absoluten Macht. Hitler dezimiert die SA*. Arte F (2020).
Kai Christiansen, *Der gute Göring*. ARD/Arte (2016).
George Clooney, *The Monuments Men*. Columbia Pictures/Fox 2000 Pictures/Smokehouse Pictures (2014).

SOURCES AND FURTHER READING

Florian Henckel von Donnersmarck, *Werk ohne Autor*. Walt Disney Pictures (2018).

Ernst Marischka, *Sissi* trilogy, Beta Film (1955–7).

Martin Scorsese, *The Age of Innocence*. Columbia Pictures (1993).

Books, chapters, articles and transcripts

Fabrice d'Almeida, *High Society in the Third Reich*. London (Polity) 2008 [Paris (Perrin) 2006].

Götz Aly & Michael Sontheimer, *How Julius Fromm's Condom Empire Fell to the Nazis*. New York (Other Press) 2009.

Benedict Anderson, *Verbeelde gemeenschappen/Imagined Communities*, Amsterdam (Jan Mets) 1995 [New York (Ithaca) 1983/1991].

Norman Angell, *The Great Illusion*. New York (Cosimo) 2007 [1909].

——, *Peace with the dictators? A Symposium and Some Conclusions*. London (Hamish Hamilton) 1938.

Dolores Augustine, *Patricians & Parvenus. Wealth and High Society in Wilhelmine Germany*. Oxford (Berg) 1994.

Reinier Baarsen, *Duitse meubelen/German furniture*. Amsterdam/Zwolle (Rijksmuseum Amsterdam/Waanders) 1998.

Richard Barkeley, *The Road to Mayerling: Life and Death of Crown Prince Rudolph of Austria*. London (Macmillan) 1958.

Julian Barnes, *The Man in the Red Coat*. London (Jonathan Cape) 2019.

Roland Barthes, *Mythologieën*. Amsterdam (De Arbeiderspers) 1975 [1957].

Heinrich Benedikt, *Damals im alten Osterreich*. Vienna (Amalthea) 1979.

Horst Bienek, *Birken und Hochöfen. Eine Kindheit in Oberschlesien*. Berlin (Corso bei Siedler) 1990.

Christian Blinzer, *Unermüdlich tätig zum Wohle der Anderen. Sozialfürsorgliches und politisches Handeln von Margit Gräfin Szapáry (1871–1943)*. Doctoral dissertation (unpublished), Karl Franzens University of Graz, 2009.

Christian Blinzer (ed.), *Unentwegt, bewegt. Margit Gräfin Szapáry (1871–1943)*. Tamsweg (W. Pfeifenberg) 2008, 2nd edn. Exhibition catalogue, 2007.

Tim Bouverie, *Appeasement: Chamberlain, Hitler, Churchill and the Road to War*. London (Penguin Random House) 2019.

Beatriz Colomina, *Privacy and Publicity: Modern Architecture and Mass Media*. London/Cambridge, MA (MIT Press) 1996.

236

SOURCES AND FURTHER READING

M. Czaja, *Der industrielle Aufstieg der Beuthen-Siemianowitzer und Tar nowitz-Neudecker Linie der Henckel von Donnersmarck bis zum Weltkrieg*. Dissertation (unpublished), Ludwig Maximilian University of Munich, 1936.

György Dalos, *Ungarn in der Nussschale. Ein Jahrtausend und zwanzig Jahre*. Munich (Beck) 2004.

Alfred Döblin, *Reise in Polen*. Olten (Walter) 1968 [Olten (Fischer) 1926].

Richard Dyer, *Stars*. London (British Film Institute) 1979.

Richard J. Evans, *The Pursuit of Power: Europe 1815–1914*. London (Allen Lane) 2016.

Orlando Figes, *The Europeans: Three Lives and the Making of a Cosmopolitan Culture*. London (Allen Lane) 2019.

W. Fock, 'Part 8, Furniture until 1900' in: *De verzamelingen van het Centraal Museum Utrecht*. Utrecht (Central Museum) 2005.

Claudia Fräss-Ehrfeld, *Kärnten und Böhmen, Mähren, Schlesien*. Klagen furt (Geschichtsverein Landesmuseum Kärnten) 2004.

Arno Geiger, *Onder de Drachenwand*. Amsterdam (De Bezige Bij) 2018 [Munich (Carl Hanser) 2018].

William D. Godsey, *Aristocratic Redoubt: The Austro-Hungarian Office on the Eve of the First World War*. West Lafayette, IN (Purdue University Press) 1999.

Maria Godyn (ed.), *Colour, Culture, Science*. Krakow (Jan Matejko Academy of Fine Arts) 2018.

K., A. & J. Heitzmann (eds), *Tamsweg. Die Geschichte eines Marktes und seiner Landgemeinden*. Tamsweg (Pfeifenberg) 2008.

E.J. Hobsbawm, *The Age of Capital, 1848–1875*. New York (Scribner) 1975.

Isabel Hull, *The Entourage of Kaiser Wilhelm II, 1888–1918*. Cambridge (Cambridge University Press) 1982.

Marion Kaplan, *The Marriage Bargain: Women and Dowries in European History*. New York (Haworth Press) 1985.

Wim Kayzer, *Nauwgezet en wanhopig. VPRO televisievertelling in 4 delen. 1989 (2 April, 9 April, 16 April, 23 April)*. (Transcription of spoken texts, part 4), Hilversum (VPRO) 1989.

François Kersaudy, *Hermann Göring. Le deuxième homme du IIIe Reich*. Paris (Perrin) 2013 [2009].

Ian Kershaw, *To Hell and Back: Europe 1914–1949*. Houten (Spectrum) [London (Penguin)] 2015.

SOURCES AND FURTHER READING

Elisabeth Kinsky-Wilczek, *Hans Wilczek erzählt seinen Enkeln Erinnerungen aus seinem Leben*. Graz (Leykam) 1933.

Volker Knopf & Stefan Martens, *Görings Reich. Selbstinszenierungen in Carinhall*. Berlin (Ch. Links) 2019 [1999].

János Köbányal, *Agnes Heller. Het levensverhaal van de Hongaars-Joodse filosofe*. Amsterdam (Boom) 2002 [Budapest, 1998].

H. Kreisel & G. Himmelheber, *Die Kunst des deutschen Möbels*, vol. 1. Munich (Beck) 1973.

Monika Kubrova, 'Vom guten Leben. Adelige Frauen im 19. Jahrhundert' in: Heinz Reif (ed.), *Elitenwandel in der Moderne*, vol. 12. Berlin (Akademie) 2011.

Yme Kuiper, Nikolaj Bijleveld & Jaap Dronkers (eds), *Nobilities in Europe in the Twentieth Century: Reconversion Strategies, Memory Culture and Elite Formation*. Leuven (Peeters) 2015.

Ella Leffland, *The Knight, Death and the Devil*. New York (William Morrow) 1990.

Les archives diplomatiques & Jean-Marc Dreyfus, *Le catalogue Goering*. Paris (Flammarion) 2015.

Judith Listowel, *A Habsburg Tragedy: Crown Prince Rudolf*. London (Ascent), 1978.

Adolf Loos, *Sämtliche Schriften*, vol. 1. Vienna (Glück) 1962.

Laurin Luchner, *Schlösser in Österreich. Zweiter Band*. Munich (Beck) 1983.

Stephan Malinowski, *Vom König zum Führer*. Frankfurt (Fischer) 2004 [2003].

Roger Manvell & Heinrich Fraenkel, *Goering*. London (Greenhill) 2005 [1962].

Sándor Márai, *Gloed*. Amsterdam (Wereldbibliotheek) 2002 [1942].

Sándor Márai. *Journal. Les années hongroises 1943–1948*. Paris (Albin Michel) 2019 [*A teljes Napló*, 1943–1948, Budapest Helikon Kiadó].

Sean McMeekin, *The Berlin–Baghdad Express: The Ottoman Empire and Germany's Bid for World Power*. Cambridge, MA (Harvard University Press) 2010.

Pauline Metternich, *Erinnerungen*. Vienna (Cark Uberreuter) 1988.

Robert Musil, *De man zonder eigenschappen*. Amsterdam (Meulenhoff) 1996 [Hamburg (Rowohlt) 1970 (1930–52)].

Odile Nouvel-Kammerer (ed.), *L'Extraordinaire Hôtel Païva*, Paris (Les Arts décoratifs) 2015.

Richard Overy, *Goering*. London (Phoenix) 2000 [1984].

SOURCES AND FURTHER READING

Jonathan Petropoulos, *Royals and the Reich: The Princes von Hessen in Nazi Germany*. Oxford (Oxford University Press) 2006.

Eva Philippoff (ed.), *Die Doppelmonarchie Österreich-Ungarn. Ein politi sches Lesebuch (1867–1918)/L'Autriche-Hongrie. Politique et culture à travers les textes (1867–1918)*. Villeneuve d'Ascq (Presses universitaires du Septentrion) 2002.

Martyn Rady, *The Habsburgs: The Rise and Fall of a World Power*. London (Allen Lane) 2020.

M. Rasch, *Der Unternehmer Guido Henckel von Donnersmarck. Eine Skizze*. Essen (Klartext) 2016.

Jan Romein, *Op het breukvlak van twee eeuwen*. Amsterdam (Querido) 1976.

Joseph Roth, *On the End of the World*. London (Pushkin) 2019.

P. Rother, *Chronik der Stadt Königshütte Oberschlesien*. Munich (Laumann) 1994.

Virginia Rounding, *Grandes Horizontales: The Lives and Legends of Marie Duplessis, Cora Pearl, La Païva and La Présidente*. London (Blooms bury) 2003.

Hans Dieter Rutsch, *Das Preussische Arkadien*. Hamburg (Rowohlt) 2014.

Felix Salten, *Bambi. Een levensgeschiedenis uit het bos*. Leusden (ISVW) 2014 [Vienna 1923].

Philippe Sands, *East West Street*. London (Weidenfeld & Nicolson) 2017.

Alexander von Schönburg, *Die Kunst des stilvollen Verarmens*. Hamburg (Rowohlt) 2006.

Merlijn Schooneboom, *Een kleine geschiedenis van de grootste Duitse worstel-ing*. Amsterdam (Querido) 2019.

Peter Sloterdijk, *Je moet je leven veranderen*. Amsterdam (Boom) 2011 [Frankfurt 2009].

Laura Starink, *Duitse Wortels. Mijn familie, de oorlog en Silezië*. Amsterdam (August) 2013.

Jonathan Steinberg, *Bismarck: A Life*. New York (Oxford University Press) 2011.

Josef Steiner-Wischenbart, *Burg Finstergrün im Lungau*. Graz (Paul Cies lar) 2011.

Tatjana Tönsmeyer & Lubos Velek (eds), 'Adel und Politik in der Habsburgermonarchie und den Nachbarländern zwischen Absolutismus und Demokratie' in: *Studien zum Mitteleuropäischen Adel. Vol. 3. Adel und Politik*. Munich (Meidenbauer) 2011.

Karina Urbach, *Go-Betweens for Hitler*. Oxford (Oxford University Press) 2015.

SOURCES AND FURTHER READING

Edmund de Waal, *The Hare with Amber Eyes*. London (Vintage) 2010.

Nora Watteck, 'Gräfin Margit Szapáry. Ein Lebensbild' in: *Mitteilungen der Gesellschaft für Salzburger Landeskunde* vol. 119 (1979), pp. 261–79.

Arnout Weeda, *Het mysterie van Wenen*. Amsterdam (Bezige Bij) 2011.

Sebastian Wienert, *100 Jahre Fürst Donnersmarck-Stiftung 1916–2016*. Berlin (FDST) 2016.

Alison Wilson, *Changing Women's Lives: A Biography of Dame Rosemary Murray*. London (Unicorn) 2014.

LIST OF ILLUSTRATIONS

SLA = Salzburg Provincial Archives (Salzburg Landesarchiv), Countess Margit Szapáry estate papers.

1. Countess Margarethe Henckel von Donnersmarck, 1899. Courtesy of the SLA.

2. Margarethe's parents, Count Hugo II and Wanda. Public domain / Wikimedia Commons.

3. Brynek Palace, as rebuilt by Hugo II. Photo by Autostopowicz / CC BY-SA 3.0 PL https://creativecommons.org/licenses/by-sa/3.0/pl/deed.en / Wikimedia Commons.

4. Sándor Szapáry, painted by Margit. Public domain / source unknown.

5. 'Uncle' Guido Henckel von Donnersmarck at Neues Neudeck. Courtesy of the SLA.

6. Room at Finstergrün Castle, painted by Margit. Courtesy of the SLA.

7. Margit's identity card, c. 1910. Courtesy of the SLA.

8. Margit with friends, 1920s. Courtesy of the de Vos van Steenwijk family.

9. Interior at Finstergrün Castle, 1920s. Courtesy of the SLA.

10. Blanche, La Païva. Public domain / CC BY-SA 4.0 https://creativecommons.org/licenses/by-sa/4.0/ / Wikimedia Commons.

11. La Païva's ornate bed. Courtesy of Sotheby's. Lot 22, Sale *Erotic: Passion & Desire* (2017). © Sotheby's Image Archive.

12. Hermann Göring, 1917. Public domain / Staatliche Landesbildstelle (State Media Centre), Hamburg.

LIST OF ILLUSTRATIONS

13. Göring telegram to Margit, 1938. Courtesy of the de Vos van Steenwijk family.

14. Wedding of Yvonne Szapáry and Karl of Hesse. Public domain / Dutch National Archives, Anefo collection, CCo, 2.24.01. 05, 919–0449.

15. Margit's four-poster bed. Courtesy of Burghausen Castle.

Photos of Finstergrün in the text © Pauline Terreehorst.

LIST OF NAMES

Royals are listed by their given name; nobles are listed by their surname.

Alice, Princess of Greece and Denmark (born Princess von Battenberg), 188, 189, 195
Anne-Marie, Queen of Greece (born Princess of Denmark), 189
Angell, Norman, 151–2
Anna, Princess of Sayn-Wittgenstein-Sayn, 124
Atzél von Borosjenö, Gabrielle *see* Szapáry, Gabrielle

Bartók, Béla, 84
Baudry, Paul, 70–71
Beatrix, Queen of the Netherlands, 187–90
Benedikte zu Sayn Wittgenstein-Berleburg (born Princess of Denmark), 188–9
Berlage, Hendrik, 73, 75
Bienek, Horst, 54
Bismarck, Otto von, 14
Blinzer, Christian, 8, 199
Blome, Carola, 114–15
Böhler, Julius, 164
Bouverie, Tim, 140

Bruckner, Anton, 8
Buber, Martin, 205

Camilla, Queen Consort of the United Kingdom, 200
Carnegie, Andrew, 87
Catt, Carrie Chapman, 111
Cézanne, Paul, 171
Chamberlain, Austen, 118
Chamberlain, Joseph, 153
Chamberlain, Neville, 118, 151, 152, 154
Charles III, King of the United Kingdom, 200
Clark, Christopher, 86
Clemenceau, Georges, 89
Clonfero, Wilhelm, 78
Constantine II, King of Greece, 189–90
Courbet, Gustave, 171
Curie, Marie (born Sklodowska), 47

d'Almeida, Fabrice, 170, 190
Dante Alighieri, 69
de Goncourt, *see* Goncourt
de Heem, Cornelis, 163
de Montesquieu, Charles, *see* Montesquieu
de Rothschild, James, 69

243

LIST OF NAMES

de Vos van Steenwijk family
　de Vos van Steenwijk, Clara
　　(née van Pallandt), 183, 199
　de Vos van Steenwijk, Godert
　　Willem Senior, 125, 181,
　　188, 189, 198
　de Vos van Steenwijk, Godert
　　Willem Junior, 125, 183,
　　197
　de Vos van Steenwijk, Ursula,
　　see Szapáry, Ursula
Delacroix, Eugene, 67
Derby, Edward Stanley, 14th
　Earl, 42, 67, 210
Disney, Walt, 24
Ditfurth, Nuisella, 114
Döblin, Alfred, 57
Dollfuss, Engelbert, 128, 130,
　141, 153
du Cane, Isabel, 133, 135, 137,
　141, 150
Dumas, Alexandre, 41–2, 67

Edward VIII, King of the United
　Kingdom, 140
Eisenhower, Dwight, 197
Elisabeth (Sisi), Empress of
　Austria, Queen of Hungary
　(born Princess of Bavaria), 11,
　82, 88, 194, 212
Elizabeth II, Queen of the United
　Kingdom, 188, 200
Emmanuel III, King of Italy, 196
Epenstein, Elisabeth (Lilli) (born
　Schandrovich Edle von
　Kriegstreu), 105, 142, 148,
　154, 174, 176, 183
Epenstein, Hermann (later
　Epenstein Ritter von

Mauternburg), 100, 103–8,
　144, 147, 167–70, 171
Ephrussi, Charles, 173

Farnsworth, Edith, 79
Fischer, Hedwig, 43
Flaubert, Gustave, 67
Fokker, Anthony, 105
Fontane, Theodor, 50
Fox, John, 72
Franz Ferdinand, Crown Prince
　of Austria, 28, 85, 88, 91
Franz Joseph I, Emperor-King of
　Austria-Hungary, 6, 11, 22, 28,
　82, 142–3, 151
　death (1916), 89, 96
　dual monarchy, 84, 87, 143
　Epenstein, knighting of
　　(1908), 100, 103
　Finstergrün statue, 142
　furniture, 57
　horse guard, 15
　Lueger, relationship with, 88
　sixtieth anniversary (1908), 62
Frederick the Great, King of
　Prussia, 50–52, 105, 139, 152
Freud, Sigmund, 12, 17, 75, 87
Friedländer-Fuld, Milly, 43
Friedrich, Caspar David, 49–50,
　62
Friedrich III, Kaiser of Germany,
　188
Friedrich Leopold, Prince of
　Prussia, 164
Fromm, Julius, 175–7, 183
Fürstenberg, Aniela, 43

Gambetta, Leon, 71

LIST OF NAMES

Gandhi, M.K. (Mahatma), 117
Garzarolli-Thurnlackh, Karl, 156
Gautier, Théophile, 67
Gerbeaud, Emile, 12
Glöckl, Otto, 128
Goncourt, Edmond de, 67, 71
Goncourt, Jules de, 67, 71
Göring, Carin (formerly von
    Kantzow, née Fock), 106–7,
    121–6, 147, 148, 195
Göring, Edda, 154, 169, 182
Göring, Emmy (née Sonnemann),
    154, 171, 182, 195
Göring, Franziska (Fanny), 103
Göring, Heinrich, 103–4
Göring, Hermann, 8, 100–108,
    121–6, 147–57, 159, 161, 182,
    183, 195–7
    Beer Hall Putsch (1923),
        121–2
    Carinhall, 126, 148, 154, 156,
        164, 167–74, 195, 211–12
    Finstergrün, expropriation of,
        8, 144–5, 147–57, 168, 174,
        179, 197, 198
    Fromm's, expropriation of, 176
    Mauterndorf, ownership of,
        182, 183
    stolen art, acquisition of, 164–
        6, 173–4, 182
Grabowski, K., 189
Grandauer, Karl, 164

Helbing, Hugo, 159
Henckel von Donnersmarck
    family, 13–15, 26, 31, 34, 37,
    39–48, 57, 79, 94, 136, 166,
    186, 208–11

Artur, 44, 207
Blanche (née Lachmann), 40,
    42, 45–6, 54, 66–73, 124
Edgar, 33, 45, 80, 136, 156,
    207
Florian, 14
Guido, 14, 39–48, 53–4, 66–
    73, 124, 206
Guidotto, 94, 124–5, 136,
    162, 211
Hugo I, 14–15, 17, 30, 44, 47,
    53–4, 58, 60, 95, 98, 156,
    186, 206, 209–11
Hugo II, 14, 30, 44, 136, 156,
    206, 207
Hugo III, 33, 45, 136
Irmgard, 33, 133, 136
Johan, 207
Karl, 156, 207
Karolina, 208–9
Katharina (née von Slepzow),
    42
Kraft, 42, 124
Lazarus I, 14
Lazarus IV, 44, 207
Margarethe, *see* Szapáry,
    Margit
Sara, 33, 34, 37, 45, 133, 136
Wanda (née von Gaschin von
    und zu Rosenberg), 31, 32
Henderson, Neville, 154, 172
Hermine, Kaiserin of Germany
    (born Princess Hermine Reuss
    of Greiz), 125
Hermsen, Dorus, 164
Herz, Henri, 42, 66, 68
Hess, Rudolf, 107
Hesse, House of

245

LIST OF NAMES

von Hessen-Kassel, Christoph, 104, 191, 195
von Hessen-Kassel, Karl, 187–90, 192–3, 195, 197
von Hessen-Kassel, Philipp, 104, 195
von Hessen-Kassel, Sophia (born Princess of Greece and Denmark), 188, 191, 195
von Hessen-Kassel, Yvonne (née Szapáry), 181, 183, 185, 186, 187–201
Hitler, Adolf, 9, 88, 107, 116, 119, 121–6, 128, 140–41, 147–8, 152, 156, 191
  Anschluss (1938), 143–4, 149–50
  art collection, 160, 164, 165, 173
  Beer Hall Putsch (1923), 107, 121–3
  chancellorship, accession to (1933), 119, 121–6, 159, 176, 208
  Czechoslovakia annexation (1939), 154
  Mein Kampf (1925), 123, 152
  Prinzenerlass decree (1940), 195–6
Hobsbawm, Eric John, 61, 62
Hofer, Walter Andreas, 174
Hoffmannsthal, Hugo von, 134
Holzinger, Simon, 77, 79, 94
Hopp, Meike, 160
Horthy, Miklós, 180
Huygens, Stan, 187–8, 190

Jacobs, Aletta, 110

Jordaens, Jacob, 163
Joyce, James, 13
Juan Carlos, King of Spain, 189
Jud, Anna, 95

Karl I, Emperor-King of Austria-Hungary, 89, 96, 127
Kawakubo Rei (of Comme des Garçons), 4
Kodály, Zoltán, 84
Kokoschka, Oskar, 114
Kraus, Karl, 17, 87
Kreisel, Heinrich, 164–5
Kröller-Müller, Helene, 79
Krupp von Bohlen und Halbach, Bertha, 39
Kubrova, Monika, 34, 46

La Païva, *see* Henckel von Donnersmarck, Blanche
Lachmann, Pauline Thérèse (Esther Blanche), *see* Henckel von Donnersmarck, Blanche
Lackner, Johann, 113
Lagarde, Christine, 210
Leffland, Elle, 168, 170
Lefuel, Hector, 39, 72
Lenin, Vladimir, 12, 77
Leyster, Judith, 163
Limberger, Gisela, 155
Liszt, Frans, 66
Lohse, Bruno, 174
Ludwig II, King of Bavaria, 165, 212
Ludwig III, King of Bavaria, 39
Lueger, Karl, 88

Mafalda, Princess of Italy, 196

246

LIST OF NAMES

Mahler, Gustav, 8, 13, 17
Manet, Édouard, 71
Manguin, Pierre, 66, 68, 69
Marie-Antoinette, Queen of France (born Princess of Austria), 169
Marie Christine, Princess Michael of Kent (née von Reibnitz), 15
McGill, John, 179
Meurent, Victorine, 71
Michael of Kent, Princess, *see* Marie Christine
Miedl, Alois, 174
Mies van der Rohe, Ludwig, 79
Miyake, Issey, 4
Moleschott, Jacob, 40
Monet, Claude, 171
Montesquieu, Charles de, 203
Morny, Comte de, 53
Mosselman, Alfred, 53
Mozart, Wolfgang Amadeus, 134, 142
Murray, Rosemary, 141
Musil, Robert, 143, 203
Mussolini, Benito, 107, 122–3, 155, 196

Nicholas II, Tsar of Russia, 87
Nobel, Alfred, 87

Otto, Crown Prince of Austria, 127, 131

Païva, Marquis Albino de Araujo, 42, 67
Pallavicini family, 180
Perko, Manfred, 204
Petropoulos, Jonathan, 190

Pius XI, Pope, 128
Philip, Duke of Edinburgh (born Prince of Greece and Denmark), 188, 195
Phipps, Eric, 172
Polgar, Alfred, 143

Ramek, Rudolf, 113
Rasch, Manfred, 42
Raubal, Geli, 126
Reed, Carol, 184
Reinhardt, Max, 134
Reinhold, Friedrich Philipp, 62
Reinitz, Maximilian, 114
Richthofen, Manfred von, 105
Riegele, Olga (née Göring), 155
Rousseau, Jean-Jacques, 16
Röhm, Ernst, 107
Roselius, Ludwig, 164
Roth, Joseph, 143–4
Rothschild family, 69, 119, 164, 173
Rudolf, Crown Prince of Austria, 11, 24, 27–8, 88, 97
Rudolf II, Holy Roman Emperor, Archduke of Austria & King of Hungary, 14
Ruskin, John, 79
Rutsch, Hans Dieter, 49

Sabatier, Apollonie, 53
Sainte-Beuve, Charles-Augustin, 67
Salten, Felix, 24, 28, 129
Salvator, Joseph Ferdinand, 142
Scheffel, Hans, 115
Schnitzler, Arthur, 17, 87
Schubert, Franz, 142

LIST OF NAMES

Schulz, Josef, 114
Schuschnigg, Kurt, 130–31, 140, 143–4, 153, 173
Schwarzenberg family, 63, 83, 184
Schwarzenberg, Eleonore, 7
Seyss-Inquart, Arthur, 143–4
Simon, Ludwig, 28, 30, 58, 66, 73
Sisi *see* Elisabeth (Sisi)
Sisley, Alfred, 171
Sloterdijk, Peter, 10
Sophia, Queen of Spain (born Princess of Greece and Denmark), 188–9
Steiner, George, 203
Strauss, Richard, 134
Stresemann, Gustav, 118
Szapáry de Muraszombath, Széchysziget and Szapár family, 8–9
Szapáry, Béla Jr
  birth (1901), 58
  Canada, life in, 7, 97, 136, 180, 182
  Christmas (1930), 133
  death (1993), 198
  education, 97
  finances, 136, 157
  Finstergrün, sale of (1972), 197–8
  Göriach, move to (c. 1966), 197
  Hungarian nationality, 81–2, 86, 99, 138
  inheritance, 161
  Netherlands, move to (1950), 185–6

Second World War (1939–45), 179–81
  war memorial construction (1949), 185
  Yvonne's wedding (1966), 188
Szapáry, Béla Sr, 16
Szapáry, Gabrielle (née Atzél von Borosjenö), 16, 81
Szapáry, Jolanta, 5, 7–8, 10, 58
  birth (1902), 58
  Christmas (1930), 133
  death (1987), 182, 198
  education, 93, 96–7, 117–18, 133, 136
  Finstergrün, sale of (1972), 197–8
  Göring, relationship with, 147, 161
  inheritance, 161
  MPO membership, 131
  Netherlands, move to (1950), 185
  nursing career, 97, 117–18, 133, 136–7, 157, 179
  postcard albums, 86, 118, 130, 154
  Schuschnigg's letter (1942), 144
  Second World War (1939–45), 179, 181–2
  war memorial construction (1949), 185
Szapáry, Margit (née Henckel von Donnersmarck), 6, 8–9, 12, 36, 183–4
  Anschluss (1938), 150–52
  auction of property (1941), 156–7, 159–66, 198

248

LIST OF NAMES

children, raising of, 81–2
conservatism, 76–7, 81, 87, 127
Countess of Lungau, 8, 9, 60, 108, 149, 169
CWO membership, 81, 109–16
death (1943), 181
education, 36, 47
family tree, 13–15, 46, 86
finances, 34, 36, 47, 59–60, 80, 91, 95–6, 112, 119, 133, 136–7, 155
Finstergrün renovation, 21–30, 57–64, 65–6, 73–80, 81, 94, 111, 167, 195
First World War (1914–18), 86, 88, 91–7, 108–9
Göring, relationship with, 8, 144–5, 147–57, 168, 169–70, 173, 174, 179, 197, 198
guests, hosting of, 133–7
Habsburg identity, 64, 82, 87, 89, 96, 126–7, 131, 139
health problems, 96, 142, 151
Hungarian nationalism, views on, 82, 89, 96
marriage proposals, 37, 46
mother, relationship with, 31–3
Nazism, views on, 126–7, 137–45, 153, 197
Order of Elisabeth, 82, 96
Order of the Starry Cross, 96
philanthropy, 60, 63–4, 91–100, 108–14
religious views, 77, 81, 109–16
Sándor, death of (1904), 59, 62, 65, 77, 150

Sándor, marriage to, 13, 16, 25, 26, 33–4, 37, 45, 46–7, 57, 59, 161
Schuschnigg's visit (1937), 130, 140, 153, 173
Szapáry, Péter, 16, 82
Szapáry, Sándor, 12, 13, 15–17
death (1904), 59, 62, 65, 77, 150
Finstergrün renovation, 21–30, 57–62, 66, 167
Hungarian nationalism, 81–2
hunting, 17, 19, 21–3, 24, 25, 27–9, 58, 201, 205
Knight of Finstergrün portrait, 76
Margit, marriage to, 13, 16, 25, 26, 33–4, 37, 45, 46–7, 57, 59, 161, 206
Szapáry, Ursula (née von Richthofen), 125, 181, 185, 188, 197, 198
Szapáry, Yvonne (Pinky), *see* von Hessen-Kassel, Yvonne

Taine, Hippolyte, 67

Urbach, Karina, 190–91

van Pallandt, Clara, *see* de Vos van Steenwijk, Clara
van Riel, Harm, 189
Voltaire, 50
von Amsberg, Claus, Prince of the Netherlands, 187–90
von Aretin, Erwein, 164
von Behr, Kurt, 174
von Bismarck, Otto *see* Bismarck

249

LIST OF NAMES

von Buddenbrock, Marianne, 98
von Dirksen, Viktoria, 125
von Hoffmannsthal, Hugo *see*
  Hoffmannsthal, Hugo
von Kageneck, Clemens, 208–9
von Kantzow, Carin, *see* Göring,
  Carin
von Kantzow, Nils, 106
von Reden, Friedrich, 51–2
von Richthofen, Manfred, *see*
  Richthofen, Manfred
von Richthofen, Ursula, *see*
  Szapáry, Ursula
von Richthofen, Wally, 125, 181
von Rosen, Carl, 106
von Schönburg-Glauchau,
  Alexander, 200
von Schönburg-Glauchau, Irina
  (née von Hessen-Kassel), 200
von Suttner, Bertha (née von
  Kinsky), 86–7, 112
von Tiechler, Max Mann, 76
von Weizsäcker, Richard, 55
von Wenzel, Adolf, 61
von Werner, Anton, 61
von Wilamowitz-Moellendorff,
  Fanny, 106

Wagner, Otto, 73, 75
Wagner, Richard, 66
Watteck, Nora, 75, 91
Weinmüller, Adolf, 159–64, 198,
  212

Welles, Orson, 184
Wilczek, Hans, Lord of
  Moosham, 22–4, 162, 167–8
  Festakademie (1936), 142
  Finstergrün renovation and,
    26–30, 58, 74, 76–7, 88,
    134, 162
  Kreuzenstein, 23, 24, 74, 76,
    88, 103, 162
  Mauterndorf renovation and,
    168
  Moosham Castle, 23–4, 27–9,
    58, 100, 103, 107, 142, 167,
    207
  World War I (1914–18), 94,
    97
Wilhelm I, Kaiser of Germany,
  27, 71
Wilhelm II, Kaiser of Germany,
  6, 35, 43, 80, 191
Wilhelmina, Queen of the
  Netherlands, 87
Wilm, Hubert, 163
Winkelhofer, Martina, 34, 46
Wittelsbach family, 212

Yamamoto Yohji, 4

Zinckgraf, Friedrich, 164
Zingg, Adrian, 62
Zita of Bourbon-Parma, Empress-
  Queen of Austria-Hungary, 89,
  127, 131

INDEX

Abbazia, 11–12, 16, 34, 37, 45, 59, 80, 137, 150, 206

Alsace, 71

Amsterdam, 3, 5, 9, 155, 170, 174, 183, 187, 189, 192, 198, 199

Anschluss (1938), 143–4, 149–50, 151, 152, 160, 163, 173, 180, 185

antisemitism, *see* Jews

appeasement, 140, 151, 154

architecture
  Bauhaus, 79, 129
  eclectic, 57, 78–9
  French, 61
  Germanic, 170
  Gothic & Neo-Gothic, 7, 30
  mediaeval, 7, 29, 57, 62, 73, 77, 165, 167
  Napoleon III, 62
  quasi-Renaissance, 78
  Renaissance, 122
  Tudor, 61

Arlington House (London), 73

Arrow Cross Party of Hungary, 180

Aryanisation, 155, 159–60, 163, 173–6

Auschwitz, 56, 206

Austria, 60
  Allied occupation (1945–55), 181, 184–5, 196–7
  Anschluss (1938), 143–4, 149–50, 151, 152, 160, 163, 173, 180, 185
  corporatist state (1934–8), 127–31, 135, 137–44, 151, 155, 180
  dual monarchy (1867–1918), 11, 16, 82–5
  First Republic (1919–34), 113, 116–17, 118–19, 122, 127–8
  First World War (1914–18), *see* First World War
  influenza pandemic (1918–20), 109
  nationalism, 81, 141, 153
  nobility, *see* nobility
  Ostmark (1938–45), 144, 163
  Prussian War (1866), 23, 84, 138
  Second World War (1939–45), *see* Second World War
  women's suffrage (1918), 110

Austrofascism, 127

Austro-Prussian War (1866), 23, 84, 138

INDEX

Bambi (Salten), 24, 28, 129
Beuthen (Bytom), 14–15
Beer Hall Putsch (1923), 107, 121–3
Belgium, 32, 52, 53, 131, 193
Berlin
  Battle of Berlin (1945), 55, 209
  Fromm in, 174–6
  Görings in, 103–4, 107, 123–5, 148, 154, 155, 195
  Guido in, 39, 42–3, 54
  Wall, fall of (1989), 83
Blücher Palace, 42–3, 209
Blühnbach Castle, 28, 136
Bloomsbury Group, 65
bourgeoisie, 43, 111, 163, 175
Budapest, 84, 110, 157, 179–81, 185
Bolshevism, 97, 112, 140
Bratislava *see* Pressburg
Breslau, 33, 45, 47, 50, 176
Brynek Palace, 30, 44–6, 61–2, 80, 136, 156–7, 206–9
Burghausen Castle, 212, 216

Canada, 7, 97, 136, 180, 182–3
Carinhall, 126, 148, 154, 156, 164, 167–74, 195, 211–12
Catholicism, 95–6, 99, 104, 116, 117
  associations, 111, 142
  Catholic Women's Organisation (CWO), 81, 109–10, 115, 116, 129–31
  Jewish people and, 104
  nobility and, 14, 39, 42, 46, 47, 50, 95–6, 139, 140, 180, 184, 203

Order of the Starry Cross, 96
  Protestants, conflict with, 14, 39–40, 46, 47, 139
  socialism and, 111, 127–9
Celtic mysticism, 106
Champs-Élysées, 41, 66, 68, 70
Château Pontchartrain, 41, 68
Credit-Anstalt, 119, 173
Christian Socialist Party (CSP), 111–13, 122, 127–8, 153
corporatist state, 127–31, 135, 137, 139–40, 143, 151, 155, 180
cosmopolitanism, 17, 54, 128, 143, 168
Count Hugo Henckel Memorial race, 29
Czechoslovakia, 89, 138, 152, 154, 163, 207

diplomats, 25, 35, 44, 54, 103, 169, 172, 181, 183, 185
Drey art dealership, 134

Edelweiss Society of Sweden, 106, 126
Eulenburg Affair, *see* Liebenberg Circle
European identity, 153
Evangelical Youth Organisation, 197

Fatherland Front, 127–31, 140–42
Finstergrün Castle, 7–9, 17–19, 73–80
  auction of contents (1941), 156–7, 159–66, 198

252

INDEX

brochures, 65, 77, 205

dining room, 76

four-poster beds, 75, 87, 148–9

furnishings, 29, 74–5, 76, 81, 133–4, 147–9, 156–7, 159–66, 167

Göring and, 8, 144–5, 147–57, 168, 169–70, 173, 174, 179, 197, 198

guests, 114–15, 117, 130, 133–45, 182

heating, 93, 136

kitchen, 92

library, 87

Maria Elend altarpiece, 134

Nazi Party ownership (1942–5), 166, 179, 181, 207

ornamentation, lack of, 73–4

paying guests, 65, 133–45, 182

portraits in, 76

postwar years, 185, 194–200

religious objects, 76–7, 134

renovation, 21–30, 57–64, 65–6, 73–80, 81, 94, 195

Sabbionara frescoes, 76, 78, 137

sale of (1972), 197–8

Schuschnigg's visit (1937), 130, 140, 153, 173

sketches of, 36, 75, 78, 182

staff, 93, 114, 156

theft from, 114, 133–4

vistas, 73, 78

walls, 78

war memorial at, 185

First World War (1914–18), 6, 11, 55, 85–6, 88–9, 91–2, 96, 99, 166

causes, 25, 28, 71, 85, 138

Göring's service, 105, 107, 147, 171

Guido's philanthropy, 210

Margit's philanthropy, 91–7, 108–9

Fittleworth, 133

Fiume, 11, 12, 85

Fleur Blanche, La (Paris), 70

France, 3, 7, 15, 52, 53, 54

fashion in, 3, 67

First World War (1914–18), 105

interior design in, 61, 62

Locarno Pact (1925), 118

Prussian War (1870–71), 71–2, 84, 138, 210

Second World War (1939–45), 165, 211

Treaty of Versailles (1919), 89

Friedrichshof Castle, 188–9, 192–7, 200, 210

Frohnau (Berlin), 210–11

Fromm's Rubber Works, 175–7, 183

Fürst-Donnersmarck Foundation, 216

Germany

Allied occupation (1945–9), 108, 165, 182

colonialism, 72

East Germany (1949–90), 11, 174, 209

First World War (1914–18), 55, 85–6, 99, 105

253

INDEX

Franco-Prussian War (1870–71), 71–2, 84, 210
Locarno Pact (1925), 118
nationalism, 72, 81, 139, 141, 149, 171
Nazi period (1933–45), *see* Nazi Party
nobility, 34–5, 191, 195
Romantic movement (1797–1830), 50, 62
Silesia and, 49–50, 55
Second World War (1939–45), 55, 156, 165, 179, 180, 196, 206, 208–9
Treaty of Versailles (1919), 55, 89, 107, 112, 151
unification (1866–71), 54, 55, 72, 84
Weimar period (1918–33), 107, 118–19, 121–2
West Germany (1949–90), 174, 209
Ginori porcelain, 133, 136
Gleiwitz, 51, 66
gymnastics associations, 116–17

Habsburg monarchy, 11, 14, 17, 36, 47, 50, 87, 99, 127
aristocracy, 5, 16, 17, 23, 25–6, 87, 96, 130, 140, 203
dual monarchy, 11, 16, 82–5
First World War (1914–18), 85, 86, 88, 89
Order of Elisabeth, 63
Order of the Starry Cross, 96
religion in, 47, 139–40, 203
Hague, The, 87, 174, 185, 187, 189, 192, 211

Heimatschutz movement, 118
Heimwehr, 127
Hessian House Foundation, 210
Home Guard, *see* Heimwehr
Hotel Kronprinz (Merano), 150
Hotel Païva (Paris), 41, 66–73, 76, 79, 80, 209–10
Hungary, 11, 13, 82–5
dual monarchy (1867–1918), 11, 16, 82–5
First World War (1914–18), 11, 25, 85, 88, 89
Kingdom of Hungary (1920–46), 99, 138, 152, 179–80
nationalism, 82, 84, 85, 88, 89, 96, 99, 138, 180
nobility, 13, 15, 24, 83–4, 96
Second World War (1939–45), 179–80
hunting, 3–4, 7, 22, 25, 45, 77, 83, 201
artistic representations, 69
Béla, 197
commoners, 99
erotic symbolism of, 24–5
Franz Ferdinand, 28
Göring, 104, 106, 148, 154, 168–70, 172
Kaiser Wilhelm, 43
Margit, 91, 99
Nazism and, 170, 172
Sándor, 17, 19, 21–3, 24, 25, 27–9, 58
Wilczek, 22, 29, 77
Yvonne, 194–5

influenza pandemic (1918–20), 109

INDEX

interior styles
  Biedermeier, 57, 61, 175
  eclectic, 76
  Empire, 61
  Georgian, 61
  Germanic, 61
  Gothic, 7, 30, 77, 148, 168
  Louis XV, 61
  mediaeval, 74, 76, 78, 106,
    137, 204
  realism, 70
  South Tyrolean, 75, 150
  Swedish, 61
International Criminal Court,
  211
Italy, 3, 7, 18, 137, 152
  Fascist regime (1922–43),
    107, 122–3, 127, 138, 152,
    196
  First World War (1914–18),
    88, 92
  interior design and, 69, 74,
    76, 78, 122–3, 133, 137,
    162, 165
  nationalism, 84, 85
  Sabbionara Castle, 76, 78, 137
  Second World War (1939–
    45), 179, 190, 191

Jeu de Paume (Paris), 155
Jews, 41, 69, 85, 88, 103, 104,
  107, 121, 122, 124, 135, 143,
  171
  Aryanisation policy and, 155,
    159–60, 163, 173–6
  Catholic Church and, 81, 129
  departure tax, 176
  Edward VIII and, 140

Holocaust (1941–5), 55–6,
  175, 179, 184, 196
Nuremberg Laws (1935), 140
Russian pogroms (1881–2),
  48, 54
socialism and, 128, 184
Jockey Club (Vienna), 16, 29, 43

Karl-Marx-Hof (Vienna), 127
Kenilworth Castle, 7
Königgrätz, Battle of, 84
Königshütte, 52–3
Kreuzenstein Castle, 23–4, 74,
  76, 88, 103, 162
Kronberg Castle, 188, 210
Krowiarki Palace, 17, 26, 30, 33,
  36, 37, 44, 58, 61, 207
Kunsthaus Drey, 134

landscaping, 36, 45, 209
Laurahütte, 15, 53
Leuchtenberg Palace, 159–60,
  162
liberalism, 11, 41, 84
Lichterfelde (Berlin), 104–5, 121,
  195
Liebenberg circle, 35
Locarno Pact (1925), 118
London, 5, 67, 72, 95, 134, 141,
  177, 210
  salons, 125
  social housing in, 73
London Nursing School, 117
Lorraine, 71
Lungau, 8, 17–19, 21, 24, 81,
  110, 118, 161
  agriculture, 92–4, 99
  Anschluss (1938), 149–50

INDEX

Christianity in, 98, 110, 115–17, 129
hunting in, 17, 19, 22, 24, 170
national socialism in, 129, 130–31, 135
paper industry, 63, 118
railway connections, 81, 151, 184
remoteness, 17, 22, 81, 110, 151
Second World War (1939–45), 179, 181
women in, 110, 115–16
Lutheranism, 14, 39–40, 46, 197

Martin list, 55
Maternity Protection Organisation, 130
Mauterndorf Castle, 100, 103–4, 107–8, 121, 144, 147–8, 154, 167–9, 174, 207
Epenstein's purchase of, 103, 107–8
interior design, 167–8
US occupation (1945), 182–3
Meissen porcelain, 133
Merano, 150
Metz, 71, 164
mining and steel industries, 40, 44, 46, 50–55, 60, 83, 136, 152, 156
blast furnace, 15
in Britain, 51, 52, 53
calamine, 52
cast iron, 40, 44, 51, 52
chemistry and, 40
coal, 11, 28, 51–2, 55, 66, 98, 136
coke, 51

iron ore, 52, 55
phosphate, 40, 94
potassium, 94
railway network and, 52, 206
steel, 40, 44, 51–3, 60, 94, 98, 136, 152
steam engines, 51
zinc, 52, 55, 206
Moosham Castle, 23–4, 27–9, 58, 100, 103, 107, 142, 167, 207
Munich, 8, 34, 76, 103, 105, 106, 107, 159, 199
Beer Hall Putsch (1923), 107, 121–2
Central Collecting Point, 183
Kunsthaus Drey, 134
Sotheby's, 198
Weinmüller Auction House, 159–64, 198, 212
Munich Agreement (1938), 154
Murray Edwards College, Cambridge, 141

national socialism, 116, 124, 126, 129, 130, 141
see also Nazi Party
nationalism, 88
Austrian, 81, 141, 153
English, 153
German, 72, 81, 139, 141, 149, 171
Hungarian, 82, 84, 85, 89, 96, 99, 180
Italian, 84, 85
Nazi Party; Third Reich, 49, 121–6, 137–43, 205, 211
Anschluss (1938), 143–4, 149–50, 151, 152, 160, 163, 173, 180

256

INDEX

artworks, theft of, 159–60, 163, 165, 171, 183

Aryanisation, 155, 159–61, 163, 173–6

BeerHallPutsch(1923),107,121–2

Brynek, ownership of (1939–45), 208

Carinhall receptions, 169

contraceptives, ban on, 176

Czechoslovakia annexation (1939), 154

'degenerate art', policies on, 148, 171

Fatherland Front, relations with, 128, 130, 131, 138, 153

Finstergrün, ownership of (1942–5), 166, 179, 181, 207

Gestapo, 160, 161, 163, 173, 181

Hitler Youth, 141, 156, 179, 190, 208

Holocaust (1941–5), 55–6, 175, 179, 184, 196, 206

hunting and, 170, 172

Italy, relations with, 121–3

Luftwaffe, 172, 179, 191, 208, 211–12

Margit and, 139, 141, 166, 200

Mother's Cross, 179

nobility and, 123–6, 164, 181, 184, 191, 195, 196

Nuremberg Laws (1935), 140

Prinzenerlass decree (1940), 195–6

Research Bureau, 172, 195

salon spies, 123, 125, 181

Second World War (1939–45), 55, 165, 179, 180, 196, 206, 208–9

Wehrmacht, 165, 185, 190, 191, 196, 206, 208

Nemzeti Casino (Budapest), 180

Netherlands, 9, 13, 61, 65, 111, 183, 184–5, 192, 197–200

artworks in, 155, 167, 170, 173, 174

royal weddings (1966), 187–90

Second World War (1939–45), 138, 184–5

Sotheby's in, 3, 5

Neues Neudeck Palace, 14, 38, 39, 40, 42–3, 45, 72, 209

nobility

apanage, 59

administration, 96

beauty ideals, 37

British, 34, 49

family, 17, 35, 46

family assets, 59–62

Fideikomiss (entailed property), 60

First World War and, 96

Gutsherrin, 35, 37, 91

Habsburg empire, 11, 16, 17, 23, 25, 130, 140, 203

hunting, 22, 25, 83

and Jews, 85, 124

marriage, 16, 17, 37, 46–7

modern, 11, 47, 194

national socialism, 124–6

noblesse oblige (social duty), 194

past and, 10

257

INDEX

philanthropy, 97–8
political insight, lack of, 25
religion and, 14, 77
reputation and, 36
social capital, 180
traditions, 47, 191
women, 34–7, 46–8, 60–61
North Pole, 23

Opatija, *see* Abbazia
Ostmark, 144, 163
Ottoman Empire (1299–1922), 83, 85

Palace of Peace (The Hague), 87
Palais Garnier (Paris), 70
Paris, 17, 39, 40–41, 72, 84, 143
artwork theft in, 155, 164, 170, 173–4
commerce in, 53
fashion in, 67
Hotel Païva, 41, 66–73, 76, 79, 80, 209–10
interior design in, 62, 69
La Fleur Blanche, 70
La Samaritaine, 84
liberalism, 41
Louvre, 39
Palais Garnier (Paris), 70
salons, 43, 125
sewers, 84
Pariser Platz (Berlin), 42, 209
pogroms, 48, 54, 83
Poland, 11, 47, 55, 83, 89, 139, 156, 165, 173, 206–9
Pour le Mérite, 105
Premhaus, 75, 93, 114, 166, 179, 181, 198, 200

Pressburg, 16, 26, 27, 29, 58, 81–4, 86, 92
Protestantism, 14, 39, 43, 47, 50, 136, 139
Prussia (1525–1947), 41, 43, 47, 49, 50, 52, 55, 125, 126, 138–9, 144, 152, 167
Austro-Prussian War (1866), 23, 84, 138
Franco-Prussian War (1870–71), 71, 84, 138, 210

Ramingstein, 7, 21, 58, 63, 133, 166, 182, 184, 195, 198
Anschluss (1938), 144, 150
CSP in, 112
CWO in, 109
Margit's philanthropy in, 63
Premhaus, 75, 93, 114, 166, 179, 181, 198, 200
paper factory, 63, 118
school, 63, 95, 205
railway connections, 81, 184
rehabilitation centres (veterans), 109, 207, 211
republicanism, 71, 89
Rijeka, *see* Fiume
Ringstrasse (Vienna), 15, 17, 44, 58
Red Cross, 6, 81, 94
'Red Vienna', 115, 127, 129
Rudolfinerhaus (Vienna), 97
Russian Empire (1721–1917)
anti-Jewish pogroms (1881–2), 48, 54
First World War (1914–18), 85, 92, 95
Revolution (1917), 97
Turkish War (1877–8), 86–7

258

INDEX

see also Soviet Union

salon culture, 41, 43, 66, 67, 87, 91, 123, 125, 198

Salzburg, 7, 8, 18, 21, 27, 28, 182
  CWO, 81, 112
  First World War (1914–18), 93–4, 95, 109
  Provincial Archive, 31, 34, 65, 182
  salt mines, 212
  transport connections, 134, 151

Salzburg Festival, 134–5

Salzburg State Mortgage Bank, 137, 154, 155, 156

Samson, 98–9, 116

Schutzbund, 118

Scotland, 6, 7, 182, 194

Secession (art), 133

Second World War (1939–45), 55, 138, 156, 165, 177, 179–85, 190, 204, 206, 208–9
  aerial battles and bombings, 179
  artworks, theft of, 159–60, 163, 165, 171, 182, 183
  Battle of Berlin (1945), 55, 209
  Finstergrün Castle and, 166, 179, 181, 207
  Holocaust (1941–5), 55–6, 175, 179, 184, 196, 206
  nobility and, 180, 194, 196, 206
  Silesia expulsions (1945), 55, 204

sewers, 79, 84

Siemianowicz Palace, 26, 31, 32, 36, 38, 39, 44, 45, 47, 62, 66, 206

Silesia, 31, 32, 47, 49–56
  German expulsions (1945), 55, 204
  Jewish migration to, 48, 54, 56
  mining and steel industries, 11, 40, 44, 46, 50–54, 66, 94, 98, 124, 156
  national identity in, 47, 72

Social Democratic Party of Austria (SD), 128

social housing, 73, 129

Sotheby's, 3, 5, 6, 10, 70, 183, 198, 215, 216

Soviet Union (1922–91), 55, 89, 140, 183
  Second World War (1939–45), 55, 165, 175, 177, 180, 181, 191, 192, 196, 207–9

Spectator, The, 137, 138, 141, 153

St Hubertus hunting lodge, 79

St Stephen's Cathedral (Vienna), 73, 96

Starry Cross, Order of the, 96

steel industry, *see* mining and steel industries

Stockholm, 106, 126

Stolperstein, 175

Sweden, 52, 61, 87, 105–7, 123, 147

Tamsweg, 21, 63, 74, 91, 98, 109, 112, 130, 141, 148, 179, 185, 197, 199

Tarnowskie Góry, 38

Tauern mountains, 8, 18, 80, 86, 94, 99

Tegernsee, 124, 126, 160, 162, 210

INDEX

Thermohaus GmbH, 184
tourism, 3, 18, 134–5, 137, 206–7, 210
Tories, 210
Travellers Club, 43, 210
Treaty of Versailles (1919), 55, 89, 107, 112, 151
Tyrol, 75, 147, 150, 165

Ukraine, 52, 54, 55, 208
United Kingdom 95, 118, 133
  appeasement policy (1935–9), 140–41, 151–2, 154
  bison dispatch (1934), 172
  colonialism, 72
  country houses in, 45, 49, 61, 62, 72
  Finstergrün guests, 135
  First World War (1914–18), 85, 105, 147
  interior design in, 61, 62
  mining industry, 51, 52, 53
  Munich Agreement (1938), 154
  nationalism in, 153
  nobility, 34, 49
  royal family, 15
  Second World War (1939–45), 211
  social housing in, 73
  Treaty of Versailles (1919), 89
United States, 41, 179, 181–3, 191, 192–3, 209
  Austria, occupation of (1945–55), 181, 184–5, 196–7
  Finstergrün guests, 135
  Germany, occupation of (1945–9), 108, 165, 182
universal suffrage, 110–12

Upper Silesia, *see* Silesia

Veldenstein Castle, 104, 107, 108, 121
Venice, 11, 27, 122
Versailles, Treaty of (1919), 55, 89, 107, 112, 151
Versailles Palace, 38, 41, 61, 68, 72, 169, 209
Vienna, 15–17, 19, 23, 25, 33, 43, 83, 87, 89, 96
  Allied occupation (1945–55), 184
  Anschluss (1938), 144
  artwork theft in, 170
  Aryanisation in, 173
  balls in, 33, 46
  government buildings, 61
  International Electrical Exhibition (1883), 27
  Jockey Club, 16, 29, 43
  'Red Vienna' (1918–34), 115, 127, 129
  Ringstrasse, 15, 17, 44, 58
  Sacré Coeur Institute, 96–7
  salons, 43
  St Stephen's Cathedral, 73, 96
  working classes, 118
Villa Rosalia, 11, 12, 206

Weinmüller, Adolf, 159–64, 198, 212
Wolfsberg Castle, 15, 26, 30, 58
women's rights, 46–7, 81, 85, 86, 97, 110–12, 128–9, 176
Wrocław, *see* Breslau

Young Fatherland, 142

260